BSF

THE EYES AND EARS OF INDIA

B S F

THE EYES AND EARS OF INDIA

Authors
Sanjiv Krishan Sood
Inderjeet Singh
Monojit Das

ADROIT

Adroit Publishers

NEW DELHI • KATHMANDU

ISBN : 978-81-87393-78-8

2022

Second Edition

Published by
ADROIT PUBLISHERS 4675/21, Ganpati Bhawan, Ansari Road,
Daryaganj, New Delhi-110 002 Phone : 011-23266030
adroitpublishers@gmail.com

Typeset in Garamond Premier Pro by Arun, Akriti Graphic Solution, Delhi-110081 E-mail: arun263923@gmail.com, Ph: 9999414390

Printed at Nutech Print Services - India

Contents

Appendix and Annexure

जनरल (डा.) विजय कुमार सिंह
पीवीएसएम, एवीएसएम, वाईएसएम (से.नि.)

GEN. (DR) VIJAY KUMAR SINGH
PVSM, AVSM, YSM (Retd)

सत्यमेव जयते

राज्य मंत्री
सड़क परिवहन एवं राजमार्ग मंत्रालय
भारत सरकार, नई दिल्ली

Minister of State for
Road Transport & Highways
Government of India, New Delhi

FOREWORD

Raised on 1st December 1965, the Border Security force is the largest border guarding force. It stands tall and proud among the galaxy of Border Guarding forces. As a harbinger of peace, tranquillity and stability on the most volatile borders in South Asia, BSF stands apart for its acumen.

Mandated to guard the extremely sensitive borders of India with Pakistan and Bangladesh, the terrain in which BSF operates varies from the extremely cold snow clad mountains of Kashmir to the scorching hot deserts of The Thar in Rajasthan enduring a temperature variance from -50 to +50. In the Eastern theatre the force faces the challenge of guarding the water logged mangroves of the Sunderbans to the dense evergreen forests of the North East.

BSF has displayed exceptional professional competence in inculcating a sense of security amongst border population by ensuring sanctity of Borders and undertaking meaningful "Border area development" and "Civic Action Programmes", thus facilitating their integration in the mainstream.

Designated as the first line of defence, it faced the first burnt of enemy attack during the 1971 war with Pakistan. The force acquitted itself admirably both on the eastern and western frontiers. Not yet 6 years old, the force performed its war time role admirably through exceptional acts of bravery, leadership qualities and improvisation. Contribution of the force has been recognised by award of several gallantry medals - including one "Mahavir Chakra" and several "Vir chakras" to its personnel.

Often called upon in aid to civil authorities, the force played a stellar role in controlling insurgency in Nagaland and militancy in Punjab and J&K. Large contingent of the force is also deployed in central India to control the threat emanating from Maoist insurgency.

This book, "BSF, The eyes and ears of India" aims to highlight the evolution of Border Management structure in India and the contributions of Border Security Force in ensuring sanctity of the borders of India and Internal Security.

Written in simple language, the book will be extremely useful in enhancing the visibility of the force amongst masses and enabling them to comprehend the challenges and constraints that it faces in performance of its tasks.

[General (Dr.) V.K. Singh]

Transport Bhawan, 1, Sansad Marg, New Delhi-110 001

Office Tel.: +91-11-23731522, 23715159 Fax : +91-11-23718568, Web : http//www.morth.nic.in

Anandiben Patel
Governor, Uttar Pradesh

सत्यमेव जयते

Raj Bhavan
Lucknow - 226 027

08 July, 2020

Message

I am indeed happy to learn that the book 'BSF: The Eyes and Ears of India' is going to be published.

Border Security Force is the largest border guarding force of the world. It has displayed exceptional professional competence in inculcating a sense of security amongst border population by ensuring sanctity of Borders and undertaking meaningful 'Border area development' and 'Civic Action Programmes'.

I am sure BSF will always play a major role in maintaining the security and integrity of the Nation.

(Anandiben Patel)

Telephone : 0522-2236497 Fax : 0522-2239488 Email : hgovup@nic.in Website : www.upgovernor.gov.in

RAJ BHAVAN
GUWAHATI

The BSF in its glorious existence of over five decades, has emerged as an elite force having excelled in its duties during peace and war time. Its mission 'any task, anytime and anywhere' has enabled its rank and file to live up to its motto that is **'Jeevan Paryant Kartavya'.**

Guarding India's land border and preventing transnational crime along the border in extreme conditions require the highest degree of dedication, determination, discipline and fortitude. The Border Security Force through its unrelenting endeavour in border management during peace or war time has instilled a sense of security among the people living along the border areas. Taking serious note of the role of BSF and its unflinching sagacity in guarding our borders with Pakistan and Bangladesh, the special initiative of Sri Sanjiv Krishnan Sood, Dr. Inderjeet Singh and Sri Monojit Das in bringing out a book christened "BSF, The eyes and ears of India' will definitely add a new feather to its kitty.

The book I am sure will highlight the evolution of border management structure in India and the contribution of BSF in ensuring sanctity of the borders. In this book the writers have given an articulated account of the challenges that the personnel of BSF face and the endearing manner in which the challenges are converted into glorifying opportunities to give a new shining chapter in the narrative of border management and its protection.

In this backdrop, I appreciate Sri Sanjiv Krishnan Sood, Dr. Inderjeet Singh and Sri Monojit Das for bringing out this book to give the much needed visibility about the BSF and its selfless services to the public in general. I hope the book informs and inspires many in days to come.

Dated: August 24, 2020 **(Prof. Jagdish Mukhi)**

Sarbananda Sonowal

सत्यमेव जयते

Chief Minister, Assam
Guwahati

Dispur
25.6.2020

MESSAGE

I am happy to know that Mr. Sanjiv Krishan Sood, Dr. Inderjeet Singh and Mr. Monojit Das have co-authored a book titled "BSF: The Eyes and Ears of India" highlighting the stellar role played Border Security Force (BSF) in maintaining security and stability on India's borders.

As the book attempts to showcase the contribution made by BSF in the security matrix of the country and management of Indo-Pakistan and Indo-Bangladesh international borders, it is imperative that the authors have to shoulder the responsibility to make the general public aware about the hardships and challenges faced by the Force in the line of duty while upholding its motto of 'Jeevan Paryant Kartavya'.

BSF also has an outstanding history in guarding the international border with Bangladesh in Assam, fighting insurgency in Northeast and helping the overall law and order situation in the region and I hope the book becomes successful in highlighting the work ethic and dedication of the Force while at the same time glorifying the supreme sacrifices made by its personnel in discharging their duties.

I extend my best wishes to the authors of "BSF: The Eyes and Ears of India" for this endeavour and hope the book would be able achieve the desired goals.

(SARBANANDA SONOWAL)

Acknowledgements I

At the outset, I am grateful to Shri S. S. Mand Commandant (presently posted at Subsidiary Training Centre BSF, Hoshiarpur), who sometime in 2017 suggested that I write a book on BSF with the aim of spreading awareness about this great organisation among general public. I immediately agreed to the suggestion and he introduced me to Dr. Inderjit Chahal, the then Head of Department of Defence Studies at Punjabi University, Patiala and Shri Monojit Das a student of Dr. Chahal and is presently, a research scholar at Goa University.

I acknowledge the contribution of both of them in framing an outline for the book and deciding on the scope of issues to be covered. Contribution of both of them in preparation of this book has also been immense by permitting uninterrupted use of their vast libraries. Insights gained by them as academicians through extensive field visits helped me overcome my professional bias and look at things dispassionately. Understanding gained by them through these field visits also helped them in writing many portions of the book.

Contribution of my wife, Surekha, in completing the project not only by helping out with Grammar and spellings but also through prompt supply of unending cups of tea must be acknowledged. But for her, the project would have taken much longer to complete.

My small little granddaughter, Ishaanvi – all of four years now – often provided me with much needed relief from the monotony of reading unending pages of literature by simply closing my laptop and directing me in her small voice "*Dadu* hide and seek". Completing the project at the earliest also became imperative as I was left with no answers to regular queries from Shaurya and Kabir "*Nanu aapki* book *kab complete hogi*?"

Acknowledgments are also due to my daughter Shweta and son-in-law Rajat Kohli, son Shashank and daughter-in-Law Karishma for the support they have extended.

Acknowledgments are also due to my batch mate Shri Bhola Nath Sharma, IG BSF Retired; Shri Parveen Bakshi, Commandant (Presently Operations Directorate BSF); Shri Jagdish Maithani, Commandant (Presently commanding 07 Battalion BSF at Karimganj); Dr. Raj Kumar Arora, Commandant (Presently Professor at Centre for Peace and conflict studies, Sardar Vallabh Bhai Police University, Rajasthan);and Second-In–Command Manoj Kumar (Presently at Subsidiary Training Centre Latur, Maharashtra), who have helped me out through various inputs in shape of data and ideas.

This book is dedicated to the memory of my late parents Shri Krishan Kumar Sood and Shrimati Bimla Sood.

I also dedicate this book to unsung fellow border men who uncomplainingly secure our borders to ensure that we sleep peacefully.

Sanjiv Sood

Additional Director General (Retd.)

Border Security Force (BSF)

Acknowledgements II

It is my pleasure to put on records my heartfelt gratitude for cooperation and assistance that I received from all those for publication of this book. At the outset, I would like to express my sincere thanks to both the co-authors Shri Sanjiv Sood for agreeing to the proposal and guiding us for the way forward and Mr. Monojit Das for his idea to bring out this publication, I appreciate his sincerity,hard work and contribution towards the publication of the book. I also express my respect to my mother Smt. Harnam Kaur and father S. Harnam Singh and place sincere thanks to my wife Manpreet Kaur and my son Rajvansh Singh for their encouragement, co-operation and moral support extended by them. I am also thankful to the Department of Defence and Strategic Studies, Punjabi University, Patiala, my teachers from the department Prof. R. N. Mishra, Prof. K. S. Siddhu, Prof. R. K. Datta, Col. Nagendier Singh whose teachings are source of knowledge which I cherish till date. I place special thanks to Comdt. Sukhminder Singh Mand for his well wishes and support to know more about the Bordermen.

At the end, I wish to convey my deep appreciation to the Bordermen for keeping us safe.

Dr. Inderjeet Singh Chahal
Associate Professor
Dept of Defence and Strategic Studies
Punjabi University, Patiala

Acknowledgements III

I would like to express my gratitude to many well-wishers, who saw me through this book to all those who provided me support editing, proofreading and design especially Akhil Sharma and Gracy Samjetsabam.

My contribution in this book is dedicated to my mother Smt. Rina Das and father Mr. Murari Mohan Das, they are the ones because of whom I am what I am!

I would like to thank Shri Sanjiv Sood and Dr. Inderjeet Singh to have confidence on me and take me in the team to lay respect the brave men who dedicate their youth and life for all of us.

Further, I express my thanks to all my teachers from Defence and Strategic Studies fraternity across the country whose guidance have enabled me to reach here starting Dr. PA Ghosh, Sir Ramesh Raut, Dr. Inderjeet Singh, Dr. Umrao Singh, Prof Kamal Kinger, Dr. Krishan, Prof Uttam Kumar Jamadhagni, Dr. E Prabhakaran, Dr. Venkataraman.

I place my special thanks to my Ph.D. supervisor Prof. Rahul Tripathi, for guiding me in every walk of life and Prof Shilpa Tripathi for being well wisher, I thank Dr. Prakash Desai, Dr. Alakananda, Ravaji Sir for extending support always whenever needed.

It will be incomplete without thanking my friends Mikaila, Nur, Sudam, Tinku, Reshma and brother Akshay for their support and good wishes.

Last and not the least, I beg forgiveness from all those whose names I failed to mention here who have been with me over the course of the years but will always remain in heart.

Special thanks to Jugal Kishore Agarwal ji, for getting us know the history of 1971 closely at North Bengal including arranging interactions with the fighters who have fought it.

Finally, to the Bordermen family I dedicate this work and hope it can be an ode to the duty they perform everyday that is difficult even for the sake of an adventure activity by an ordinary citizen.

Monojit Das

CHAPTER ONE

Evolution of Borders of India

Introduction

At the University of Oxford in 1907, Lord Curzon in his Romanes lecture lamented that the history and politics of the frontiers have long tended to be neglected subjects. He further pointed out that "Frontiers are the chief anxiety of nearly every Foreign Office in the civilized world, and are the subject of four out of every five political treaties or conventions that are concluded . . . ."[1] Yet, very little literature is available on this vitally important subject. Situation after a lapse of over 110 years is better only marginally.

India shares its land borders with seven of its neighbours. These are Afghanistan, China, Pakistan, Bangladesh, Nepal, Bhutan and Myanmar. Afghanistan is not directly connected to India but a part of Pakistan Occupied Kashmir (PoK) is in between India and Afghanistan. So, we can consider Afghanistan a neighbouring country, although it does not directly share borders with India.

India also has a long coastline and shares maritime border with Sri Lanka.

Statistical data along with a map of India's border is given below.[2]

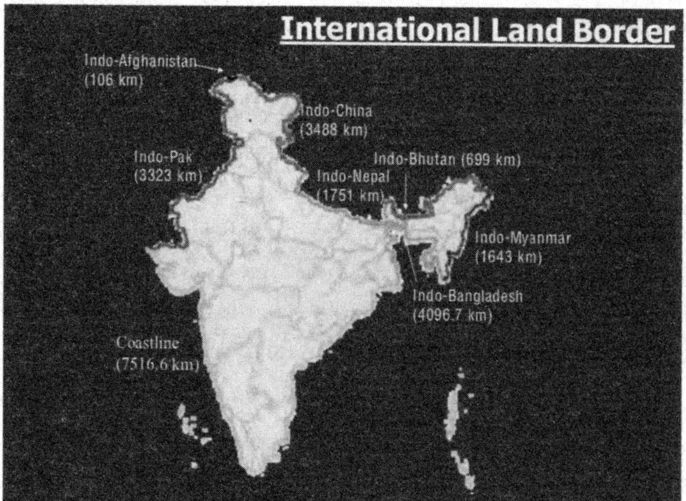

Figure 1.1: International Land Border

1. Lord Curzon of Kedleston D.C.L., LL.D., F.R.S. (1907) *The Romanes Lecture (1907) Frontiers, delivered in the Sheldonian Theatre, Oxford*. Clarendon Press, Oxford.
2. Annual Report Border Management (2019). New Delhi: Government of India, Ministry of Home Affairs, p.34.

LAND BORDER

Name of Country Length of Border in Km

PAKISTAN	3323.00
AFGHANISTAN	106.00 (Along PoK)
CHINA	3488.00
NEPAL	1751.00
BHUTAN	699.00
BANGLADESH	4096.70
MYANMAR	1643.00
TOTAL LAND BORDERS	**15106.70**

Besides, the above land borders India has a long coastline of 7516.6 kms, which comprises 5422 kms along mainland and, the Lakshadweep and Andaman Nicobar Islands extends to 132 kms and 1962 kms, respectively.

Both the land borders and the coastline need to be defended during the times of war and guarded during the peacetime. During war, the defence forces viz the Indian Army, the Navy and the Air Force are responsible for defending the borders whereas, in peacetime, the responsibility is on the four forces that guard the borders, i.e. the Border Security Force (BSF), the Assam Rifles (AR), the Sashastra Seema Bal (SSB) and the Indo Tibetan Border Police (ITBP).

The Group of Ministers (GoM) set up after the Kargil war in 1999, had recommended adopting the policy of "One Border One Force".[3] In accordance with this policy, the BSF is mandated to guard the India-Pakistan Border and India-Bangladesh Border, the ITBP to guard the India-China border, the SSB to guard the India-Nepal Border and the India-Bhutan Border whereas, the AR is given the responsibility for guarding India's border with Myanmar. All these forces operate based on the command from the Ministry of Home Affairs (MHA) except the Assam Rifles. The Ministry of Defence (MoD) commands on the Assam Rifles for operation.

India also has its "Coast Guard" to guard its long coastline. There is now a thinking that the country should have coastal police posts deployed along the coastline.

Evolution of Borders of India

British declared India's independence on 15 August 1947. Modern India came into being as an independent state but with independence the sub-continent was divided

3. Vifindia.org. (2001). *Report of the Group of Ministers on National Security*. https://www.vifindia.org/sites/default/files/GoM%20Report%20on%20National%20Security.pdf

into two dominions – independent India and independent Pakistan. The boundaries of India at that time had no exact coincidence with those of any pre-colonial state in the sub-continent. India was never a united empire before the British times except when the Mauryas and later, when the Mughal Dynasties ruled over India.

On the basis of inscriptions on the Ashokan Rock Edicts and Pillars, it can be concluded that the Mauryan Empire after its expansion by Ashoka in the third century BC extended well into Afghanistan on the west, but had not expanded to the south as much as the British Empire.

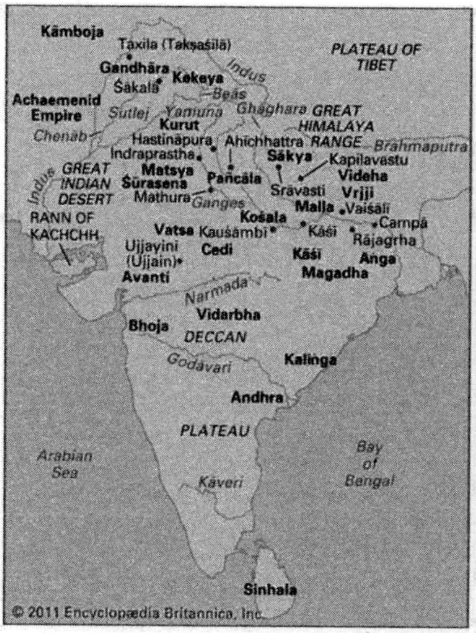

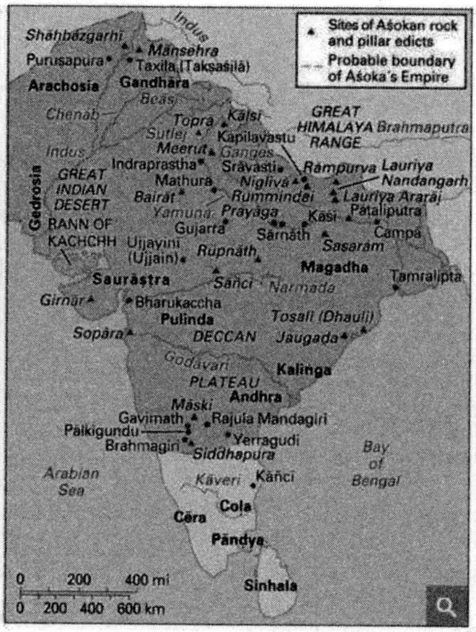

Figure 1.2: Map of the Ashokan Empire[4]

In its time, the Mauryan empire constituted one of the mightiest empires of the world. In the peak of the empire it extended to the Himalayas in the north, into portions of Assam in the east, and to the West reaching out to Baluchistan that is part of south-west Pakistan and south-east Iran and to present day Afghanistan along the Hindu Kush mountains.

Chandragupta and Bindusara expanded the Empire into central and to the southern regions of India. Their conquest spared an insignificant portion near Kalinga (now in Odisha) that consisted uncharted tribal areas and forest regions. Within half a century after the end of Ashoka's rule, the Mauryan empire disintegrated in185 BCE, upon which the Shunga dynasty laid its foundation in Magadha.

4. The Editors of Encyclopaedia Britannica (ed.). (2011). *Mauryan empire ancient state, India.* Encyclopædia Britannica, Inc. https://www.britannica.com/place/Mauryan-Empire

The next major dynasty to rule over a large land area of India was the Gupta Empire, which ruled from 320 to 550 CE, approximately and occupied large parts of northern India.

The Gupta period is considered the Golden Age of India as peace and prosperity was thought to be prevalent during the period.

Figure 1.3: Gupta dynasty map[5]

Chandragupta I, Samudragupta, and Chandragupta II were some of the most prominent rulers of the Gupta dynasty, who according to Kalidas, the famous fourth century poet had conquered about 21 kingdoms.

5. The Editors of Encyclopaedia Britannica (2011). *Gupta dynasty Indian dynasty.* Encyclopædia Britannica, Inc. https://www.britannica.com/topic/Gupta-dynasty

At the height of their power, the Mughal empire during the sixteenth and the seventeenth centuries AD went farther west than the British empire but not quite so far south as the British.

A map of the Mughal empire during Aurangzeb's regime is reproduced below.[6]

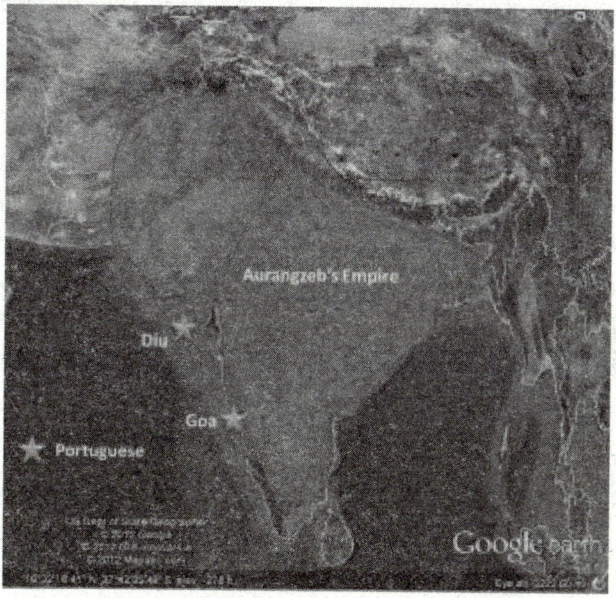

Figure 1.4: The Mughal empire during Aurangzeb's regime

The Mughals like the British were outsiders. Hence, there were no indigenous parallels for the British Raj in terms of the expanse of the empire, except for the Maurya and Gupta dynasties. However, small Hindu states have always impacted upon the boundary structure of India even though it may have been merely internal influence.

The states of Kerala, Mysore and Tamil Nadu (earlier Madras) have origins in various dynasties of southern India. These states are generally organised along linguistic lines and assert their regional and linguistic identity, which therefore often lead to unrest when any attempts to impose Hindi (a language mostly spoken in northern India) in these parts.

The British, therefore can be credited with constructing a frontier system and bringing together a number of language groups, which even though shared a tradition of the Hindu civilisation, had never been unified politically.

6. Mughal-Empire-Map-Aurangzeb (2019). *Mughal empire map Aurangzeb.* (image): https://www.globalresearch.ca/wp-content/uploads/2015/05/Mughal-Empire-Map-aurangzeb.jpg

It may be said that the British Raj brought about political union of a diverse and hitherto separate regions within the sphere of its power.

It did so by a two-fold process, first the Hindu heartland was occupied, and secondly, the centers of the Hindu civilisation like the north-west, the former Hindu regions, which had come under the Islamic domination. On the East, the frontier belt stretched from the Arabian Sea to the hills of Northern Burma (modern day Myanmar), all the population within these areas were included in the new region. There were Buddhists along the foothills of the Himalayas having traditional cultural ties with Tibet, which is a region under the influence of China. Some of the inhabitants like the Khasis, the Lushais and the Nagas had entirely distinct cultural identity. The population of North-East Frontier had come under the influence of the European and American Christian missionaries and had acquired a sense of their own cultural and national identity. They saw British rule as a protection for that identity and regretted the British departure. It is this conflict of identity, which led the Naga Rebellion against Indian republic soon after independence.

India shares a long border with China, which have more or less remained unchanged over centuries. There are many disputes along India's border with China or what is referred to as the Tibet autonomous region. India also share borders with Nepal and Bhutan in the North. There are no border disputes with Bhutan and Nepal except for some minor issues with Nepal. However, the scope of this book being restricted to the borders guarded by the BSF, a detailed discussion about India-China, Indo-Bhutan and Indo-Nepal borders is not being done.

Separation of Burma

In 1937, British Burma was separated from British India, thus becoming a separate colony. On April 1, 1937, the boundary between Assam and Bengal on the one hand and Burma on the other, ceased to be an internal boundary of the Indian empire and became a boundary between two distinct British colonies. A portion of this boundary, which was contagious to India became the boundary between India and Burma (now Myanmar).

India consisted of Princely states or states, which were not fully and formally part of British India. These portions were under indirect rule or were subjected to subsidiary alliances as these areas were not conquered or annexed by the British.

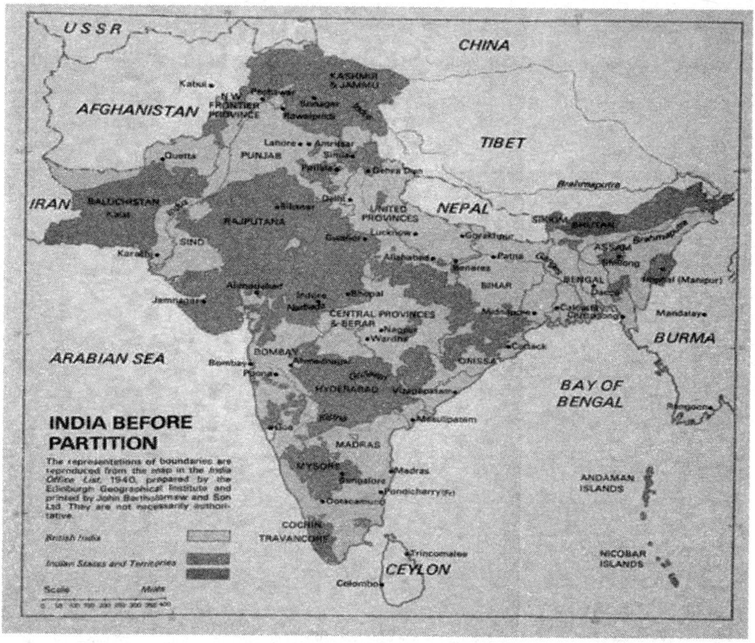

Figure 1.5: Indian borders before partition[7]

The shape of borders of India just before partition as depicted in the map in Figure 1.5 is of native states which comprised 564 princely states and these states were not wholly or formally a part of British India. These portions of the Indian subcontinent were not yet conquered or annexed by the then British empire but were subjects under indirect rule or subsidiary alliance.

The British divided India and left on 15 August 1947 leaving a legacy of disputes, which continue to fester even till date.

Genesis of these disputes lies in the manner of division of India. Sir Cyril Radcliff was tasked to draw boundaries of two new dominions in just six weeks. Lawyer by profession, he had never visited India and did not possess knowledge of local conditions, geography or of boundary making process. The sole term of reference he employed was dividing the country on religious majority basis and at the same time to minimize the disruption of the existing infrastructure.[8] All these factors led to the formation of most unnatural boundary.

---

7. Pinterest (2019). *A map of India before partition of 1947.* (image) https://i.pinimg.com/236x/24/45/fe/2445febbcd3d9865227ba567e2a083b6--maps-history-gandhi.jpg
8. Nayar, K. (2018). "I nearly gave you Lahore": When Kuldip Nayar asked Cyril Radcliffe about deciding Indo-Pak border. *Scroll.in*. https://scroll.in/article/891693/i-nearly-gave-you-lahore-when-kuldip-nayar-asked-cyril-radcliffe-about-deciding-indo-pak-border

Thus was created Pakistan, a unique country whose boundaries were decided on religious basis by partitioning the then British India in such a manner that the Muslim majority areas in and contiguous to Punjab and Bengal were joined together as one political entity.

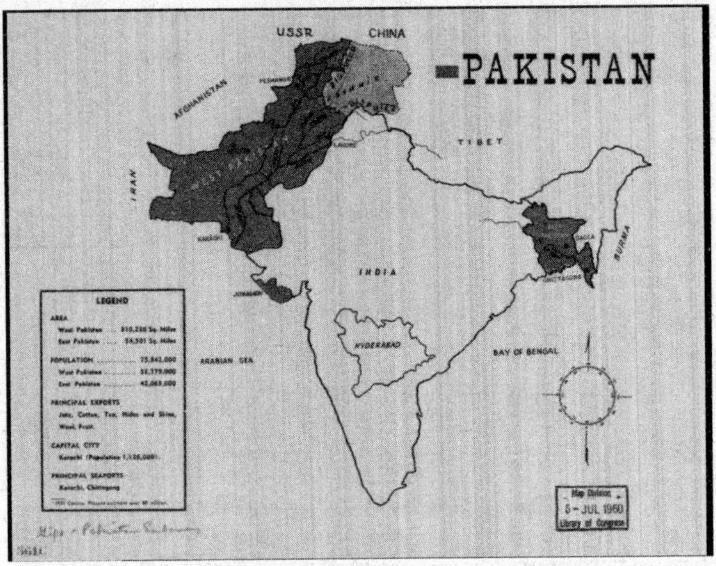

Figure 1.6: Boundary of India with Pakistan (erstwhile East and West Pakistan)[9]

The West and East Pakistan apart from Islam had nothing in common. They were ethnically and culturally different and geographically widely separated from each other.

These differences coupled with exploitation of resources of East Pakistan without corresponding development and political domination by West Pakistan led to the civil war and the creation of Bangladesh in 1971. The boundaries that Bangladesh shared with India were no different from those with East Pakistan.

Merger of Princely States

The era of the princely states effectively ended with the independence of India in 1947. By 1950, almost all of the principalities contagious to India had acceded to India. The accession process was largely peaceful, except in the cases of three princely states.

First being Jammu and Kashmir (J&K), where its ruler opted for independence but acceded to India following an invasion supported by Pakistan. However, by the time

9. Library of Congress (1960). *From minor village to world metropolis: Karachi in maps.* Library of Congress. https://blogs.loc.gov/maps/2018/04/from-minor-village-to-world-metropolis-karachi-in-maps/

this could happen, a large portion of the state had been occupied by Pakistani raiders. India and Pakistan have entered into four wars predominantly on the Kashmir dispute. Pakistan continues to foment trouble via militancy, sponsored and launched from its soil. A large portion of J&K continues to remain under Pakistani occupation by the name Pakistani Occupied Kashmir (PoK), wherein a de-facto border called Line of Control (LoC) separates PoK from Jammu and Kashmir in India.[10]

The second state was Hyderabad, whose ruler opted for total independence in 1947, followed the process a year later by the police action (Operation Polo invasion) and annexation by India.[11]

The third state was Junagadh, which initially acceded to Pakistan, but was annexed by India and the princely state was merged with India.

The states of Tripura and Manipur agreed to accession only in late 1949[12], after the Indian conquest of Hyderabad.

Maharaja Jagaddipendra Narayan, the ruler of Cooch Behar, which was a princely state acceded to join India on 12 September 1949. Cooch Behar eventually became part of West Bengal on 19 January 1950.[13]

Goa, Daman and Diu

The next stage of realignment of Borders of India occurred with the annexation of the Portuguese Indian territory of Goa, Daman and Diu in December 1961 through an armed action by the Indian armed forces codenamed as "Operation Vijay," which was executed for 36 hours. After the liberation, these territories were placed under the military administration which was finally replaced by civilian administration on 8 June 1962.

Puducherry

Till 1954, like Goa Puducherry (earlier Pondicherry) continued to remain a French

10. J&K (n.d.). *Instrument of accession of Jammu and Kashmir State.* [online] The Law Department J and K. http://jklaw.nic.in/instrument_of_accession_of_jammu_and_kashmir_state.pdf
11. Desai, H. (2019). Sardar Patel initiates Operation Polo.*Asian-voice.com.* https://www.asian-voice.com/Opinion/Columnists/Hari-Desai/Sardar-Patel-initiates-Operation-Polo
12. Sanajaoba, N. (n.d.). Instrument of accession executed on 11-8-47 between Governor-General of India and His Highness the Maharajah of Manipur. *E-PAO.* http://e-pao.net/epSubPageExtractor.asp?src=news_section.Oja_Naorem_Sanajaoba.Sanajaoba_Articles.Problem_of_1949_Annexation_of_Manipur_Part_3_By_Naorem_Sanajaoba
13. *Coochbehar.nic.in.* (n.d.). Royal history of Cooch Behar. http://coochbehar.nic.in/Htmfiles/royal_history.html

territory. The French East India Company in 1674 established Pondicherry as its headquarters. There was often a shift of power on Puducherry between the France and the Britain. In the later 1850s, as the British expanded their control on almost the entire span of India, French were allowed to retain parts of their settlements in India. Mahé, Pondicherry, Yanam, Chandernagor and Karaikal were under French India up to 1954, after which these territories were part of the Indian Union as well as of French India.

In the general election held on 18 October 1954 out of 178 people, Pondicherry Municipal as well as the Commune Panchayat, 170 favoured independence. A mere eight went against the vote. On 1 November 1954, the French Indian territories experienced a de facto transfer from France to India and became Pondicherry, which was a Union territory. Further, it was on 16 August 1962 that a formal de jure agreement between France and India was signed for the transfer of the territory.[14]

Kutch

The next realignment of the borders with Pakistan took place with the resolution of the Kutch dispute in 1968. Dispute arose because Radcliff did not take into consideration the regional boundary claims and counter claims between the Maharaja of Kutch and the Maharaja of Sind, while drawing the Radcliff line in that region. India claimed that the entire Rann of Kutch is in the Indian territory as it was part of Kutch and was further validated by the accession of entire Kutch to India on 1 June 1948. Pakistan was of the contention that jurisdiction was exercised over the northern parts of Kutch under Sind from when it, came under the annexation of the British.[15]

There was a brief skirmish between the Indian and the Pakistani armies in April 1965. A cease fire was made possible through international pressure on 30 April 1965. Harold Wilson, the then British Prime Minister was successful in convincing the two nations to put an end to the ongoing hostilities and instead, to resolve the dispute, set up a tribunal in June 1965. The tribunal on 19 February 1968 awarded 90 per cent of the area of Rann to India and yielding just about 10 per cent of the area to Pakistan.

---

14 Ministry of External Affairs (1956). Treaty establishing De Jure Cession of French Establishments in India (MEA. *Mea.gov.in*. https://mea.gov.in/bilateral-documents.htm?dtl/5302/Treaty+establishing+De+Jure+Cession+of+French+Establishments+in+India

15. United Nations (1965). Agreement between the Government of India and the Government of Pakistan relating to cease-fire and the restoration of the status quo as on 1 January 1965 in the Gujarat/West Pakistan Border and determination of the border in that area. *United Nations. Peacekeeping United Nations*. https://peacemaker.un.org/sites/peacemaker.un.org/files/IN%20PK_650630_Agreement%20to%20CeaseFire%20and%20Restoration%20of%20the%20Status%20Quo.pdf

Both the countries welcomed the UN secretary general's announcement of awarding the Indo-Pakistan Western Boundary Case Tribunal. Pakistan originally claimed about 9,100 square kilometres, but was awarded just about 910 square kilometres out of it.[16]

Sir Creek

The Sir Creek border alignment is disputed between India and Pakistan and is yet to be resolved. Sir Creek is located at 23°58' N 68°48'E approximately and is a tidal estuary of 96 kms that falls on the India and Pakistan border. The estuary passes through Gujarat in India and through the Sindh Province in Pakistan, thus dividing India and Pakistan and finally falling into the Arabian Sea. Besides this, the Kori Creek is one other tidal estuary in the Indus River Delta that lies at about 34 kms south east from Sir Creek.

The long-lasting disagreement prevents the actual demarcation of Sir Creek from the mouth to the top and from the top of the Creek eastward towards a designated point on the Western Terminus of the line. The boundary from this point onwards is fixed according to definition provided by the Kutch Tribunal Award of 1968.

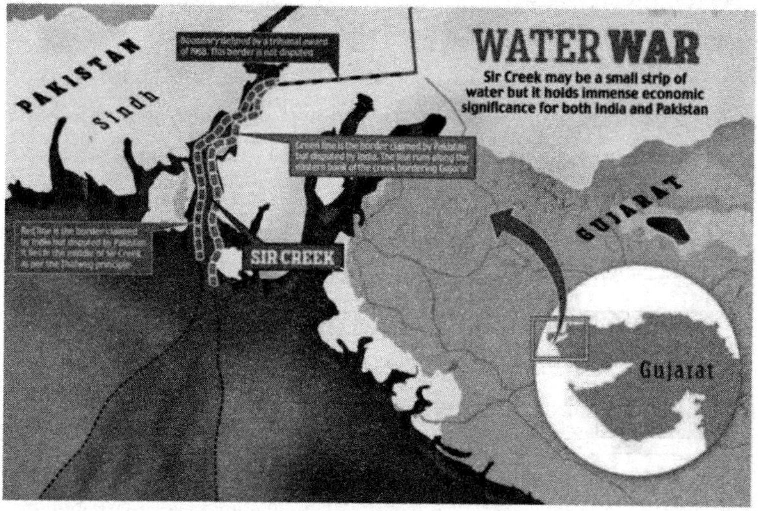

Figure 1.7: Sir Creek dispute [17]

A major area of dispute is the interpretation of maritime boundary between

16. Misra, A. (2010). The Rann of Kutch dispute and the resolution process. In: India-Pakistan. Palgrave Series in Asian Governance. Palgrave Macmillan, New York. https://doi.org/10.1057/9780230109780_5
17. Joshi, M. (2012). The troubled waters of Sir Creek: Gujarat CM's demand for a freeze on the disputed creek complicates issue. *India Today*. https://www.indiatoday.in/india/north/story/sir-creek-dispute-gujarat-chief-minister-narendra-mod-rann-of-kutchmaritime-boundary-124418-2012-12-16

Pakistan and India.[18] The disputed area prior to India's independence was within British India, but post-independence, in 1947, Sindh joined Pakistan and Gujarat joined India.

Pakistan claims Sir Creek to be part of Pakistan in accordance to what is stated on paragraph 9 and 10 of the Sind Government Resolution of 1914, which was signed between the then, Government of Sindh and the Maharaja (Maharao) of Kutch.[19] The resolution on the demarcated boundaries includes the Creek as part of Sindh that settles the demarcation as the eastern flank. But India maintains that according to a map of 1925 prepared on the basis of the 1924 mid-channel pillars installation, the boundary is mid-channel. India cites the Thalweg doctrine in international law to support its stance.[20] The law upholds that river boundaries can follow the mid-channel division if the two states agree. Pakistan does not contest on the 1925 map but insists that the doctrine applies to non-tidal rivers and that it does not apply on Sir Creek as it is a tidal estuary and not a non-tidal river. India on the other hand disagrees with Pakistan on the grounds that at high tides the Creek is navigable, in some international boundaries of tidal waters the Thalweg principle is applicable and that fishing trawlers use the Creek to move to big seas. Additionally, Pakistan is concerned about the notable changes in the Creek's course in recent times. Both India and Pakistan would have to bear lose although in small proportion on its wetland territory that are part of the respective provincial histories, if the Thalweg principle is to be applied in the present channel and boundary. Furthermore, it would be a loss for Pakistan to accede to India's claim as it would deprive Pakistan of its Exclusive Economic Zone under the United Nations Convention on Law of the Sea by several thousand square kilometres, which in turn will prove to be a shortcoming to its land shift or sea terminus in kilometres.[21]

India and Pakistan have had 12 rounds of talks with no advancement since 1967. In June 2012, the 12th round identified measures for the resolution of the dispute that could be employed including demarcation, allocation, administration and delimitation.

---

18. Dabas, M. (2016). Everything you need to know about the dispute over Sir Creek between India and Pakistan. *indiatimes.com*. https://www.indiatimes.com/news/everything-you-need-to-know-about-the-dispute-over-sir-creek-between-india-and-pakistan-260071.html
19. Lagergen, G., Entezam, N. and Bebler, A. (1968). The Indo-Pakistan Western Boundary (Rann of Kutch) between India and Pakistan (India, Pakistan). *legal.un.org*, Reports of International Arbitral Awards, United Nations, pp.336–357. https://legal.un.org/riaa/cases/vol_XVII/1-576.pdf
20. Merriam-webster.com. (n.d.).*Definition of THALWEG*.https://www.merriam-webster.com/dictionary/thalweg
21. *Un.org.* (1982). Overview - Convention & Related Agreements. https://www.un.org/Depts/los/convention_agreements/convention_overview_convention.htm

As none was ready to concede ground, India proposed a conclusion on the maritime boundary demarcation first based on the provisions of Technical Aspects of Law of Sea (TALOS).[22] But Pakistan refused the proposal as it was more inclined to resolve the dispute first. Pakistan supported an international arbitration option and urged India to opt for the same, which India rejected. India continues to advocate no third party intervention to resolve any bilateral disputes between the two countries. Since 2012, very less progress is made on Sir Creek negotiations.

Land Boundary Agreement between India and Bangladesh 2015

In 2015, India and Bangladesh signed a land boundary agreement at the time when India's Prime Minister visited Bangladesh.[23] This agreement was implemented in July 2015. The implementation brought finality to the Land Boundary Agreement of 1974 along with the protocol of 2011 to this agreement. Thus, India and Bangladesh border attained a finality.

Enclaves

As discussed above, accession of Coochbehar to India came with the peculiar problem of Enclaves. The origin of these enclaves is attributed to the practice of gifting away of pieces of land by the Rulers of Coochbehar and neighbouring Rangpur (Now in Bangladesh) to each other after losing in the game of "Chaupar"[24] or whenever they visited each other. The enclaves can be depicted diagrammatically as below.

---

22. Reddy, B. M. (18 January 2005). Joint survey of Sir Creek completed ahead of schedule., *The Hindu*. https://web.archive.org/web/20060304033412/http://www.hindu.com/2005/01/18/stories/2005011804971200.htm
23. *Mea.gov.in*. (2015). Exchange of enclaves between India and Bangladesh. https://mea.gov.in/press-releases.htm?dtl/25565/Exchange+of+enclaves+between+India+and+Bangladesh
24. Brown, W. N. (1964). The Indian games of pachisi, chaupar, and chausar expedition magazine. *Penn.museum*. https://www.penn.museum/sites/expedition/the-indian-games-of-Phisi-chaupar-and-chausar

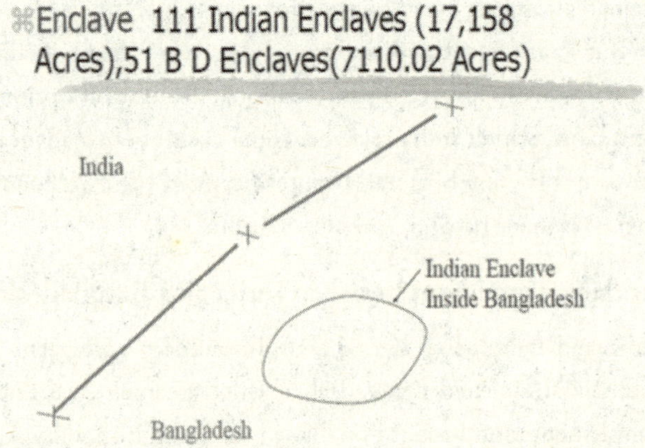

Fig 1.8: Enclaves

Details of the enclaves were a result of the joint comparison and reconciliation from the records as maintained by both India and Bangladesh according to the Land Records and Survey authorities. It was prepared at the Indo-Bangladesh Boundary conference held from 9 to12 October in 1996 at Kolkata and during the joint field examination at Jalpaiguri in West Bengal, India and Panchagarh sector in Bangladesh from 21 to 24 November in 1996.

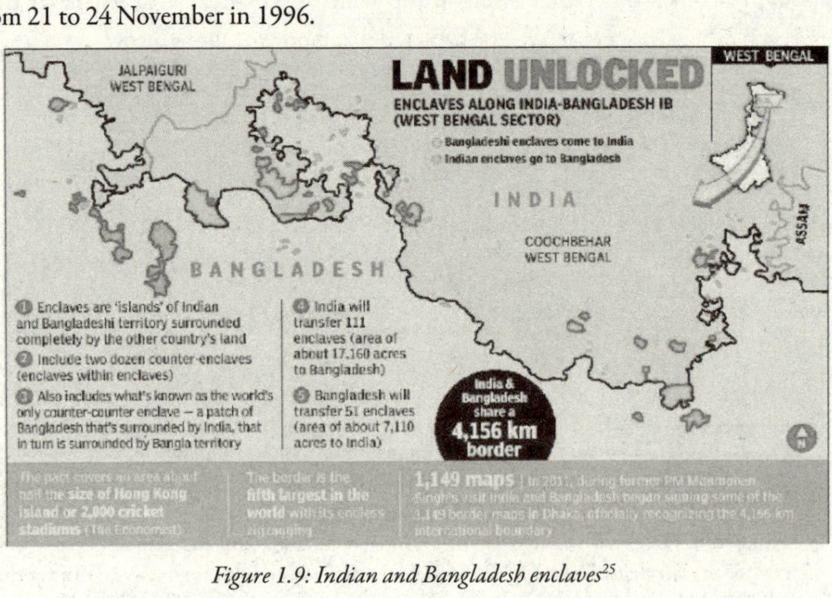

Figure 1.9: Indian and Bangladesh enclaves[25]

25. *Times of India* (2015). Historic enclave swap: 68 years after Independence, another freedom at midnight. https://timesofindia.indiatimes.com/india/Historic-enclave-swap-68-years-after-Independence-another-freedom-at-midnight/articleshow/48302901.cms

It was observed that there was a count of 111 Indian enclaves on the side of Bangladesh and of 51 Bangladeshi enclaves on India's side.

The existence of enclaves and residents therein meant that there were nationals of both countries not having any contact with the mainland of the country of which they were nationals. For example, residents of Indian enclaves in Bangladesh could not cross over to India as they had to pass through the Bangladeshi territory. They could not officially come out of the enclave to go even to marketplaces or send their children for education outside the enclave. These people almost had a stateless existence.

Existence of the enclaves also had implications on border management as the security forces could not enter them, being a foreign territory. The criminals thus had a safe place to hide after committing a crime on the mainland.

Being located away from mainland, the security forces of the parent country could not come to the help of residents of these enclaves in case of any eventuality as it involved passing through the land of the other country.

Implementation of land boundary agreement has resolved this issue and all the enclaves have been merged in the country in which they are located, except for the "Dahagram-Angrapota" enclave which continues to remain with Bangladesh. The Indira Mujib boundary accord of 1974 and later protocol to that accord signed between the then, India's Prime Minister Manmohan Singh and Bangladesh's Prime Minister Sheikh Hasina Wazed in 2011 provided for the residents of these enclaves to opt for nationality of either country upon merger of enclaves. Accordingly, the residents were given the option. All the residents of Bangladeshi enclaves in India opted for Indian nationality whereas 201 families consisting of 922 persons opted to come to India from Indian enclaves in Bangladesh.

Dahagram-Angarpota Enclave

The agreement and the protocol both provided that the Dahgram-Angarpota enclave will continue to remain with Bangladesh. Sketch of this enclave is given below. It has an area of 18.68 sq. km (border length of 33 km). This Bangladeshi enclave is situated near the border in Cooch Behar, West Bengal. The agreement offers that Bangladesh retains Dahagram–Angarrapota enclave with no compensation of any additional area from it and India retains Berubari union in return.

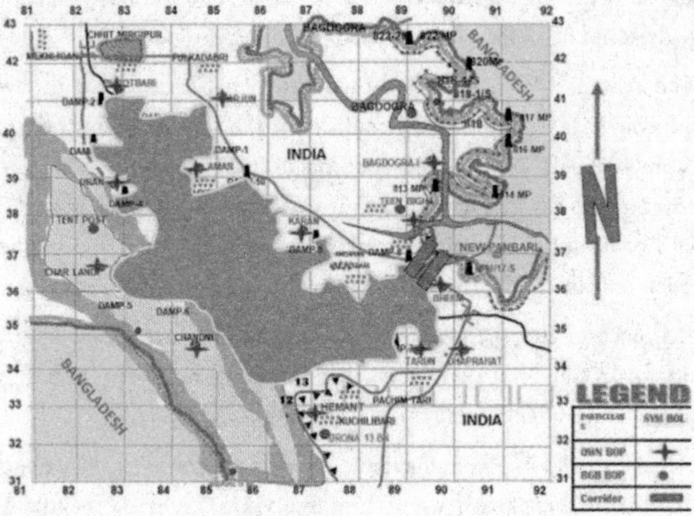

Figure 1.10: Dahagram-Angarpota enclave

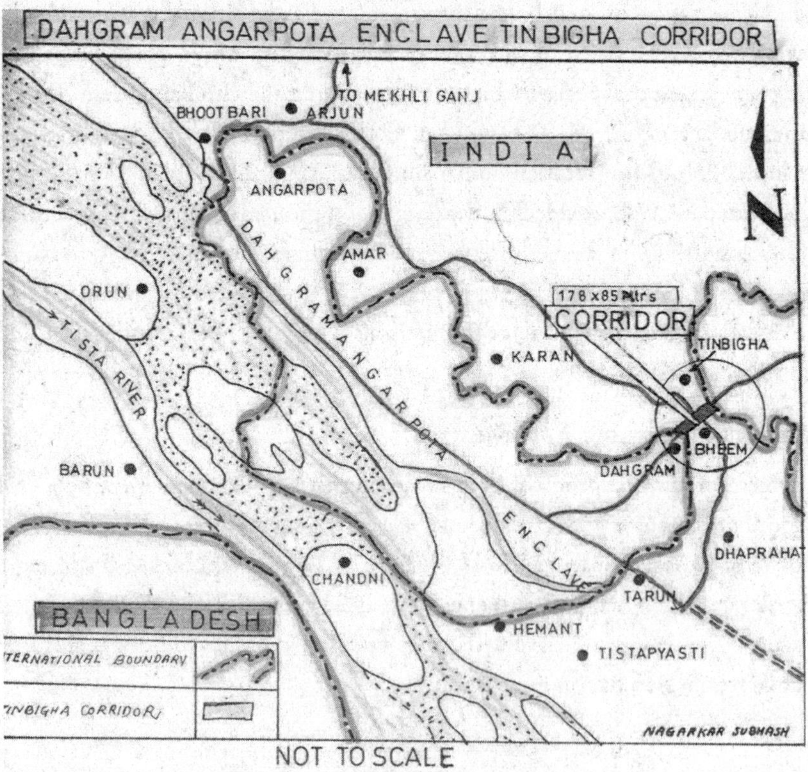

Figure 1.11: Tin Bigha corridor[26]

26. Image BSF Handbook, BSF Academy, Tekanpur.

The agreement on a corridor that connects this enclave to the Bangladesh mainland was arrived at in order to help Bangladesh carry out a proper administration of the enclave. On 7 October 1982, foreign ministers of India and Bangladesh signed an agreement to lease an area of size of three "Bighas"[27]. The corridor has been made and Bangladesh is given lease in perpetuity. Detailed lease and use modalities on the corridor is given in the 1982 agreement as is mentioned above. The prime minister of Bangladesh inaugurated the Teen Bigha corridor during her visit to the enclave in September 2011. 24 hours movement was allowed through this corridor from then on.

Adverse Possessions

There were several places along the Indo-Bangladesh border where the land falling on the Indian side of the demarcated IB i.e., de jure boundary was under Bangladesh occupation and vice-versa. Thus, adverse possession occurred when the de facto and de jure boundaries did not coincide. Land that lies between the de jure and de facto boundary was called adverse possession.

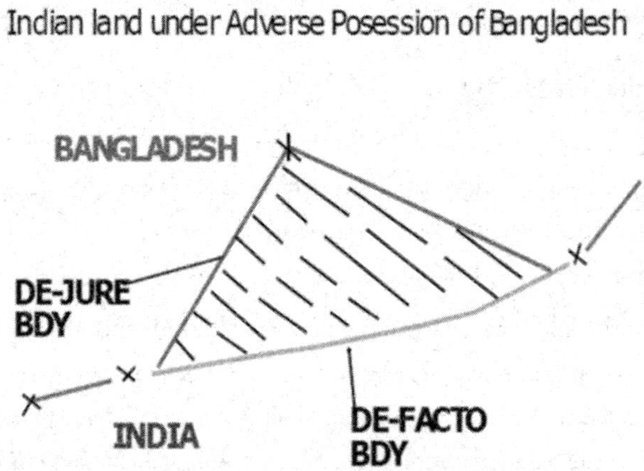

Figure 1.12: Indian land adverse possession of Bangladesh

The genesis of the problem of adverse possession lies in the fact that, Sir Radcliff's scalpel ran through villages, fields and even houses leaving farms divided and falling on either sides of the border. Thus, at numerous locations along the international border lands that belong to resident of one country would lie on the other side of the de jure boundary.

27. *Lexico Dictionaries* | English. (n.d.). *Bigha* | Meaning of Bigha by Lexico. https://www.lexico.com/en/definition/bigha

There were 42 places where Bangladesh land was under possession of Indian nationals and 35 places where the Indian land was under adverse possession of Bangladesh. The total size of, adversely possessed or held areas by India and Bangladesh were 3017.16 and 2587.25 acres, respectively as measured during the survey in 1996 as mentioned above.

The implementation of land boundary agreement with Bangladesh in July 2015 has finally put an end to these problems. Enclaves have been exchanged and merged with the country within whom they are located. Similarly, adverse possessions have also been retained by the residents of the country, who were cultivating such land and de jure boundary realigned accordingly.

Implementation of the agreement also has facilitated formal demarcation of boundary on ground thus resolving all contentious issues relating to borders with Bangladesh.

Appendix A gives details of enclaves and adverse possessions, the Land Boundary Agreement of 1974, the Protocol to 1974 agreement signed in 2011 and the Land Boundary Agreement signed in 2015.

New Moore Island Dispute

New Moore or South Talpatti island is located in the Bay of Bengal along the far side of the coastal region of the Ganges-Brahmaputra Delta and is a tiny uninhabited sandbar island. After the Bhola cyclone in 1970, the island surfaced in the Bay of Bengal and disappeared after a while.[28]

There were speculations that the island was rich in oil and natural gas and so both India and Bangladesh claimed sovereignty over the area even if there were no inhabitants or permanent settlers in the location. The dispute on the issue of sovereignty of this island is linked to the bigger dispute on maritime boundaries between the two countries, which is based on the Radcliffe Award methodology of settlement.

On 7 July 1947, the Permanent Court of Arbitration (PCA) declared arbitration on the Bay of Bengal maritime boundary between India and Bangladesh and resolved the matter. The Government of Bangladesh case file of October 2009 at the Permanent Court of Arbitration (PCA) was upgraded the status of settled. The PCA order went in favour of Bangladesh and was not open to appeal. Hence, 19,467 km^2 (7,516 sq mi)

---

28. Arnoldy, B. (2010). Global warming as peacemaker? Disputed island disappears under rising sea. *The Christian Science Monitor*. https://www.csmonitor.com/World/Asia-South-Central/2010/0324/Global-warming-as-peacemaker-Disputed-island-disappears-under-rising-sea

out of the total of 25,000 km^2 (9,700 sq mi) according to the PCA verdict was awarded to Bangladesh.[29]

Katchatheevu Island[30]

Katchatheevu is an uninhabited island and is under the administration of Sri Lanka. The island was disputed territory which India claimed was under it till 1976. Located between Neduntheevu in Sri Lanka and Rameswaram in India, fishermen from both the countries have traditionally been using the island area.

In the 14th century, a volcanic eruption gave birth to the island. India takes cognizance of Sri Lanka's ownership of the island in accordance with the 1974 conditional agreement. Both the countries had a role it the administration of the island under the British Raj. Legality of the ownership transfer was challenged at the Supreme Court of India as the Indian government did not ratify its recognition. The island is vital for fishermen from both the nation. According to the Indo-Sri Lankan agreement, Indian fishermen can fish in and around Katchatheevu and the island can be used for drying their nets. However, difficulties were faced due to Sri Lankan navy deployment in the area to prevent the rebel LTTE from smuggling weapons through the area. Furthermore, a Catholic shrine in the island attracts devotees from both the countries.

The Govt of india took a stand in the court that the dispute is settled as per agreement of 1974 after taking into consideration the historical and legal aspects. It took a stand that none of the territory belonging to India was ceded nor the sovereignity compromised.

Conclusion

Any further realignment of borders of India is subject to resolution of Jammu & Kashmir problem and Sir Creek issue with Pakistan and the border issues with China.

There are several complexities along the borders of India both in terms of terrain and prevailing operational environment. The borders lie across all type of terrain that include mountains, plains, deserts, riverine and jungles along with a variety of habitation and ethnic mix inhabiting along the boundary. Border residents share family relations with residents across i.e. on the other side of the borders. With the exception of states situated on the western frontiers, most of the border states are underdeveloped and

29. PTI (2014). Respect UN court award on maritime boundary with Bangladesh: India. *Zee News*. https://zeenews.india.com/news/nation/respect-un-court-award-on-maritime-boundary-with-bangladesh-india_946119.html
30. Arun Janardhanan (2014). Explained: An island marooned. *The Indian Express*. https://indianexpress.com/article/india/india-others/explained-an-island-marooned

experience physical isolation from the mainland. This isolation varies in degrees due to relatively poor communication and transport infrastructure. The North Eastern states vary culturally from the mainland or other parts of Indian union. The border population feels alienated because of slow economic development. Such conditions prevailing on borders with ethnic ties across fence makes these borders porous.

Complexity of managing Indo–Pakistan and Bangladesh borders further gets aggravated because of the mixed nature of border viz Line of Control (LoC), well demarcated or disputed borders. The strategy to manage a particular border therefore has to vary according to its nature. Some borders have therefore more militaristic management systems in place compared to others, which are soft borders.

Nature of problems and crimes on different borders also vary drastically. The problem of insurgency in J&K and attempts by Pakistan to facilitate infiltration of militants into India makes the LoC and IB in Jammu Sector one of the most live borders with daily exchange of heavy fire. Borders in Punjab, Rajasthan and Gujarat on the other hand are prone to smuggling of drugs. The borders in the East and North East are prone to cattle smuggling and other petty crimes. The border management practices adopted are therefore varied in nature.

CHAPTER TWO

Concept of Border Management and Evolution of Border Management in India

Border Management – The Concept

> The first boundary was traced on the ground by the first being that understood his position in face of his neighbours. From individual property it passed to the collective sovereignty, i.e. to the household, from the household to the city, from the city to the province, and from the province to the country. Everything has limits, lanes, fences, walls or some other designation that defines the characteristics of the material possessions, of some being, be that a man or a social entity.
>
> Castillos Goycochea[31]

History is replete with examples of walls and fortifications constructed on the frontier areas by states, big or small. Instances include the Great Wall of China in China, the Hadrian's Walls in Great Britain, the Willow Palisade in Mongolia, the Maginot Line and the Siegfried Line in France, the Berlin Wall in Germany, or the McNamara Line in Vietnam. The Great Wall of China,[32] the first physical linear boundary in Asia was constructed to "exclude what could not be included". Japanese Sakai or water parting were first employed as natural boundary in Japan. The peace treaties of Westphalia in 1648 harbingered the concept of modern nation-state.[33] The 1659 treaty of the Pyrenees in which France and Spain partook was the first boundary treaty on the basis of watershed principle ever recorded.[34] The word "Natural" was applied to give meaning to elements that brought in a natural region be it sociological, economic, linguistic, cultural or racial.

Commonly understood concept of territory is just about 300 years old. Before that the territory of a nation would be the land on which the governments could exercise their sovereignties.

31. Krukoski, W. (n.d.). *Frontiers and Boundaries.* (Translated by Jose A. Krukoski). Lncc.br. http://info.lncc.br/artigoi.html
32. History.com Editors (2010). Great Wall of China. *HISTORY.* https://www.history.com/topics/ancient-china/great-wall-of-china
33. Cavendish, R. (1998). The Treaty of Westphalia. History Today. *Historytoday.com.* https://www.historytoday.com/archive/months-past/treaty-westphalia
34. *Treaties United Nations.* (n.d.). Treaties and international agreements filed and recorded from 28 March 1979 to 8 August 1979 No. 838. https://treaties.un.org/doc/Publication/UNTS/Volume%201142/volume-1142-II-838-English.pdf

The limits of territory started being defined with landmarks (like the border pillars) constructed on ground only in the 18th Century after the treaties of Madrid and Saint Ildefonso divided the continent of South America,[35] into the Spanish domains and the Portuguese domains.

Borders can be linked to geographic boundaries of political entities or legal jurisdictions that include governments, sovereign states, federated states, and other subnational entities. Political or social entities can come to agreements to establish borders that authorizes control over the areas; these kind of agreements are known as boundary delimitation.[36]

Borders are formed in many ways:

(a) The countries concerned may agree to define the extent of their respective jurisdictions through formal treaties.

(b) The stronger country may impose the border on a weaker one.

(c) Third parties may impose the border, e.g.: an international organisation, etc.

(d) It may be inherited from a former state, colonial power or aristocratic territory or,

(e) It may be inherited from a former internal border, for example as was within the former Soviet Union.

Defined lines to demarcate borders were not a norm in the past. Claimed or disputed areas known as marchlands or buffer zones were intervened or fought for to claim ownership,[37] e.g., the Saudi Arabian–Iraqi neutral zone from 1922 to 1981 and similar declaration of Saudi–Kuwaiti neutral zone from 1922 until 1970.

Even in the present times, there are many borders which are not formally defined. Additionally, there could be a de facto military ceasefire line in many cases as is in the case of a number of portions in the borders of India and China and in the case of India and Pakistan on the border of J&K.

When borders follow a natural physical feature such as a river, mountain, etc. these are said to be natural borders and the other borders fall in the category of unnatural borders.

---

35. Encyclopedia ed., (n.d.). San Ildefonso, Treaty of (1777). *Encyclopedia.com*. https://www.encyclopedia.com/humanities/encyclopedias-almanacs-transcripts-and-maps/san-ildefonso-treaty-1777
36. Laine, J. and Kolosov, V. (2015). Introduction to Border Studies. *absborderlands, Far Eastern Federal University*. pp.14–61. https://absborderlands.org/wp-content/uploads/2013/04/Introduction-to-Border-Studies-2.pdf
37. *Sheppardsoftware.com*. (n.d.). World Statistics and Facts: Borders of the World. http://www.sheppardsoftware.com/worldgeographymainpage/worldstatistics3.htm

At international levels there are three distinct sets of borders namely the land borders, the maritime boundaries and the air space. The land border makes two neighbouring countries contagious, whereas the maritime boundaries separate two littoral states of a particular ocean while the air space has no defined boundaries.

Some borders are totally open for movement, whereas others are subject to different levels of control in regard to movement of persons, animals, goods and stores. The internal borders of states and sometimes among states – are open and unguarded like Schengen countries.[38] The borders of India with Nepal and Bhutan are similarly open for movement without requirement of any documents. Check posts and guard stations are generally put up to control and channelize movements across controlled borders.

The borders in modern times are generally, clearly defined and demarcated. Almost every country maintains some sort of border control laws or norms. Countries experiencing acute problems of illegal migration, infiltration, trans-border smuggling of contraband like drugs, weapons fake currency, etc. have put up permanent barriers like walls and fences and instituted formal border control procedures. On the other hand, some borders are totally indistinguishable from each other. Free movement is possible through such "porous" borders.

Before we go on to discuss the concept of Border Management, we must understand the difference amongst three terms, "Boundary," "Frontier" and "Border," which are often used interchangeably.

"Boundary" is the line of demarcation between two countries arrived at through a formal process as explained in subsequent paragraphs. Boundaries thus indicate the limits of legal and administrative jurisdiction of states and have international legal significance. Boundaries must be defended during war.

Boundaries determine the prospects of co-operation and discord between states. It would not be exaggeration, if we say that borders between two countries can "either be used to build bridges or create barriers between them". According to Lord Curzon, "frontiers are indeed the razor's edge on which hang suspended the modern issues of war and peace."[39] Fredrich Ratzel in 1896 said, "secured and developed borders are symbolic of national development, power and security."

Boundaries are measured as a framework of a nation. It is necessary and inevitable to have a frame to create a structure and so are boundary essential. Location of the

38. *European Commission*. (2013). Schengen Area. https://ec.europa.eu/home-affairs/what-we-do/policies/borders-and-visas/schengen_en
39. Lord Curzon of Kedleston D.C.L., LL.D., F.R.S. (1907) *The Romanes Lecture (1907) Frontiers, delivered in the Sheldonian Theatre, Oxford*. Clarendon Press, Oxford..

boundary regulates the rules and laws to be followed by the population, their culture and many other such things. Boundaries are termed good or bad depending upon whether there is dispute between states located on both sides of the boundary. The boundaries are important to people of all professions and walks of life. Historians study it to analyse causes of past disputes. Geography being an important factor for determining boundaries, the geographers get interested in them. Politicians, bureaucrats and lawyers are involved as boundaries determine political, administrative and legal jurisdiction.

Old historic notifications, agreements, revenue records, traditional rights of group, etc., are considered while deciding boundary, besides the strategic consideration of strengthening security of countries that are involved. These principle were not considered while partitioning India. Other considerations in the boundary making include leaving similar ethnic groupings on one side, ensuring viability of economies of the countries on either side, aligning it along a well-defined geographical feature to facilitate easy identification and elimination of possibilities of conflicts at the later stage. Historic considerations like claims to territory by either side based on the historical facts are another consideration. Thus, eliminating chances of conflict to a great extent.

The above factors contribute majorly in deciding the boundaries, which is carried out diplomatically through mutual dialogue, signing of treaties, etc. Arbitration by international bodies as happened in case of Kutch award is another method used to decide the boundaries.

"Border" designates the area inwards from that of the boundary. The depth of the border differs on the basis of the area's terrain and geopolitical location. In general, a border area's administrative infrastructure is not different from the rest of the country. Keeping guard of the border during peacetime is a prime responsibility of respective border guarding force of a country.

"Frontier" is a loosely defined term. The basic difference between Border and Frontier is that while the border is normally under full control of the civil administration, the frontier is generally a troubled area along the boundary, where the writ of the government has often to be enforced by force of arms. The classic examples in the pre-independent India were the North West Frontier Province (NWFP) and the North East Frontiers Area (NEFA). Area alongside Indo-Myanmar Border where the boundary in spite of being demarcated, holds little sanctity for the tribal people and they can move across borders freely, falls in same category. This free movement across the boundary has, in fact, been given legal sanction by permitting the tribals to move up-to 16 Kms inside the Indian borders on the Indo-Myanmar borders. As per the demand of the situation, the writ of a government is usually enforced by border guarding forces and armed forces of a country.

In short, the boundary is to be defended in the time of war and the border is to be patrolled during peacetime in order to ward off illegal immigration, control smuggling, control trafficking, etc. Consolidation of frontier is required along with the evolvement of appropriate socio–economic and political policies.

Friedrich Ratzel in *Political Geography*[40] (*Politische Geographie*) in 1897 introduced the concept of lebensraum (living space), which considered an empire or a state as a living organism that has internal organs, protective boundaries at the external with an inherent drive for expansion. For Ratzel, borders were insignificant. An advancing, developing, and thus successful and dominant, state had to continuously seek to enlarge its life-space through annexation of territories controlled by adjoining, less powerful states. Ratzel rejected the static concept of borders. His conception of a border was thus not a fixed rigidly defined boundary-line, but rather a zone of transition and a peripheral organ.[41]

National borders have now become more or less permanent. However, boundary disputes keep arising and are one of the most contentious issues facing the world, especially the developing countries.

Therefore, it is to be reiterated that boundaries designate the line of physical contact between states and are frameworks of nations which are also important cause of discord and co-operation.

Types of Boundary

Two types of boundaries can be identified according to their legal status:

(a) *De Jure Boundary:* It is the legal boundary, decided and ratified by the involved national governments and demarcated by numbered pillars. In some cases it may be difficult to demarcate the boundary for example, the terrain configuration being such, it is difficult to demarcate large portions of boundary between China and Nepal, and China and Bhutan.

(b) *De Facto Boundary:* It is the alignment on ground decided by two opposing force commanders, delineated on maps and signed by both as token of acceptance.

---

40. Farinelli, F. (2000). Friedrich Ratzel and the nature of (political) geography. *Political Geography, 19*(8), pp. 943–955. https://www.sciencedirect.com/science/article/pii/S0962629800000366
41. Abrahamsson, C. (2013). On the genealogy of Lebensraum. Research Gate. https://www.researchgate.net/publication/274054319_On_the_genealogy_of_Lebensraum

Being purely a working arrangement to maintain peace, it does not commit any party to de jure claim. It is also called "working Boundary". LoC along PoK in J&K and LAC with China are examples of such boundary.

Both the de jure or de facto boundary can be:

(c) *Fixed Boundary:* Alignment is defined by permanent landmarks like erecting pillars on ground.

(d) *Seasonal Boundary:* Alignment is defined by erecting temporary pillars, which need to be demarcated regularly (e.g.: Murshidabad/Rajshahi Sector on Indo-Bangladesh border following general alignment of river Padma) until signing of the Indo Bangladesh Border Agreement in 2015.

The boundaries can also be defined based on whether or not they are aligned to a natural geographical feature.

(e) *Natural Boundary:* The term denotes such boundaries which follow natural geographical divides without cutting through concentration of people having similarity in religion, language or social customs and does not disturb the administrative or communication set up of the region.

(f) *Unnatural Boundary:* A boundary is unnatural, if it does not follow well-defined geographical divides and cuts through ethnic groups and thereby affecting the administrative or communication set up of a region.

Demarcation of Boundary

After boundary has been decided, the next step is to identify its exact position on the ground. The process of locating and marking of the boundaries can technically be complex and legally contentious. The entire process, finally, leading to demarcation of the boundary on ground goes through following steps

(a) The first step is listing of territories into those belonging to one side and those to the other side, i.e. allocation of territories. This process also is referred as determination. The process involves identifying the co-ordinates of different places/landmarks through, which the boundary line will pass. A list of these co-ordinates is exchanged by the countries involved.

(b) The second step involves the description of alignment of the boundary in a narrative form. This is necessary to remove any ambiguity and to resolve any disagreements at a later stage. This is specially resorted to when the boundary is decided through arbitration or by an appointed commission to resolve disputes.

The process is called "Delimitation". The credit for inventing this word goes to Lord McMahon.[42]

(c) The third step is to mark the line, of the defined boundary, on the map. This is called "Delineation". The process is preferably done on large scale maps, so that there is no ambiguity in its interpretation at the time of final demarcation.

(d) The fourth step in the boundary making is "Ratification" i.e., formal approval or sanction of the mutually agreed delineated boundary by the governments involved. In the case of India, the ratification is done by Parliament.

(e) The fifth step involves "signing" of the boundary agreement by the plenipotentiaries (authorised signatories) on behalf of respective sovereign Heads of state.

(f) At the sixth stage, the actual task of "Demarcation" of boundary on the ground starts. This is done by locating ground markers along the alignment identified after a joint survey and identification of the co-ordinates described in the process of delimitation and delineation. The ground markers so constructed are called Border Pillars. These pillars may be of different shapes and sizes agreed to by the respective countries.

(g) After the boundary has been demarcated by construction of pillars, the survey authorities of the countries that are involved have to conduct another joint survey in order to ascertain the correctness of the location of the pillars. After verification of correctness, the international boundary is considered to have been finally accepted by the two countries.

Function of Boundary Line

(a) The boundaries represent the extreme territorial jurisdiction of a country and separate it from the neighbouring country. Sovereignty of one country ends at the boundary and that of the other starts. The nations have full rights to exploit the natural and economic resources lying on their side of the boundary. People

---

42. The distinction between "delimitation" and "demarcation" is all-important in the discussion of boundary questions. It was first drawn in 1897 by Sir Henry McMahon, who later put it in these words: "The laying down of boundaries comprises two distinct and important stages, 'Delimitation' and 'Demarcation' ... 'Delimitation' I have taken to comprise the determination of a boundary line by treaty or otherwise, and its definition in written verbal terms; 'Demarcation' to comprise the actual laying down of a boundary line on the ground, and its definition by boundary pillars or other similar physical means." (Sir McMahon, Henry's inaugural Address as the President-Elect to the Royal Society of Arts, 1935. *JRCS*, Vol. LXXXIV) Gupta, K. (1971). The McMahon Line 1911–45: The British Legacy. *The China Quarterly*, 47, 521-545. doi:10.1017/S0305741000006214

of that nation also have the freedom to move right up to the extreme edge of the border i.e., the boundary line.

(b) The boundary generally restricts free movement of the population across the countries. Movement across the boundary is regulated by international bilateral regulations, which may involve obtaining passport, visa, etc. Some countries do not impose any such restrictions on the movements of their citizens.

(c) Any infringement of boundary line is a violation against the sovereignty of the country. The infringements may be in the shape of physical occupation of land belonging to the neighbouring country or, intrusion or, illegal entry of the nationals of one country into other. These violations may involve the security force personnel or the border community or border criminals. Violations of the boundary, whether major or minor lead to several border problems and disputes leading to difficulties in proper management of borders during peacetime. Further, if the violations are not controlled or if they are state sponsored by a neighbour who is an adversary, they may lead to a full-fledged war.

Border Management

Border Management is a recent concept, scope of which is much wider than simple border guarding. Its ambit includes the function of creating security measures for border population through prevention of crime, ensuring infrastructure development in border areas and bring improvement in the quality of life. It also includes providing employment opportunities to border residents. The larger aim of effective border management thus is to ensure social, cultural and economic integration of population of remote border areas with that of hinterland.

In 1999, the Kargil Review Committee (KRC) was set up by the Government of India. It concluded that transgressors or criminals have a tendency to look for gaps on land, whether it be along the coast or from air. Incidents such as the Purulia incident of 1995,[43] Kargil episode of 1999 and Mumbai attacks of 2008[44] have demonstrated our vulnerability from the air, land as well as sea. Hence, adopting a holistic approach to border management is vital. The review committee recommends a wide interpretation

43. *Times of India* (2011). Purulia Expose: India's best kept secret. https://timesofindia.indiatimes.com/india/Purulia-Expose-Indias-best-kept-secret/articleshow/8106795.cms

44. ET Online (2019). *Revisiting the night of Mumbai terror attack: When 10 Pak terrorists attacked India's financial capital. The Economic Times*. https://economictimes.indiatimes.com/news/defence/revisiting-the-night-of-mumbai-terror-attack-when-10-pak-terrorists-attacked-indias-financial-capital/articleshow/72235424.cms

of the idea of border management and that it is accomplished through coordination amongst leadership at the political level, the administrative level,, taking up diplomatic measures, enhancing cooperation amongst agencies that include the legal, intelligence, security, regulatory and economic factors.

In "the words of Gerald H. Blake,[45] the world's 315 or so land boundaries display a huge variety of characteristics, and approaches to boundary management are similarly diverse. It is impossible to prescribe in detail how boundaries must be managed, but it is possible to identify some emerging principles of good management. Surprisingly, little systematic thought has been given to boundary management in the past. Some management related aspects such as boundary delimitation and demarcation have been well documented and scientifically implemented. Boundary demarcation is not the end of the process however, but the beginning and subsequent quality of boundary management can fundamentally affect relations between states and the welfare of border population on either side. Bearing in mind that many of the world's boundaries were superimposed by imperial powers, it is not surprising that many boundaries are inherently difficult to manage".

In political geography, there is no agreed definition of the term Border Management. Till recently management of land borders implied to most of us, a need to ensure their sanctity against military aggression and early settlement of our border issues, which again for a common man meant territorial issues. It is only recently that our concepts and attitudes towards the management of our borders in general and land borders in particular have undergone a radical change. The Kargil, conflict has forced us to interpret the term management of our land borders in its widest sense to employ co-ordination between various segments of the government machinery. After Kargil War, the KRC remarked on the complexities of border management in recent years and therefore, a detailed study on it is the need of the hour so that the evolving contours of the force structure and procedures in it are recognised and its improvement is ensured. In doing so, it can bring a speedy reduction in the inflow of illegal migrant, arms, narcotics and terrorist.

Post Kargil War, a Group of Ministers (GoM) Committee was set up to suggest reforms to the National security system. It mainly focused at concerns of border management. The report states that border management be carried out broadly through the use of co-ordination and intensive action via political leadership, execution of administrative activities, diplomatic means, security measures, intelligence activities,

45. Blake, G. (1998). The Objective of Land Boundary Management. *Durham University*. https://www.dur.ac.uk/ibru/publications/download/?id=137

regulations or economic agencies in the country to safeguard its frontiers and to subserve the country's best interest. Therefore, border management can pose a major challenge. Border management, at the strategic level is thus tasked to integrate border lands and border people with mainland and mainland people through diverse projects and programmes to be undertaken individually and jointly by civil and military/border guarding authorities. The guiding principle is to seek sustainable development of the sensitive border regions. In tangible terms, this is to say that it is to achieve socio-economic prosperity and emotional integration of the border inhabitation which is vital to consolidation of security interest of the nation. As such, an integrated and holistic approach is needed for the multi-dimensional development and progress of these areas and people, which, in turn, becomes important for their active involvement in national security issues and plans. As such, border management is an all-encompassing programme oriented towards the formulation of nation's policy for keeping its borders vibrantly secured.

According to Gerald H. Blake's *The Objective of land Boundary Management* the national foreign policy objectives primarily determines the objectives of the boundary management strategy. The boundary could be instrumental to foreign policy, predominantly if the neighbours have poor relations. Good boundary management is planned to help realize: (a) International peace, (b) Security at the local and the national levels, (c) Prosperous borderland, and (d) Effective local government.

Blake further goes on to state that the boundary management begins with a clear legal framework, which describes the alignment clearly. He states that different aspects of boundary management include - (a) Access management, (b) Security management, (c) Environment management, (d) Trans boundary resource management, and (d) Crisis management, which is: (i) at the national level by not allowing the incidents along the borders to escalate, and (ii) on prompt settlement of local problems like straying of animals, etc.

Prakash Singh,[46] former Director General of the Border Security Force identifies border management to be a fluid concept that is to mean that the efficacy of border security management is linked and as such depends on the political, economic ties, ethnic and religious relations amongst the border population on both the sides of the borders. However, border management indicates a wide-ranging spectrum that includes:

(a) To guard the borders during peacetime.

(b) To defend the borders during war time.

---

46. Singh, P. (2001). Border management. *BSF Journal*, *1*(1), pp. 11–23.

(c) To ensure restrictions of unauthorized movements of men.

(d) To take steps that eliminates smugglings of narcotics, arms, ammunitions, explosives, and other contraband items.

(e) The use of advance technology and devices to complement human effort.

(f) Coordinating the intelligence inputs from various agencies.

(g) Promoting welfare of the border population.

The above explanation of the term Border Management is particularly relevant for the agencies guarding the borders.

In modern times, border management has acquired even wider meaning and explanation, the above becomes complete if we include the aspect of interaction of the counterpart border guarding forces with each other to resolve local disputes and problems of the border population. This is important for maintaining peace and will also facilitate better coordination for resolving problems like repatriation of border people erroneously straying into the territory of other country and retrieval of strayed cattle, etc.

The scope has further widened with increasing realisation of enhancing trans-border cooperation and thus, also extends to include cooperation amongst trans-border and intra-border agencies like customs, immigration authorities, etc. to facilitate trans-border movement of persons and goods.

Border Management Vs Border Security

Border Management as discussed above has a wider canvas in terms of areas of interest, engagement and action. Forces of globalization, mass-media revolution and technological development in various fields have had a lot of impact on the border management framework. The agencies involved need comprehensive planning and coordination in order to achieve peace and progress in the border areas. Thus, border management is inclusive of border security.

Border security and border management are mutually re-enforcing and interdependent. Peacetime apparatus on borders includes border security and is significant for the physical security of boundary line, borders and border population. By preventing trans- border crimes and other dangerous activities of opposing border guarding forces or civilian population, it strengthens and instills sense of security amongst own people on the border and its prime objective boils down to accomplishing security of population living in the border area.

Border management is not a single agency work, but is function of the collective effort of the forces that guard the borders, the people who live in the area, and the other security agencies of the government including the local police and the state administration both from the state and the centre. Border security is crucial to any viable management plan on the borders, both at the macro and micro level

The Rise of the Border Guarding Forces in India

After India's independence, India adopted policy of peaceful settlement of border related issues. India continues to maintain friendship, peace and wants boundary agreements with its neighbours. However it has maintained its physical presence on its borders. To begin with, the state police forces were entrusted the responsibility to guard the borders.

India after its conflict with China worked on improving and revitalising preparedness of the defence of the country and therefore, worked on strengthening its borders. The Chinese conflict brought into sharp focus the necessity of guarding against the Politico – strategic threat that China posed and need to take preventive measures. The conflict forced the Indian national security apparatus to work on a dispassionate assessment of larger national obligations and perspectives.

In 1954, with the signing of the Sino-Indian trade agreement came the Indo-Tibetan Border Police (ITBP), which was given the responsibility of providing security to check posts situated at the Indo-Tibetan border. After the 1962 India-China war, expansion of the force was carried out to enable it to work as a guerrilla force. The responsibility of guarding the borders with China at the borders in its North-Western and Central sectors was entrusted to it.

Up to 1965, the responsibility of guarding India's borders along with Pakistan was under the State Armed police. Need to deploy a regular border guarding force specifically for peace time border guarding was felt after April 1965 misadventure by Pakistan in the Kutch area.[47]

The first Director-General of the Border Security Force (BSF) Shri K. F. Rustamji on the birth of the force states that in April 1965 Pakistan made a deliberate and calculated move and made an incursion in the Indian territory in the Kanjrakot area in the Rann of Kutch after which, Lal Bahadur Shastri, the then Prime Minister of India called for a detailed review on the security arrangements of the borders with Pakistan and raise a centrally controlled force.. The Chief of the Army Staff Gen J. N. Choudhary and

47. Nayyar, S. (2018). Brief history of how India's BSF was born after CRPF defeated Pakistan's soldiers. *Dailyo.in*. https://www.dailyo.in/voices/crpf-pakistan-army-bsf-border-security-force-1965-india-pakistan-war/story/1/23129.html

K. F. Rustamji, IP worked closely and diligently to raise the BSF. General Choudhary, expressed great concern after the Pakistani aggression. As reproduced in Operational Manual of BSF, General Choudhary wrote, "The recent happenings along the Kutch-Pakistan border and in fact, continuous incidents along the Sino-Indo-Pak border as a whole, bring into prominence the whole question of how such a border should be looked after, in peace, in Cold War and when threat of Cold War hots up." Thus, BSF came to be raised and deployed along the International Border (IB) with Pakistan (Now Pakistan on the west and Bangladesh on the East). Some units of newly raised force were also deployed along LoC in Kashmir.

Necessity of raising a specialized force for border guarding arose because the State Armed Police Forces were unable to provide the standard of security expected of them during the Indo-Pakistani War of 1965. Major deficiencies noted are listed below:

(a) *Resources:* The states did not have adequate number of units to provide the desired standard of security. Even the units deployed on the border were often thinned out for dealing with the law and order situations. The states also lacked resources in terms of equipping these units to the desired level.

(b) *Training:* The State Armed Police Forces were basically designed to handle the law and order situation and their training was oriented accordingly. The duties on the border required greater element of militarisation essential to enable them to handle minor skirmishes along the borders and to supplement the war efforts of defence forces in case where it is required. The states did not have the wherewithal to train them in this manner.

(c) *Uniformity*: The State Armed Police Forces of different states differed in their organisation, equipment, and training methodology. Therefore, they could not be expected to function in a uniform manner which was particularly important when operating to assist the war efforts of defence forces. The aspect of uniformity in dealing with the counterpart was also an important consideration for raising a centrally controlled force.

(d) *Integration:* Lack of uniformity and integration of different State Forces deployed along the border had obvious disadvantages as discussed above. It was therefore essential to integrate all the forces responsible for guarding the borders at that time into a single centrally controlled force.

The above factors coupled with the effects of developmental activities and associated social changes contributed to strategists focusing on improving security environment along the borders of the country. The need for effective border guarding coupled with requirement of proper integration with the Defence forces in war effort compelled the planners to conceive of a centrally controlled professional force, organized, equipped and trained, accordingly.

With this backdrop the government of India constituted a study group to go over various aspects of guarding borders. The study group recommended formation of a border police force at national level to take responsibility of guarding the borders of India with Pakistan and, thus, was born the BSF.

Raised on 1 December 1965, the BSF was deployed along the Indo-Pakistan Borders (Now Indo-Pakistan on the west and Indo-Bangladesh on the east). Few units of the force were also deployed along the LoC in the state of Jammu and Kashmir under the operational control of the Army.

Till about the late 1980s, border guarding mostly relied on human effort. The deployment of troops on the ground was also thin because of a limited number of units. The militancy in Punjab and Kashmir in the 1980s and 1990s compelled the planners to rethink the strategy for guarding the borders specifically in the context of the Indo-Pakistani borders because the militants were getting the monetary support and arms ammunition from Pakistan. Limited number of units and absence of any technological assistance were making the task of border guarding and preventing infiltration very difficult.

A three-pronged strategy was adopted to tackle the problem. Firstly, many more units of BSF were raised in order to increase the troop density. Secondly, modern technological devices were inducted to assist the troops in observation and detection of infiltrators. And, thirdly, a decision was taken to fence the borders with Pakistan to prevent and/or channelise militants/infiltrators. The fence proved to be very effective in cutting of the channels of weapons and finances to the militant organization from Pakistan. The fence was slowly extended to cover the entire western borders and later along the Borders with Bangladesh. The fence is being continuously strengthened with measures like flood lighting, installing early warning devices and also equipping the troops with better surveillance devices.

Next major overhaul of border management strategies took place after the Kargil conflict. Review of the security situation along the borders once again brought into focus the importance of proper coordination of border management efforts amongst different agencies. It was realised that border management cannot be a single agency function. All the stakeholders had to work in coordination with each other to ensure the well-being of the population in the border area.

The "Group of Ministers"[48] set up after Kargil War made several important recommendations to improve management of borders of India.

One recommendation was related to the need to set up a department of border management within the MHA. The department sought to take the responsibility for coordination of any activity related to the borders. In 2006, a land ports authority came up with the objective to build land ports on India's borders that would ensure secure, seamless and efficient systems for cargo and movement of passengers, to decrease dwell time and costs of trade transaction, to endorse regional trade and people-to-people contact and aim to incorporate the best international practices.

One important recommendation was "One Border One Force" which entailed that the responsibility of guarding different borders be entrusted to different forces. Thus, while BSF was responsible for Indo-Pakistan and Indo-Bangladesh Borders, ITBP for India-China border, they recommended raising new forces for guarding Indo-Nepal, Indo-Bhutan and Indo-Myanmar borders.

Thus in June 2001, the "Special Service Bureau" which was raised in 1963 in the aftermath of the India-China War, with the aim of achieving "Total security preparedness" in the far-flung border areas for carrying out a "stay-behind" role during war time was transformed into a border guarding force and was given the role of guarding the Indo-Nepal and the Indo-Bhutan borders. The force was given the name - Shashastra Seema Bal (SSB).[49] Similarly, the responsibility of guarding the Indo-Myanmar border was entrusted to Assam Rifles.

The Recommendations also introduced the concept of "Lead Intelligence Agency" which implied entrusting the responsibility of coordinating efforts of different Intelligence agencies to the respective border guarding forces for respective borders under their responsibility.

The committee placed a lot of emphasis on developing infrastructure in border area, keeping the importance of ensuring wellbeing and necessity of integrating border population with rest of the country. Lot of emphasis was therefore placed on implementation of "Border Area Development Programme (BADP)"[50] which aimed at the development of infrastructure and enhancing employment opportunities in the

48. *Kargil Review Committee* (2000). From surprise to reckoning: The Kargil Review Committee report. New Delhi: Sage Publications.
49. SSB (2019). Sashastra Seema Bal, Ministry of Home Affairs, Govt. of India. *Ssb.nic.in*. https://ssb.nic.in
50. Department of Border Management, Ministry of Home Affairs (2015). *Border Area Development Programme (BADP): Modified Guidelines*. https://badp.mha.gov.in/sites/default/files/Guidelines_badp.pdf

border areas. The committee also recommended greater involvement of the Border Guarding Forces in the planning and implementation of this programme.

Thus, the scope of border management has become wider and now includes several stakeholders towards achieving a singular aim of integration of the border and the border population in the mainstream.

In this book, we shall restrict our discussion to the various aspects of border management along the Indo-Pakistani and Indo-Bangladesh borders.

Border Guarding

India's border guarding systems along the border with Pakistan are militaristic in nature and designed to work as barriers. Along the Line of Control (LC) regular Army is deployed in classic defensive role on Forward Defended Localities (FDLs). BSF is deployed under the Army operational control. The militaristic methodology is necessitated because the infiltrators equipped with lethal weapons are actively aided by Pakistani forces with cover fire. The infiltrators themselves react aggressively on being intercepted. The contact between counterparts is extremely limited.

On the international borders in Jammu, Punjab, Rajasthan, and Gujarat the BSF operates by establishing the "Border Out Posts (BOP)" for conducting border domination operations. Normal border guarding operations like Patrolling and deployment of observation posts is carried out during the day time, besides Patrolling and ambushes during the night. "Kissan guards" are deployed in area ahead of the fence for surveillance and protection of farmers working in their fields.

Figure 2.1: A Kissan Guard in Operation

BSF also carries out certain special operations to dominate the area ahead of the fence especially, at night to prevent trans-border criminals and infiltrators from contacting and breaching the fence. The smugglers at times adopt methodology of conceal and clear that involves hiding the contraband in area ahead of the fence to be cleared by their accomplices and brought to own side by hiding it in their tractors, bullock carts and other implements. Frequent search operations are carried out by BSF to prevent this from happening. Implements and personnel are also searched thoroughly at the fence gates when going out or coming, in order to prevent contraband from crossing over.

Earlier it was difficult to search women folk going across the fence gate for work. However, with the induction of women constabulary in BSF, this problem has been resolved to a great extent. Proper gate management during the day time is crucial for ensuring that contraband does not crossover to own side of the fence. This also is important for maintaining cordial relations with the border population.

Figure 2.2: Troops regulating entry and exit from Fence Gates

The riverine border in Sir Creek area south of Gujarat is dominated by Water wing of BSF which has evolved its own drills for dominating the border.

General nature of border guarding along Bangladesh border is similar to that on west however, these are less militaristic due to friendly relations with Bangladesh and high density of population residing very close to borders.

The riverine borders in the Bay of Bengal, Brahmaputra river and other smaller riverine area are dominated by the Water wing in the same manner as in Sir Creek on the West.

Figure 2.3: Troops dominating Riverine border with Patrol Boat

Cattle smuggling is a major crime on the Indo-Bangladesh borders and is a cause of many causalities on the borders, often leading to diplomatic furore. In view of this, the BSF has adopted a "less lethal strategy" on these borders which implies the use of less lethal weapons like Pump Action Guns (PAG), Stun Grenades, Chilly Grenades, etc. This has gone a long way in reducing the causalities and ensuring better relations with counterpart.[51]

Border Guarding – Legal Provision

The BSF while performing its role of preventing border crimes has to operate as per the procedures laid down by the Law. Section 139 of the BSF Act 1968 provides for conferment of powers and duties on the members of BSF under various Central and State Acts. These legal powers have been conferred under various Acts by way of several notifications issued by the central and State Governments. The powers are mainly confined to the arrest, search and seizure and as such these are justiciable and to be exercised judiciously.

The powers conferred include Police powers under *Criminal Procedure Code (CrPC) 1974* for search and seizure in specified areas. These powers can be exercised in the entire states of Manipur, Tripura, Meghalaya, Mizoram, and Nagaland and area within the belt of 80 kilometres from the borders in the state of Gujarat, 50 kilometres

51. Singh, A. (20 July 2019). Non-lethal strategy effective but smugglers emboldened on India-Bangladesh border. *Uniindia News Service*. http://www.uniindia.com/non-lethal-strategy-effective-but-smugglers-emboldened-on-india-bangladesh-border/east/news/1671834.html

from the borders in the state of Rajasthan and 15 kilometres from the borders in the states of Punjab, West Bengal and Assam.

Such Police powers with consent of the Union Territory (UT) Government are also conferred on members of the BSF for the entire UT of J&K under the *Jammu and Kashmir Code of Criminal Procedure 1989*.

Various Powers under the *Customs Act, 1962* have been conferred on members of Force according to their rank – viz. Commandant and below, Subordinate officers and Under Officers. Some of the powers under Section 105 and 108 of the Customs Act can be exercised by BSF officers only when Customs officer of the rank of Superintendent or above are not posted.

Powers have also been conferred under the *Passport Act, 1967* under Section 4 of the act. These powers can be exercised within the local limits as applicable (given above) for exercise of police powers.

Under provisions of Section 37 of the *Narcotics drugs and Psychotropic Substances Act, 1985,* BSF personnel are empowered to arrest persons within the prescribed limits as applicable (given above) for exercise of police powers.

Miscellaneous other powers have also been conferred on the members of the BSF under the provisions of different state acts.

Inculcating Sense of Security Amongst Border Population

Relations with Border Community

The border community is the most important stakeholder on the borders. All other stakeholders owe their existence to border population and have to work towards their welfare and integration with the mainstream.

The BSF being deployed on remote borders is the sole visible representative of the government for the people of the border area, whom they can approach in times of need. Expectation that they can depend on the BSF for help is therefore natural. The BSF has been trying to live up-to the expectations through its deeds during normal times and also, during times of natural calamities like floods, earthquakes, etc. However, the scope for improvement always remains.

The reason for adversarial relations can be traced to the very nature of tasks carried out by the BSF. Efforts to prevent trans-border crimes and smuggling, often brings the BSF into conflict with the border population, many of whom get involved in trans-border crimes in the absence of any meaningful economic activity or employment opportunities in the border area. Smuggling is a way of life in many bordering villages, especially on the

Eastern Borders. Interventions by the BSF to control these crimes are looked upon as a deliberate disturbance in the means of livelihood for the local population.

It is therefore vital for the BSF to institutionalise targeted programmes to secure the trust of the population in the border area. This should be seen as a command function and must consider public attitude and public perception. BSF should detect problems to formulate policies and programmes of action to gain the goodwill, understanding and also, acceptance of the border community.

The BSF community relationship involves honest efforts by four major players i.e. the BSF, the local community, the state administration and the central Government in their respective areas for deeper understanding and mutual benefit. The community can vitally assist as force multiplier in replacing border management.

Relations with the border community will further improve, if the government is able to wean away the population from smuggling and other border crimes. This can happen through developing infrastructure in the border area, providing avenues for employment locally and equipping them with adequate skills to take up employment.

At its own level, the BSF also needs to take certain steps to obviate the feeling of distrust amongst the border population. This can be achieved through small effort like ensuring that the troops are aware of the local language and culture of the people. Better communication thus facilitated will earn a lot of goodwill and trust for BSF.

Further, there is a need for attitudinal change amongst the BSF personnel who tend to treat all the border residents as criminals. This hinders contact with local population and prevents mutual trust from developing. This also prevents the flow of information related to crimes.

Thirdly, the fence, although has proved a formidable obstacle, also has a negative impact on the relations with the border population because of restrictions imposed on their movement across the fence. BSF should try and ease these restrictions in consultation with the population without compromising with the security.

Another major step that BSF needs to take in order to improve relations with border population is to dispense with the statistical approach to measure success of operations. The current system obstructs the vision and brings forth competition wherein, public support is sought to make catches which otherwise should be employed to curtail the menace. This should be pivotal in turning the orientating of BSF towards the community.

Good relations with the public can foster, strengthen and enhance efficiency of the organisation and with enhanced efficiency; the BSF will be in position to fulfill its duties in a more professional manner and show better results.

The locals are even now being gainfully utilised in assisting on following border management functions, especially on the Eastern Borders. This is done by way of forming the Village Defence Committees (VDCs), which is to:

(a) Report any illegal activities and infiltration along the border.

(b) Keep the allotted areas under surveillance.

(c) Report any abnormal activity especially in rugged terrain.

(d) Report any subversive activity being carried out by the enemy.

(e) The local population could also employed the construction of roads, tracks and border fencing maintenance. Thus, providing them with avenues for income. Besides, during both peace and hostilities, local population can provide vital information regarding the enemy build-up and activities that happen close to the border areas.

(f) Watch groups amongst fishermen in the riverine areas can be formed. These groups in their normal course of earning a livelihood venture out to the sea up to quite a distance. Also, their other routine activity of maintenance of boats, nets and drying of the catch is carried out on the seashore. These fishermen once suitably motivated and imparted certain basic training could well turn out to be the eyes and ears of agencies monitoring the maritime boundaries. This would help overcome large gaps that exist in the surveillance cover. They would also require training, motivation. Incentives must be provided to them too for taking part in supporting the force in the mission of border management. Once this is done, they will prove useful tool to manage localized border problems.

(g) Provide local guides to the Armed Forces whenever essential.
(*For details, see: https://idsa.in/)

The BSF conducts frequent awareness programs to familiarise the border population about its tasks, duties, capabilities and constraints. This helps the force become friends of the border population. BSF must however guard against becoming unduly familiar with them. This aspect must be covered adequately in training of the BSF personnel i.e. the bordermen.

The BSF units before being inducted in an area undergo pre-induction training, wherein every borderman learns about the topography, local language, customs and social aspects besides the modus operandi of the anti-national elements and border criminals, to a reasonable standard of satisfaction before operational deployment.

Sensitivity is created on such issues from constables to officers, to ensure proper and humane responses.

Prolonged stay at one location has to be looked at rationally and a balance created so that the troops and leaders are able to maintain sustained good relations with the border population and at the same time obviating any scope of undue familiarity leading to connivance.

It is also essential for the BSF to maintain good relations with the local administration, the Police and other agencies so that minor irritants are resolved. This will also support these agencies to create an understanding on the capabilities as well as the constraints of the BSF thus facilitating a congenial working atmosphere. The role of "Lead Intelligence Agency" assigned to BSF for the Indo-Pakistan and the Indo-Bangladesh Border will further enhance the cooperation amongst agencies.

The presence of BSF in remote areas can gainfully be used to channel genuine problems of the local population and also compile their demands for onward submission. Also, the BSF can identify goals for community-oriented programmes, identification and development of projects, developing a permanent communication leading to a better understanding, to help win better trust of the public, to encourage co-operation from the public and to encourage better understanding with the public regarding the problems that the force faces and to work on mitigating their problems.

At the functional level, it helps develop civic action programmes and provide support for population control measures. Civic action is dynamic by nature and a continuous process, it aims to fulfill the local needs and aspiration. Both short-term and long-term projects are undertaken under this programme in consultation with local population and state government. Funds for civic action programme are generally allocated directly to the BSF.

Population control measures in the context of border management refer to steps taken to identify infiltrator(s), criminals, etc. and isolate them from the local population in border areas. It also implies identification of respectable persons of the border community, who have the ability to motivate the population to cooperate with the BSF.

The civic action programmes undertaken by the BSF generally relate to improvement of existing facilities like schools, panchayat houses, etc. Providing machinery like tractors, tube wells, hand pumps, ambulances, etc., also is done through these programmes. Besides, some programmes aiming to develop skills amongst youth at the borders such as motor driving, motor mechanic, cutting and stitching, computer awareness, etc., are also carried out to make them employable.

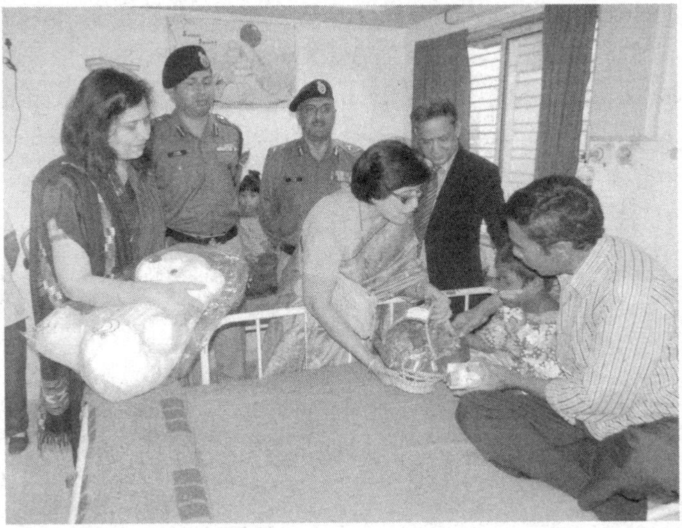

Figure 2.4: A small child with cleft lip condition being facilitated after corrective operation conducted jointly under aegis of Smile Foundation, India.

The BSF also undertakes some activities on its own without involvement of any funds. Activities like identification of villagers with physical disabilities and distributing assistive aids through aegis of NGOs and philanthropic societies and helping them out for corrective surgeries are also undertaken.

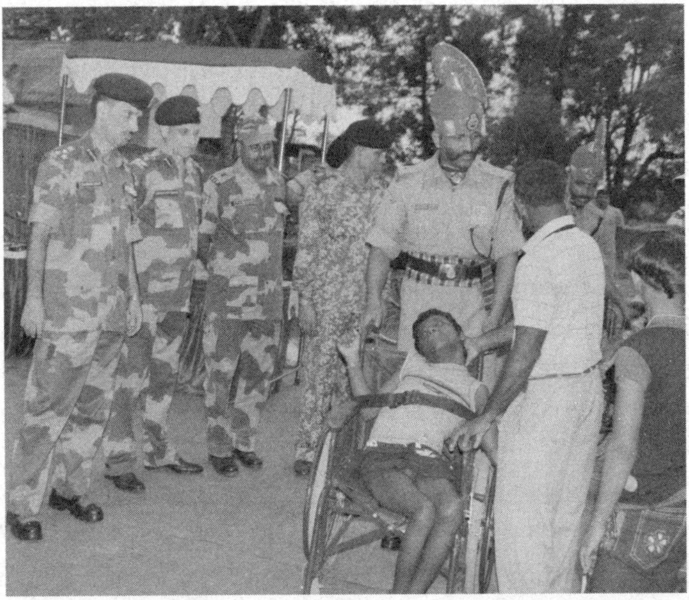

Figure 2.5: Assistive Aids Procured from Artificial Limb Manufacturing Corporation (ALIMANCO) being distributed to Physically Challenged Residents of borders

The activities also include training the youth at the border for competitive examinations like the physical and General Knowledge tests for selection in armed forces, career counselling for school children and deputing their own personnel for taking classes in schools on common as well as specialized subjects like computers, etc.

Figure 2.6: Computers provided by the BSF under the Civic Action Programme being used to impart training to students by BSF personnel classes in progress

The following additional steps also help in improving the relations with the border population: (a). Proper selection and training of bordermen, (b). Review of field procedures e.g., restrictions imposed on the bordermen on interaction with locals creates a barrier in communication with border population, (c). Training, besides focusing on enhancing operational efficiency must also endeavor to imbibe ethical values and integrity amongst personnel of the force. This should be followed up with strong action against defaulters to send a message across that the force cares about the rights of the border population. Training should be oriented to make the bordermen people-centric, so that they are able to empathise with them, (d). Grievances against the BSF personnel should be monitored and brought to logical conclusion in appropriate time frame, (e) The BSF must get as near as possible to the population without compromising on efficiency. There should be frequent formal and informal interactions and joint celebrations of religious festivals, (f). Upon induction in a new area, the commanders must gather as much information as possible and study different peculiar features relating to various aspects of life like the social structure, customs, beliefs, language, religious adaptations, economy, political leanings, etc. An analysis of the good and bad, the rich and poor, the friendly and not so friendly, the law abiding and law breakers should be carried out. (g). Fraternising through all possible help in emergencies, assisting in developmental work, group activities for youth like sports activities, personal counselling for career choices, education, etc. and participation in community development activities will support long-term measures in developing cordial relations and empathy for the force.

A very important aspect of developing good relations with the border population is proper behaviour and conduct with them. This includes image projection of the Force, respecting the sentiments of the border population, non-interference in their religious affairs, fairness in financial dealings and no forced labour, accepting invitations and attending local functions, non-interference in the local disputes or political activity, avoiding damage to the crops or other property and very importantly proper conduct with the women folk.

The expectation of public from the BSF is that everyone visiting the BOP especially, those with a grievance must be treated with courtesy besides, addressing their grievances promptly. They also expect that the money allotted for projects in their area is well-spent in consultation with them and their representatives i.e., Panchayats. These expectations can be met to a large extent through implementation of measures suggested above and through good conduct by the BSF personnel.

Border Area Development Plans (BADP)

The foremost objective of the Indian government's initiating of the Border Area Development Plans (BADP) is to enhance special developmental needs of the population residing in remote and unapproachable locations in areas that are close to the international border. The programme covers all the bordering states. These are entirely centrally funded programmes.

The schemes are required to be identified for funding through these programmes. The schemes identified are intended to pay attention to the special problems confronted by the border population and particularly those that live in rural areas. Preferences are to be given to schemes for rural and distant areas that are located along the international border over schemes that support those of the urban areas. BSF can also take up creation of security related expenditure under BADP. However, it must be ensured that expenditure relating to such schemes must not exceed 10% of the specific year's total allocation.

The Central Para-Military Forces (CPMFs) positioned in the bordering states have also been designated as one of the executing agencies under these programmes.

Individual schemes in each State require the approval of a Screening Committee which is chaired by the Chief Secretary of the State. The Screening Committee also includes representatives of the Border Guarding Force(s) functioning on the international border situated within the state, besides the representatives of other nominated agencies. BSF can play a major role in identifying the areas and schemes required to be given special attention because it is BSF which has a presence in remote border areas as the arm of Government.

The Government of India (GoI) issues guidelines for the BADP from time to time. The latest guidelines were issued in the year 2015 vide GoI, Ministry of Home Affairs, Department of Border Management, letter No. 12/63/2014-BADP dated 29 June 2015. (**Attached as Appendix 'B'**)

A list of schemes that the BADP can carry out are provided in the guidelines. It also includes a list of schemes that are not allowed to be taken up under BADP. The concerned BGFs can also suggest schemes upto 10% of the state's annual allocation as expenditure on the same. Further, a list of security related schemes permissible and non-permissible is provided in the guidelines.

Conduct with Counterpart

Interaction with counterpart border guarding force is an important aspect of border management. This is essential in order to resolve day-to-day problems within the jurisdiction of the local commanders. This also is important in order to provide a safe and secure environment to the border population to enable them to carry out day-to-day activities without fear.

Certain "Ground Rules" have been laid down by the authorities for guidance of the border guarding personnel in their interaction with their counterpart.

The first such ground rules for regulation of interaction and conduct of border guarding forces with each other on the Indo- Pakistan border were brought into force in 1960 and 1961. These were called: (a). Pakistan/Gujarat and Rajasthan (India) Ground Rules, 1960; and (b). Western Pakistan/Punjab (India) Ground rules 1961 (**Attached as Appendix 'C'**). These ground rules provide for frequency and methodology of conduct of meetings between border guarding forces at different levels, movement of armed patrols and limit of construction of defences in the vicinity of borders, etc.

After the two wars with Pakistan, these Ground rules are no longer formally recognised by the GoI. However, informally most of the provisions of these are being followed by troops on ground.

On the eastern border with Bangladesh, the first set of Ground Rules that were brought into effect in 1959 were known as the East Pakistan Border Ground Rules 1959 (**Attached as Appendix 'D'**). These were superseded by the Joint India Bangladesh Guidelines for Border Authorities 1975 after the independence of Bangladesh and the signing of the Indo-Bangladesh Boundary Agreement 1974 (**Attached as Appendix 'E'**).

In 2011, the Director Generals of the BSF and the BGB (Bangladesh Border Guards) signed a Coordinated Border Management Plan (CBMP) (**Attached as Appendix 'F'**), which is an additional set of instructions for the border guarding personnel. It provides for identification and periodic review of the crime prone areas, besides helping in effective Simultaneous Coordinated Patrolling (SCP) in which the troops of the BSF and the BGB jointly patrol the border but on the respective sides of their borders. It also provides for appointment of the Nodal Officers at different levels, who would be responsible for resolving issues cropping up at their levels.

Figure 2.7: The BSF and the BGB after a Simultaneous Coordinated Patrol

The "Border Guidelines" or "Ground Rules" can thus be said to be a formalised working arrangement between the two-counterpart border guarding forces to maintain peace and tranquility at the borders formalised through a bilateral agreement.

Border guarding authorities hold regular meetings with each other. These are held biennially between the Directorates General (DsG) of the respective border guarding forces. Such meetings are also held at prescribed frequency at the formation and the sector levels. The agenda for such meetings is exchanged in advance.

Figure 2.8: BSF, BGB Commandant Level Flag Meeting on Border

The border meetings up to the level of the Unit Commandant are called Flag meetings and are held whenever the need arises. The agenda for such meetings is not pre-decided nor any minutes kept.

A chance meeting between the patrols of the border guarding forces of the two countries also comes under the category of the flag meeting and the brief of discussions held if any are reported to higher Headquarters.

Another mode of communication with the counterpart at the local levels is through the lodging of "Protest Notes". These are initiated by the respective forces whenever they wish to inform the counterpart about any breach of guidelines, retrieval of persons and animals that may have crossed over inadvertently. Such notes are also sent to convey greetings or to call for a flag meeting, etc.

The counterpart border guarding forces also meet each other and exchange sweets on important occasions like celebration of Independence Day, Republic day and important festivals like Diwali, Holi, Eid, etc.

Facilitating Trade and Transit

Realising the importance of improving bilateral trade, India and its neighbours are opening up to possibilities of greater cooperation in Border Management. The

Department of Border Management under the MHA has set up a "Land Ports Authority". This authority is responsible for selecting locations and setting up "Land Customs Stations (LCS)" and Integrated Check Posts (ICP)". Several such LCS and ICPs have been setup along Indo-Bangladesh, Indo-Nepal and Indo-Pakistan border. Many more will be coming up in near future. These ICPs and LCS have proved very useful in easing the trade and transit. These facilities also cater to the transit trade through India to the land locked Nepal and Bhutan.

Figure 2.9: ICP Attari - Wagah on Indo-Pakistan Border

The setting up of the LCS and the ICPs involves seamless integration of all agencies involved in facilitating the border trade and transit of persons by locating them at one location, creating data bank, which is accessible to all these agencies to ensure a smooth flow of traffic. As is apparent from the nomenclature, the LCSs are meant only for import/export/transit of goods. Entry or exit of persons is not permitted from these. On the other hand, the ICPs are equipped with integrated infrastructure for transit of both goods and persons.

It is essential that the LCS and ICPs be equipped with modern facilities to avoid delays.

Smooth and hassle-free transit through the borders also necessitates that agencies deployed on the LCSs and the ICPs coordinate with their counterpart across the border. This is important because advance information of likely traffic if available to the agencies obviates any chances of delay. The BSF will have the responsibility of ensuring security and preventing contraband from passing through these facilities whose overall management rests with Customs.

It can thus be seen that border management is not just a uni-dimensional function of border guarding. It involves cooperation amongst various agencies operating in the border areas and their smooth integration for greater effectiveness. The border management is a multidimensional and multiagency function with an objective to improve the quality of life of the border population.

Border Haats Along Indo-Bangladesh Border

A foremost objective to the introduction of the concept of Border Haats[52] along the Indo-Bangladesh border is to promote trade for local products at the border area itself. These Haats share the goal of promoting the well-being of the people residing in distant or isolated areas on or across the borders of both the countries through the establishment of a marketing system that is traditional to allow marketing of the local produce and help flourish the local economy.

This marketplace arranged on both the sides of the countries is operated on a one-day-each-week basis. It does not only serve as a marketplace to buy items of daily need but also as a reunion spot for families living on either side of the border.

Figure 2.10: Border Haat at Tripura[53]

Four such Border Haats are functional at Kalaichar, Balat, (Meghalaya) and Srinagar Kamlasagar (Tripura). Further, GoI and Bangladesh have agreed to establish six more Border Haats, which include four at Bholaganj, Nalikata (Ghumaghat), Shibari and Ryngkua in the state of Meghalaya and two at Palbasti (Rangana) and Kamalpur in the state of Tripura. Border Haats can solve problem of smuggling of items of daily use to a great extent. The border population which cannot afford to take their products to bigger markets in the hinterland are thus facilitated in getting a fair price for their product without travelling to great distance.

52. Press Information Bureau (2016). Border Haats. *Pib.gov.in.* https://pib.gov.in/newsite/PrintRelease.aspx?relid=155324
53. Border Haat. (n.d.). Government of Tripura. *Southtripura.nic.in.* https://southtripura.nic.in/tourist-place/border-haat-srinagar/

Barter system is one of the method to carry out trade at the border Haats and the trade dealings are permitted to be carried out in Indian Rupees/Bangladesh Taka. The respective Border Haats have their own Haat management committee that maintain all the trading data.

Trade data reveals that these Border Haats are effective facilitators of local trade. According to data recorded by the concerned state governments, e.g., cash trade carried out at the above four border Haats for the period 2015-16 amounts to the Indian Rupees 1686.62 lakhs.[54]

The GoI has also signed a Memorandum of Understanding (MoU) with the Government of Myanmar to establish Border Haats along the border.

In addition, a proposal of 62 more Border Haats along the Indo-Bangladesh border has also been introduced.

54. Press Information Bureau (2016). Border Haats. *Pib.gov.in*. https://vifdatabase.com/wp-content/uploads/2019/04/2016-Border-Haats.pdf (https://pib.gov.in/newsite/PrintRelease.aspx?relid=155324)

CHAPTER THREE

Organisation and Role of BSF

The circumstances of the origin of the Border Security Forces (BSF) having been discussed in chapter two, we shall discuss the role and organization of BSF in this chapter.

Role of Border Security Force

The preamble of the Border Security Force Act (1968) defines the constitution of the BSF as an "armed force of the union for ensuring the security of the border of India and matters connected there with."[55]

The specific roles of the BSF have been defined in Rule 15 (1) of the BSF Rules, 1969. These are listed below as to:

(a) Promote a sense of security amongst the people living in the border areas;

(b) Prevent trans-border crimes, unauthorized entry into or exit from the territory of India, and;

(c) Prevent smuggling and any other illegal activities.[56]

Analysed in strictly technical terms, the role as defined in Rule 15, does not envisage any responsibility for the BSF in so far as the internal security and war are concerned. However, if we analyse the preamble and also, the definition of "Active Duty" given in Sec 2 (1) (a) of the BSF Act, 1968, the full scope of the intended role can be discerned.

According to the Sec 2 (1) (a) of the BSF Act (1968), "Active Duty" is defined as, "in relation to a person subject to this act, means any duty as a member of the force during the period in which such person is attached to or forms part of a unit of the force: (i). which is engaged in operations against an enemy; or, (ii). which is operating at a picket or engaged on patrol or other guard duty along the borders of India and includes duty by such person during any period declared by the Central Government by notification in the official Gazette as a period of active duty with reference to any area in which any person or class of persons subject to this act may be serving." (*For details, see: https://bsf.gov.in)

---

55. The Border Security Force Act (1968). Constitution of the force and conditions of service of the members of the force. New Delhi. http://legislative.gov.in/sites/default/files/A1968-47.pdf
56. The Border Security Force Rules, 1969 (2004). The Border Security Force Rules, 1969. New Delhi: BSF. https://mha.gov.in/sites/default/files/bsfAct&Rules_2.pdf

Sec 2 (1) (a) makes it clear that the BSF personnel can be deployed for any duty anywhere in the country which need not necessarily be on the borders and may also not necessarily involve operating against the enemy. The only stipulation being that the central government has to issue a notification declaring the period of that duty as "active duty".

Further, the enemy has been defined in Section 2 (1j) of the BSF Act of 1968, "Enemy includes all armed mutineers, armed rebels, armed rioters, pirates and any person in arms against whom it is the duty of any person subject to this act to take action". Thus, inclusion of the armed rebels and the armed rioters in the definition of enemy also gives an avenue to the government to utilise the BSF in aid to civil authority. (*For details, see: https://karaikal.gov.in/; https://idsa.in/)

Sub-rule 5 of rule 15 of the BSF Rules of 1969 also needs to be studied in this context. It states that "Any member of the force shall be liable to perform any duties in connection with safeguarding of the security of the borders of India, the administration, discipline and welfare of the force and such other duties as he may be called upon to perform in accordance with any law for the time being in force and any order given in this behalf by a superior officer shall be a lawful command for the purpose of this act." This provision implicitly covers the period of deployment of the BSF on IS duty and wartime duties. (*For details, see: https://karaikal.gov.in/; https://bsf.gov.in/)

The term "matters connected therewith" has also been given a wider interpretation to include threats to the security of the country from within, therefore, legally justifying the utilisation of the BSF for internal security duties in aid to civil authority and also in war.

The provisions of Article 355 of the Constitution of India are also relevant in this regard. It is obligatory on the part of the Central Government to defend all the states against any external aggression as well as internal disturbances and further, guaranteeing that the governance of all the states is performed in accordance to the provisions of the constitution. Therefore, the armed forces of the union including the BSF can be, on requisition by the respective state, and after the approval of the Central Government may be used for the above purpose.

The report of the study group set up in 1965 to analyse the security scenario and to recommend measures for more effective guarding of the borders goes on to expound on the role intended for the BSF.[57] The extracts given below will make it clear that the role of the BSF is to be interpreted in its wider sense as explained above:

57. *Operation Manual*, BSF Academy.

Role of Border Police Force

"It is neither possible nor advisable to man the border with the regular Army, for there are many advantages in maintaining the permanent force on the borders in the form of police. In spite of alarms and incursions, control of the border normally implies prevention of depredations, control of trans-frontier crime, prevention of infiltration, handling minor skirmishes and incursions and intermittent firing across the border. All these duties, the armed police units should be fully capable of handling and the Army should not, for obvious reasons, be involved in their direct performance. At the same time, the fact remains that defence of the country is principally a function of the defence forces, which must remain connected with border police and fully prepare for any untoward developments. The role of the border police force should therefore, be defined with clarity and should be well-understood by the police force itself, by local civil authorities on the border, the local Army commanders, the State Government and the various Central authorities, including the Defence Services Headquarters. An attempt is made in the following paragraph to define this role.

The border police force must retain its police character even though its recruitment may, to the extent necessary, include ex-army personnel in various ranks. The force will be largely employed in small detachments at the platoon and company levels and may, on occasions, be required to establish outposts of one or two sections strength. The role that has to be assigned to it, therefore, should take into account the nature of its deployment without, at the same time, giving up the concept that the Army should not be involved in minor border incidents till it becomes inevitable. The following role is suggested.

In normal times, the border police force should be expected to give a sense of security to people living in border areas, and to prevent trans-border crime, unauthorized entry into or exit from Indian territory and smuggling. To perform these functions effectively the force should be highly mobile, patrolling frequently along the border and especially in the remote and unpopulated regions where incursions can sometimes go undetected over long periods. The force should also collect such intelligence as it can in the course of patrolling, trans – border observations, and interrogation of suspects; such intelligence should invariably be passed on to the nearest Intelligence Bureau (IB) officer for effective joint coordination and national security. The force should be given the minimum necessary powers for the apprehension and arrest of criminals and suspects, for search and seizure of property, involved in crime or smuggling, and for the interrogation of intruders. It should not, however, involve itself in detailed investigation of crime or smuggling which is defined to be performed by the State Police and the Customs authorities.

There must be very close liaison with the District Magistrate and Superintendent of Police who are responsible for internal law and order and crime control in the district as a whole. While the dispositions of the border police force will be controlled by its own organization in consultation with the Army, the District authorities are likely to have a number of problems arising from border incursions, dacoities, cattle thefts, smuggling and such other incidents of a trans-frontier nature. All such information with the district authorities should be promptly made available to the Border Police Commander in the area and it should be the duty of the later to take such preventive or other action as he may consider necessary. However, the District authorities should not expect either the dispositions or the role of the border police to be altered outside the brief that may have been given to the local Border Police Commander without the specific orders of the sub-sector or sector Commander.

The border police force should also handle by itself, or with such reinforcements as may be available from its own reserves, minor skirmishes and incidents of firing across the border. However, whenever such incidents occur, very close liaison should be maintained with the local Army authorities to ensure that they are in a position to move in before the incidents grown into major clashes.

When there is a danger of massive attack either in a local area or generally along the border, and the situation becomes grave, the Army should assume operational control of the border police force. Any decision in this regard has to be taken at the highest level, but once it is decided to place operational control with the Army, such control must be complete and the responsibility undivided. It is essential, however, that in such situation only that portion of the border, with enough room for maneuver on either side should be placed in Army control as actually requires such control. The tendency to put the entire border of the State concerned under the Army should, for obvious reasons, be avoided. Once the situation has stabilised, the Army control should quickly be withdrawn and the border police placed under its own organization. Even when the Army is in operational control, it will be necessary that the normal functions of preventing crime, smuggling, infiltration, etc. and of giving assurance to the people that they are fully protected should be performed by the Border Police. This should be borne in mind when any re-deployment is ordered the administration of the force should as far as possible continue to be under its own organization. These are aspects which can cause avoidable misunderstanding and there is need for prior study of the problems in each sub-sector so that decisions are not taken in a hurry without a full understanding of the implications.

During an emergency when armed hostilities between India and Pakistan are considered highly probable, the Army will assume operational control over the border police on long stretches of the border or on the entire border, as may be necessary. This decision will again be taken at the highest level. The following general considerations will guide action following the declaration on such an emergency:

(a) Emergency should be defined as the period from the moment of alert to just short of hostilities.

(b) While the police are not designed or trained to take part in large scale Military operations of an offensive or defensive nature, they may be used along with regular troops in small scale operations. They may also be given tasks on the lines of communications, and to guard installations, bridges and depots and to carry out searches and in mopping up operations.

(c) In areas where no operations are mounted by the army the police posts will remain in position and deal with all kinds of developments mentioned in paragraph 4.2.2 above under the operational control of the Army.

(d) Any Police detachments that may be withdrawn on commencement of actual hostilities would be replaced at the disposal of the Border Police Organisation. However, the Army may still require some of these detachments for security measures such as those mentioned in (b) above." (*For details, see: https://www.mea.gov.in/)

Peacetime Tasks

The peacetime task is performed in the following manner:

(a) Guarding the borders: First step towards which is the establishment of the border out-posts (BOP) and dominating the routes of ingress and egress.

(b) Policing and patrolling the borders to ensure that borders of the country are not violated. This would also involve enforcement of any restrictive measures if promulgated by the local administration.

(c) Take effective anti–smuggling and anti-infiltration measures like establishing observation posts, laying ambushes and patrolling the borders and also by collection of requisite intelligence.

(d) Promoting a sense of security among the border population by establishing our presence in the remote border areas through measures listed above at (a), (b), and (c) and also, by getting involved in the welfare of the border community by undertaking suo moto or government sponsored programmes.

(e) Co-ordination with the counterpart to ensure peace and tranquility on the borders.

(f) Carry out Internal security duties in aid to civil authority. (*For details, see: https://idsa.in/)

War Time Role

As discussed above, the preamble, Section 4 and the Section 2 (1) (a) and Section 2 (1) (j) of the BSF Act 1968 expand the role of the BSF to include operations against the enemy. The report of the study group reproduced above also describes the expectations of the government from the BSF during war. The tasks of the BSF during war are thus, besides being derived from the above report of the study group have further been elaborated in the MHA (GOI) letter No- 20/130/67/BSF-I of 5 April 1968 (**Attached as Appendix G**). These tasks are:

(a) Holding ground in less threatened sector so long as the main attack does not develop in a particular sector, and it is felt that the local situation is within the capability of the BSF to deal with.

(b) Protection of vital installation particularly airfields against enemy commandos/ para troopers or raids.

(c) Providing extensions to the flank of main defence line by holding of strong points in conjunction with other units.

(d) Limited aggressive action against paramilitary or irregular forces of the enemy within the overall plan of the armed forces.

(e) Performing special task connected with the intelligence, including raids.

(f) Acting as guides in area of responsibility where routes are known.

(g) Maintenance of law and order in enemy territory administered under the control of own army.

(h) Provision of escorts.

(i) Guarding of prisoners of war cages.

(j) Assistance in control of refugees

(k) Anti- infiltration duties in specified area. (*For details, see: https://bsf.gov.in/)

It may, thus, be seen that the BSF is expected to perform multifarious roles. The force therefore has to be organised and trained not only to fulfill the original mandate of border guarding but also, to play a major part in the eventuality of war and also be capable of assisting the civil administration in maintenance of law and order.

Organisation

Border guarding being an essential aspect of national security, the BSF needed to be a professional force organized and trained to discharge the following functions: -

(a) Maintain sanctity of boundary line and, thereby, safeguarding of territorial limits.

(b) Provide protection to own population inhabiting the border areas.

(c) Check and prevent illegal movement of human beings across the border.

(d) To check and prevent illegal movement of article/commodities across the border.

(e) Gain information of value (intelligence) from across the border.

(f) Protection of economic resources including those within the limits of territorial waters.

(g) Enforce and regulate movement of vessels passing through own territorial waters.

(h) Maintain limited aggressive posture against hostile neighbours and handle minor skirmishes on the border.

(i) Supplement efforts of defence forces in case of war.

The war time role necessitated that organization and training of the BSF was oriented to ensure: (a). Availability of organized and trained body of troops capable of supplementing war effort; (b) Getting involved in war effort from the very beginning; and, (c). Having intimate knowledge of the border area.

The pyramidal organizational structure of the force into Frontiers, Sectors and Units ensures the following:

(a) *Organizational balance:* ensures fair amount of self-reliance at the unit level enabling easy sustenance, even in isolation, while fulfilling its assigned peacetime role. This implies that the BSF units are lightly armed and have well-organised organic administrative elements.

(b) *Easy integration:* The organisation of the BSF is such that it facilitates easy integration with defence forces in supplementing the war effort.

(c) *Compatibility of equipment:* The BSF is equipped with such weaponry, radio-sets and operational equipment which are compatible with those of defence forces to facilitate easy integration and cooperation.

(d) *Economy:* The BSF is organised in a manner to ensure favourable "Teeth to Tail" ratio and economy vis- a-vis the equivalent force level of regular defence forces.

(e) *Essential equivalence:* Essential equivalence necessitated that it be equipped with essential elements and equipment which is almost equal, if not superior in operational strength, vis-a-vis the opposing border guarding force or the counterpart, thus, enabling it to handle minor skirmishes at the borders with desired effect and without having frequent dependency on the defence forces.

Periodic review of the organisational structure is carried out in view of ever-changing operational requirements.

The BSF was raised by amalgamating 25 Battalions i.e., about 25, 000 personnel of State Armed Police Forces and just two Frontier Headquarters, one each for the eastern and western borders. The force now has almost 200 Battalions with a strength of over 2.5 lakh personnel and 13 Frontier Headquarters including two for the internal security.

A broad organizational structure of BSF is as described below.

The Force Headquarters located at Delhi headed by the Director General is the policy making Headquarter. It has several Directorates responsible for policies related to particular domains namely Operations, Intelligence, Training, Communications, Personnel, Administration, Procurement etc.

Deployment of the force on the western borders with Pakistan and eastern borders with Bangladesh are supervised by Special Director Generals located at Chandigarh and Kolkata, respectively. Besides these two, the theatre tasked for internal security is supervised by an Additional Director General located at Raipur.

There are Five Frontier Headquarters on the western borders. On the Eastern Theatre, there are six frontier Headquarters. The Internal Security Theatre has two Frontier Headquarters. Each of the Frontier Headquarter is headed by an Inspector General.

Each Frontier has three or four Sector Headquarters under their command headed by an officer of the rank of DIG.

Each Sector has three to four Battalions commanded by an officer of the rank of Commandant. Each Unit has seven companies under its command besides the Support Company. The number of companies in each Battalion was increased from six to seven in early 2000.

A large portion of India's borders being riverine, the force has been authorised a "Water wing,"[58] which mainly operates in Sir Creek, the Bay of Bengal and the

58. Business News (2016). How BSF guards the natural border between Gujarat and Pakistan. [online] Economictimes.com. Available at: https://m.economictimes.com/slideshows/infrastructure/how-bsf-guards-the-natural-border-between-gujarat-and-pakistan/water-wing-jpg/slideshow/55416757.cms?from=desktop

Brahmaputra river. Small detachments of water wing are deployed at many other places, where the border is riverine and the troops cannot operate on foot or in vehicles.

The BSF also has an Air Wing, which is equipped with both fixed wing aircrafts and Helicopters.[59] The fixed wing aircrafts are mainly small passenger or transport aircrafts used for movement of supervisory officers, troops and stores. The Helicopters are also used for these purposes, besides casualty evacuation from remote areas.

Camels are authorised as an additional resource for patrolling in the deserts of Rajasthan. Besides performing normal patrolling there, the Camel contingent and the Camel mounted band of the BSF are a major attraction during the Republic Day parade.

Figure 3.1: BSF Camel Patrol in Rajasthan

Horses have been authorised to the BSF Battalions in Punjab and Jammu, which are used for patrolling the border by troops.

59. Border Security Force. (n.d.). BSF Air Wing. [online] Available at: http://bsf.nic.in/en/air-wing.html

Figure 3.2: BSF Horse Patrol in Punjab

Each unit of the BSF is authorised Sniffer and Tracker Dogs, which are used for patrolling in conjunction with the troops or for special operations.

The BSF has three Premier Training Institutions, the BSF Academy at Gwalior, the Central School of Weapons Training at Indore and the Training Centre and School at Hazaribagh. The three training institutions are conferred Centre of Excellence by the Government of India. These institutions cater to the training needs of the officers as well as the subordinate officers of BSF. These institutions also cater for training of the BSF personal in specialized fields like weapons, support weapons, field engineering, etc.

Besides above premier training institutions there are eleven other subsidiary training institutions which cater for the induction training of the jawans. These institutions also provide preparatory training to force personnel for advanced courses at premier training institutions.

There are two signals training institutions which impart technical training to communication personnel. The BSF also has a Central School for Motor Transport, which is responsible to impart training to drivers and mechanics.

The National Training Centre for Dogs is another Centre of Excellence for training of Dogs and Dog handlers for the BSF as well as other Police forces.[60]

The Central Workshop and Stores located at Gwalior is responsible for procurement of armaments and ammunition for the force. It also is responsible for the higher advanced repair of weapons which is not within the capability of the unit and frontier level workshops.

60. *BSF Academy*. (n.d.). National Training Center for Dogs. http://acy.bsf.gov.in/ntcd.html

The Tear Smoke Unit located at Gwalior is one of its kind in Asia. It manufactures and carries out research in the field of Tear Smoke Munition. The Unit is also now manufacturing "Chili grenades," which is now extensively used as a non-lethal munitions, especially on borders with Bangladesh.

Weapons and Equipment

The BSF unit is equipped with the same weaponry as the Infantry unit viz. rifles as personal weapon, and light machine guns (LMG) 51 mm mortars in companies. Support weapons like 81 mm mortars and 7.62 mm MMGs are also authorised in battalions. This enables easy integration with infantry units in eventuality of war

Besides these weapons, a BSF unit is also authorised grenade launchers and rocket launchers for use during war time and when deployed in anti-militancy operations.

Various communication equipment are authorised to units for both forward communications with companies and rear communication with higher headquarters. Besides, the authorization of wireless communication, fixed line telephones and mobile phones are authorised. Places where mobile phones are not effective, satellite phones are provided to ensure connectivity.

Modern surveillances devices are authorized to units. These include night vision devices of different types, thermal imagers both handheld and static ones linked to a screen to enable real time tracking and reaction, Battle Field Surveillance Radars (BFSR) and Long Range Reconnaissance and Surveillance systems (LORROS). The BSF also has undertaken an ambitious programme of installing "Comprehensive Integrated Border Management systems". Once the trials succeed, the system will go a long way in reducing stress on manpower.

Adequate resources are authorized to units and higher headquarters in terms of transport for move of troops and stores. Services of railways are requisitioned in case of long-distance moves.

The Artillery regiments of the BSF are equipped with 120 MM Guns.

The water wing is equipped with floating BOPs with enough endurance for prolonged stay in deep waters. These floating BOPs act as mother ships for launching patrol boats for patrolling the riverine borders.

The air wing is equipped both with fixed wing and rotary wing aircrafts which are used for transport of troops and goods/rations for troops. Small aircrafts are used for transporting senior commanders and VIPs for supervisory visits to operational areas.

CHAPTER FOUR

Contributions of BSF in Defence of the Country

As elaborated in Chapter 2, the necessity of raising a specialised force for border guarding arose because the State Armed Police Forces were unable to provide the standard of security expected of them. It was experienced during the Indo-Pakistani War of 1965 that the State Armed Police lacked training and equipment to stand up to even minor offensive by enemy. The BSF was thus raised with expectation that it will be able to face the first burnt of enemy attack and hold ground till the time Army could stage forward. Thus, the BSF has a very important war time role as discussed in Chapter 3. War time tasks of the BSF are listed in the Government of India Letter No 20/130/67/BSF-I of 5 April 1968 **(Appendix G)** **(1)** These tasks are reproduced below:

a) Holding ground in less threatened sectors.

b) Protection of Vital Installations particularly airfields against enemy commandos/ Paratroopers or raids.

iii) Providing extension to the flanks of main defence line by holding of strong points in conjunction with other units.

iv) Limited aggressive actions against paramilitary or regular forces.

v) Performing special tasks connected with Intelligence including raids.

vi) Acting as guide in an area of responsibility where routes are known.

vii) Maintenance of law and order in enemy territory administered under the control of the Army.

viii) Provision of escorts.

ix) Guarding of prisoners of war cages.

x) Assistance in control of refugees.

xi) Anti-infiltration duties in specified areas. (*For details, see: https://bsf.gov.in/)

The newly raised BSF was put to test by fire within six years of its raising during the 1971 war with Pakistan.[61] Troops of this young force displayed their valour both on the eastern and western frontiers and won many laurels for the country and the force. Contribution of the force to the war effort was recognised by the then Prime Minister Indira Gandhi who wrote to the then, Director General BSF Shri K. F. Rustomji, "As

61. *Kol.bsf.gov.in.* (n.d.). The Role of the BSF in the Liberation Struggle – 1971. http://www.kol.bsf.gov.in/index/ctb_files/Liberation%20Struggle%20Of%20Bangladesh.pdf [

the First line of our defence, the BSF had to bear the immediate brunt of the enemy onslaught. The manner in which they faced enemy fire and the support they gave to the Army has played a crucial role in our ultimate success...."[62]

Role in Liberation of Bangladesh

The BSF got involved in the War of Liberation of Bangladesh from 25 March 1971, itself when the Pakistani Army started the genocide in East Pakistan.[63] Rustomji states that the only directive he got from the Prime Minister was, "Do what you like, but don't get caught". DG BSF was directed to deploy maximum resources at the border immediately. The tasks allotted to BSF were to ensure security of borders and supply of rations and clothing to freedom fighters and civilians besides interfering with the actions of the Pakistani Army against the freedom fighters.

Shri Golak Mazumdar[64] who was the IG of eastern frontier of the BSF was allowed complete freedom to exercise his initiative for furtherance of the aim of the Indian Armed forces. Having worked for several years in Tripura and West Bengal, Shri Mazumdar activated his contacts who proved to be instrumental in providing very useful intelligence about the Pakistani forces. He was also the person who was in direct communication with leaders of Awami League of Bangladesh and was a conduit for conveying their requirements to the Indian authorities.

The BSF also had an important role in drafting the provisional constitution of Bangladesh, which was done by then Chief Law Officer of BSF Col. M. S. Bains.

Mr. Golak Mazumdar was also instrumental in persuading the High Commissioner of Pakistan in Kolkata Mr. Hossain Ali to defect and support the cause of Bangladesh.[65] A large crowd cheered the hoisting of Bangladesh flag and taking down of Pakistani flag on the High Commission building. This was a symbolic defeat of Pakistan that led to several such defections in other parts of the world. The BSF was host to the Awami League leaders till the war ended in December 1971. Shri Golak Mazumdar was awarded the Param Vishisht Sewa Medal in recognition of his stellar contribution in the Bangladesh Liberation

62. Deshpande, A. ed., (2015). *The First Line of Defence glorious 50 years of the border security force*. Delhi: Shipra publications, pp. 15. http://bsf.nic.in/doc/history/01.pdf
63. *Dhaka Tribune*. (2017). Operation Searchlight: Genocide unleashed on Bengalis in East Pakistan. https://www.dhakatribune.com/bangladesh/2017/03/25/operation-searchlight-genocide-unleashed
64. Mannan, A. (2015). Golok Majumder his memories will live forever | daily sun. *Daily Sun*. https://www.daily-sun.com/arcprint/details/61021/Golok-Majumder-ndash-his-memories-will-live-forever/2015-07-25
65. *En.banglapedia.org*. (n.d.). Ali, M Hossain - Banglapedia. http://en.banglapedia.org/index.php?title=Ali,_M_Hossain

War. The Bangladesh government also recognised his contribution by awarding him the honorific "Friend of Bangladesh".[66]

The BSF was deeply involved in the task of training, organising and equipping the "Mukti Yodha" which was later named "Mukti Vahini". Mukti Vahini was the one involved in resisting the Pakistani armed forces till war broke out in December 1971. Brigadier B. C. Pandey the then, Director BSF Academy was tasked to organise training and advise the leadership of the Mukti Vahini in planning operations against the Pakistan Army.

Figure 4.1: Mukti Vahini Cadres Being Trained by BSF

Operations against Pakistan Army in Eastern Theatre

The training was organised at 17 locations all along the border. A senior BSF officer was made responsible for each location. Over 3, 000 Mukti Vahini cadres were imparted training at these centres.

The BSF also helped organising Mukti Vahini in different sectors with clearly defined areas of responsibility for operations.

In the first phase of the operations along the eastern sector, the BSF was involved in coordinating training of the Mukti Vahini, disrupting lines of communications of the Pakistani Army, establishing the Bangladesh force headquarters and ensuring proper administration and conduct of the operations. The BSF also established a wireless communication centre for Bangladesh, which helped disseminate correct information to the people of Bangladesh.

Many preliminary operations like disruption of communication links by destroying several bridges between the major towns in East Pakistan were carried out by the BSF

66. *theindependentbd.com*. (2015). Golak Bihari Majumdar's contribution to Bangladesh's Liberation War. http://www.theindependentbd.com/magazine/details/26864/Golak-Bihari-Majumdar's-contribution-to-Bangladesh's-Liberation-War

commando teams. A special commando group called the "Black Shirts," which inflicted considerable causalities on Pakistani troops by ambushing them at several places, was also created. They also carried out stand of attacks on nearby Pakistani positions including airfields by using high trajectory weapons.

In the second phase, the BSF was tasked to protect the border and defend the BOPs. It also continued to train the Mukti Vahini during this period.

After the outbreak of hostilities in early December 1971, the BSF fought shoulder to shoulder with the Indian Army. Tasks were initially restricted to what was envisaged in the roles and tasks, however increasingly bigger tasks were given to the BSF. Twenty-three units of the BSF functioned under the operational control of the Indian Army. At the beginning of the War, the BSF bore the brunt of well-coordinated enemy offensives and held them back.

It will be necessary to briefly describe some of the important operations conducted by the BSF during 1971 operations either independently or in conjunction with the Indian Army in order to highlight the role of the BSF in the war effort to liberate Bangladesh. Records of the operations conducted by the BSF both on the eastern and western theatre have been documented in the respective unit history and also, as a consolidated history in a compilation by the BSF Academy, Tekanpur.[67] Unfortunately, the complete sacrifice and valour of the BSF might not be known to public as most of the documents from the Bangladesh War have been shredded.[68] The operations described in succeeding paras have been extracted from these compilations.

One company of 71 Battalion BSF along with 10 Post Group Artillery (PGA) under command of Shri L. S. Negi, Assistant Commandant played a key role in the capture of Nawabganj by troops of 1 Naga Regiment. Exemplary courage displayed by the 10 PGA was appreciated by Maj. Gen. Lachman Singh, PVSM, VrC, GOC, 20 Mountain Division. In a Demi Official (DO) letter addressed to the Commander Artillery, BSF, he wrote, "The Battery of BSF from Malda area did extremely well and helped a lot in capturing Nawabganj. I am quite sure that this could not have been possible without the support of your battery. Their improvisation and will to fight deserves appreciation". (*For details, see: https://www.mea.gov.in/)

The 71 Battalion displayed resolute courage while deployed to protect the flanks of the Army unit and held its ground in spite of heavy shelling, thus enabling the Army

67. *Compilation by BSF Academy*, Tekanpur, "Role of BSF in 1971 War"
68. *Times of India* (2010). Truth lost? Most military records of Bangladesh war missing. https://timesofindia.indiatimes.com/india/Truth-lost-Most-military-records-of-Bangladesh-war-missing/articleshow/5907855.cms

units to launch offensives against the enemy. The unit was also involved in ambushing a Pakistani Army convoy after crossing the Mahananda River during the operation to capture Nawabganj. Constable Padam Bahadur Lama attained martyrdom during this operation while two others received injuries. The unit was further entrusted to proceed to Rajshahi, where it received tumultuous welcome with slogans like "Long live India Bangladesh friendship" resonating the air. The unit remained in Rajshahi, till the end of the conflict and withdrawal of the Indian forces from Bangladesh and was hailed as the force of liberation of Bangladesh.

The 77 Battalion of BSF was deployed at Hilly and surrounding areas since April 1971. It repeatedly came under heavy shelling from the Pakistani forces but held on to its defences and repulsed their fire assault with equal ferocity compelling them to call for a flag meeting on 22 April 1971, wherein it was agreed that both sides will stop resorting to firing. Determined action, highest standard of courage and discipline displayed by the BSF to counter Pakistani aggression was highly appreciated by the Divisional Commissioner.

Later, the unit launched an attack on Khanpur BOP of East Pakistan and captured it in the early hours of 12 November 1971 causing heavy causalities to the Pakistani troops. Naik Amal Kumar Mondal sacrificed his life during the operation.

Similarly, 103 Battalion BSF deployed in Cooch Behar since July 1971 displayed its valour and fighting capabilities by getting an area of approximately 1800 Sq. miles freed from the Pakistani troops.

Eighty-two Battalion BSF deployed in Panbari, Assam carried out many raids inside East Pakistani and blew off several bridges well inside their territory thus disrupting the lines of communications of Pakistani Army.

Figure 4.2: A Bridge destroyed by BSF

The operational responsibility of the northern sector along the Indo-Pakistan Border in North Bengal fell almost exclusively upon the BSF after the Army formations moved to south for operations. The BSF under the overall command of the DIG BSF North Bengal acquitted itself very well in this area. The DIG BSF North Bengal formed a "Peter Force" by pooling troops from different Units, Mortar and MMG elements and Post Group Artillery. The force took to offensive and pushed back the Pakistani troops several kilometres inside East Pakistan to Mirazgang Haat and Domar. Peter Force along with the Mukti Vahini later attacked Domar compelling the enemy to withdraw to Nilfamari. Having achieved their aim, Peter Force was asked to advance towards Kishoreganj, which it captured by 15 December 1971.

Deputy Commandant Indrajeet Singh Uppal of the 78 Battalion BSF attained martyrdom displaying exemplary bravery during what is known as "The Battle of Raiganj". Shri Uppal led two companies of the 78 Bn BSF tasked to capture the North Bank of River Phulkumari, near Raiganj. The BSF companies along with the Mukti Vahini, and troops of the Rajput Bn captured the objective. However, Deputy Commandant Uppal fell to enemy bullets. His bravery in the operation was recognised by posthumously awarding the "Veer Chakra" to him.

The 70 Battalion BSF commanded by Lt. Col. N. G. O' Connor (re-employed with the BSF) was tasked to capture Bantara and Mohanpur BOPs manned by Pakistan regular Army. They completed the task after a furious battle on 5 November 1971. Ten Pakistani soldiers were killed in the action and one was taken prisoner. Col. O' Connor leading the troops from front was awarded the Veer Chakra for exemplary bravery and leadership displayed by him. Inspector B. L. Shah, Head Constable Rai Pada Das (posthumously) and Constable Amarendra Nath Mallick (posthumously) were awarded Sena Medals for their gallant action in what is known as the "Battle of Bantara".

Figure 4.3: A BSF Sub unit advancing in battle field

The BSF deployed in Bengal repelled the enemy aggression with grit and determination and frustrated all their attempts to occupy any Indian territory. The BSF thus ably assisted the Army in its operations against the Pakistan Army.

Kilapara area in Tura, Meghalaya received almost one lakh refugees from East Pakistan including Sayed Nazrul Islam, the Vice President of provisional Bangladesh Government. The nearby BSF company at Dallu was directed to establish a post at Kilapara.

Accordingly, a Section strength BSF was deployed there. Shri B. S. Tyagi, Assistant Commandant ensured that strong defences were prepared at both Dallu and Kilapara. Defences were prepared over a long frontage in order to deceive the enemy forces. Kilapara came under heavy attack from the Pakistan Army on night intervening 24 and 25 May 1971. Eleven persons deployed at Kilapara fought gallantly till the last bullet repulsing several attacks by Pakistan. Nine of the Jawans sacrificed their lives defending the Post. Sub Inspector Kirpal Singh and Constable Mohan Das were reported taken prisoners of war. Kirpal Singh was later released from Dacca jail on 16 December after surrender of Pakistan Army. Assistant Commandant B. S. Tyagi and nine martyrs were awarded Presidents Police Medal for Gallantry (PPMG) and Fire Service Medal. At Kilapara, a memorial stands in reminiscence of the gallant BSF soldiers and, Major General Aziz Ahmed the then Director General of BGB payed homage to them in recognition of their supreme sacrifice in the war of liberation of Bangladesh.

Shri B. S. Tyagi was further involved in forcing surrender of Pakistani soldiers of 33 Punjab Regiment including their commanding officer at Nabinagar on 16 December 1971 along with their arms and ammunition including one LMG, four Chinese machine guns, seventy G-3 rifles, and forty 303 Rifles.

One company commanded by Shri M. S. Chauhan AC was tasked to liberate Kishoreganj a small town, a task that he completed on 17 December taking about 290 Razakars and Mujahids prisoners along with their weapons.

The 85 Bn BSF, deployed in Shillong area, operated deep inside the enemy territory up to Sylhet and executed a number of successful raids/ambushes and destroyed retreating columns of the Pakistan army.

One company of the 86 Battalion (deployed at Dawki in Meghalaya) along with the Mukti Vahini elements attacked Kaniarghat (manned by the Pakistan regular Army) after last light on 3 December 1971 and captured it by first light 4 December. The enemy having suffered large causalities had to withdraw. The BSF Company along with the Mukti Vahini dug in immediately and repulsed several fierce counter attacks.

Shri Lushai, Assistant Commandant and Head Constable Hari Singh were awarded Vir Chakra for gallantry displayed during the operation.

The 86th Battalion of BSF was tasked to clear a pocket of enemy resistance on the Dawki – Sylhet axis as it was hampering linking up and supply to Indian Army troops. This was achieved by one Company of the 06 Battalion in an audacious day light attack on well-organised enemy defences on 12 December 1971. SI Gopal Singh of the company, despite being injured by a hail of bullets, displayed exemplary bravery in achieving the task. His courageous action inspired his company to overrun the position.

One company of the 86th Battalion of BSF under Command Shri Shivaji Singh, Assistant Commandant was tasked to capture Kamla Bagan on 3 December 1971. This location along with an area called OP Hill are the only high features in Jaintiapur. All approaches leading to Kamla Bagan were heavily fortified by the enemy with mines and other obstacles covered by fire. However, braving all odds, the company achieved its objective in the given time frame.

Operations in the Sylhet sector were undertaken from the Cachar side. The 86, 87, and 84 battalions BSF took part in these operations. Two Companies of the 87 Battalion took part in capture of Zakiganj. One company of the 86th Battalion relieved the Army on Sylhet-Darbasth road for further operations by them. They were also tasked to clear all the pockets of enemy resistance in the nearby area. They succeeded in capturing the Hemu bridge intact after which explosive charges layed by enemy to destroy the bridge were removed.

The 104 Battalion BSF was deployed in the Khowai Sector in Tripura on different BOPs which it defended with grit and determination. The BSF troops caused heavy causalities to Pakistani troops while defending Phulbari and snatched the MMGs from the enemy in the operations in May 1971. The unit was redeployed in November 1971. It took part in the Battle of Dhalai and the bravery displayed by the troops of this Battalion was recognised by awarding a war trophy to the unit in April 1972 by the then Lt. Governor of Tripura.

The 93 Battalion was deployed in Teliamura Sector which became very active and sensitive in view of crackdown by the Pakistan Army in East Pakistan. The Commando Platoon of the Unit under command of Assistant Commandant K. R. Rao carried out several operations independently and destroyed three bridges and demolished three Pakistani BOPs opposite Jalaya sector. The Unit was also engaged in training of Mukti Vahini on its BOPs.

These companies successfully supported operations by the Indian Army and prevented any intrusion in the area by Pakistani Army. These companies also operated inside Bangladesh under operational command of the 81 Mountain Brigade.

The 92 Battalion BSF deployed in South Tripura in Belonia and Subroom sector played an important role by undertaking a series of commando raids inside Bangladesh. It was also involved in training of Mukti Vahini cadres which included top leaders of Bangladesh like Major Zia-Ur-Rehman (later President of Bangladesh), General Usmani and Capt. Huda. Further, this battalion was also handed the responsibility to protect the Shobhpur Bridge on River Fenni and helped stop the advancing enemy columns towards Commila town. Besides that, the Battalion performed numerous operations successfully opposite the Belonia sub-division during the 1971 War and was praised by the Indian Army and the Bangladesh leaders.

Thus, BSF played a significant role in the Bangladesh Liberation War from the very beginning. The stellar performance of the young force was not restricted to the eastern theater only. The BSF also made very important contribution to the war effort on the western theatre.

Operations against Pakistan Army in Western Theatre

Even before the full-fledged war broke out, the BSF had started working in close liaison with the Army. The BSF with its intricate knowledge of the terrain along the border was assisting the Army in the conduct of reconnaissance and thus, enabling them to gather useful operational information. The BSF also started extensive patrolling of the border and tasked its sources for collecting specific operational information.

The intelligence efforts met with an early success when a Pakistani spy in the garb of a *Sadhu* was apprehended in the border district of Ganganagar in Rajasthan in the second half of November 1971.[69] The spy who was involved in collecting information about Indian Air Force, revealed that Pakistan had planned preemptive airstrikes in 1971 on selected Indian Air Force bases on 3 December. The information proved very useful in averting any major damage to our air assets.

Operational task of the BSF in Gujarat was to capture Jaleli and Vingoor posts and then extend control up to Valawa bulge and Barana hill features. The First and Second Battalions of the BSF accomplished this task by 5- 6 December 1971 even though the Pakistani posts were augmented by the Pakistan regular Army. These units further

69. Deshpande, A. ed., (2015). *The First Line of Defence Glorious 50 years of The Border Security Force.* Delhi: Shipra Publications, pp. 52. http://bsf.nic.in/doc/history/01.pdf

captured many more BOPs and went on to capture the Taluka Headquarters. Virawah was captured in face of stiff enemy resistance with the help of close air support from Indian Air force. The 03 Bn BSF also operating in the same sector captured the Pak BOP Vingoor.

In view of deficiency of Artillery support from the Army, the Government sanctioned raising of 20 "Post Group Artillery" (PGA) which were raised by 1 October 1971 and equipped with 3.7-inch Howitzers and 4.2-inch Mortars held surplus with the Army. The 1,2,3 and 4 PGAs were deployed in Bhuj and Dantewada and supported the BSF units in the capture of Vingoor and Virvawah. They also provided support to 13 Grenadiers in capture of the Pakistani posts of Ranihal and Rukanwala.

Shri Joginder Singh Deputy Commandant Artillery sacrificed his life in operations against enemy in Bhuj area. His gallantry was recognized by posthumous award of Vir Chakra. Shri K. J. Thakur, Assistant Commandant OC 2 PGA was also awarded "Sena Medal" for his conspicuous gallantry.

In Rajasthan, Pakistan launched a major offensive in the Longewala sector. A handful of the BSF troops along with the troops of the Indian Army put up a heroic fight at the Longewala Post against a much larger enemy force consisting of armour and infantry that had surrounded the post. They kept the enemy at bay which was destroyed by the Indian Air force. The BSF troops also fought valiantly at the Ghotaru Post and thwarted the enemy's attempts to capture it.

A detachment of the 14 Battalion BSF along with one company of the 23 Punjab thwarted the enemy attack on Longewala post on 6 December 1971 in which L/Nk Bharon Singh single-handedly inflicted heavy causalities to the advancing enemy.

BSF was also tasked independently to launch a number of attacks and was able to capture 23 enemy BOPs inflicting heavy casualties on the Pakistani regulars and militants.

Troops of the 14 Battalion gave a sterling display of their fighting abilities and were involved in several operations in the Longewal Ghotaru area. This included, capture of Mirza Toba along with troops of the 8 Dogra, capture of Islamgarh along with troops of the 3 Raj Rif, and capture of Pakistan post Sinahta. The troops of this Battalion also effected the capture of a large number of POWs along with arms ammunition and stores.

Exceptional acts of heroism displayed by the troops of the 14 Battalion in the famous battle of "Tanot Longewala" and "Shahgarh bulge" earned them the sobriquet of "*Sentinels of The Thar*".

The 15 and the 11 Battalions of the BSF also displayed their valour in the operations in Rajasthan. Inspector Gokul Deo led a Platoon of the 11 Bn BSF and successfully raided Pakistani post Ghunewala on 4 December 1971. He was awarded "Sena Medal" for his bravery. The 11 Battalion also played a vital role in capture of Pakistani posts Salamsar, Rakanwala and Lanewaladhar deep inside Pakistan. The troops of the 11 Battalion were awarded three Sena Medals and ten PMGs for the valour displayed by them during this War.

In Punjab sector, the men and officers of the BSF displayed indomitable courage by facing up to a modern Pakistani Army equipped with the latest American technology. They continued to hold on to their positions even in the face of heavy attrition by enemy and their over-whelming superiority.

Assistant Commandant R. K. Wadhwa of the 31 Battalion of the BSF led a daring attack on Raja Mohtam post with two Platoons of the BSF and took the enemy by surprise by storming the post from the rear. The post was captured by first light 7 December 1971. However, Shri R. K. Wadhwa was killed soon after the operation during shelling of the post by the enemy.

Shri R. K. Wadhwa was posthumously awarded the Mahavir Chakra for the conspicuous bravery and leadership displayed in capture of Raja Mohtam.

BSF defended the posts with grit in Jalalabad – Fazilka Sector and frustrated enemy attempts to capture territory. In Gurdaspur – Dera Baba Nanak sector, the BSF captured as many as 17 BOPs.

The 27 Battalion BSF deployed at Amritsar repulsed four enemy attacks on Ranian post on night intervening 3-4 December 1971 and inflicted heavy causalities on them. Head Constable Mohinder Singh laid down his life fighting gallantly during this operation and was posthumously awarded Vir Chakra. Naik Charan Singh and Constable Dalbir Singh were also decorated with Vir Chakra and Sena Medal, respectively. Subsequent attacks by the enemy on the 4,5,6,7 and 17 Dec were also repulsed successfully.

The 27 Battalion BSF repulsed an enemy raid on BOP Mulakot on 4 December 1971. The enemy however succeeded in the second raid on 5 December, wherein they took Cook Dunichand as a POW. One section of the 27 Battalion volunteered to go with the Army companies to recapture the BOP Malukot. The raid was successfully carried out with Head Constable Sukhcharan Singh, Lance Naik Harnarayan Singh and Constable Baktawar Singh in the forefront of the operation. H. C. Sukhcharan Singh and Const. Baktawar Singh were injured in the operation.[70]

---

70. Unit History, 27 Bn, *BSF.*

Sub Inspector Ajit Singh of the 23 Battalion BSF in a daring day light attack on enemy post in Ajnala Sector led his platoon from front in spite of being injured and helped capture the objective. His conspicuous bravery in the operation was recognised by award of Vir Chakra.[71]

In Jammu and Kashmir Sector, the BSF was at the receiving end of enemy fire assault in Ranvir Singh Pura, Chhamb and Palanwala Sectors before being withdrawn for the tasks in-depth upon arrival of the Army. In R. S. Pura, however, the 57 Battalion BSF continued to hold most BOPs even after the War started. Eighteen soldiers of this Battalion have remained untraced and are suspected to have either been killed or captured by the enemy. Naik Operator Swarn Singh displayed remarkable courage and did not let the communications fail during withdrawal from BOP Nathan, till he attained martyrdom, having been injured in heavy shelling by the enemy.

A section of the 57 Battalion deployed at Moel BOP kept fighting alongside the 5 Sikh Battalion and repulsed several attacks by the enemy till they were ordered to withdraw and fall back to the main defences. Personnel of the 54 Battalion were co-opted for a raid on Saleem post of enemy on 13-14 December 1971 and played a crucial role in the success of the raid.

In Rajouri and Bandipura Sectors, the BSF fought a defensive battle alongside the Indian Army.

In Rajouri Sector, five BSF Battalions operated on the Line of Control under the Army Operational Control, whereas two Battalions were deployed under the DIG BSF Rajouri for anti-infiltration duties. One of the Battalions i.e., the 49 Battalion BSF held an independent sector in Mandi Mandir and captured two Pakistan Commando (SSG) infiltrators. The 44 Battalion BSF assisted the Army in the capture of the Pak FDL Druchian through the cover fire. The Unit also provided close support from the Forward Defended Locality (FDL) 495 to 11 Raj Rif in carrying out a successful raid on enemy post Tarkundi. These actions were highly commendable.

One Company of the 50 Battalion BSF as part of an operation to clear large number of infiltrators from Thanpir area on 5 December 1971, performed commendably in recovery of large number of weapons and explosives.[72]

Assistant Commandant, N. S. Dalal of the 40 Battalion BSF was posthumously awarded "Vir Chakra" for displaying conspicuous bravery defending the FDL Delta Contour in the Saujian Defended area.[73]

71. Unit History, 23 Bn, *BSF.*
72. Role of BSF in 1971 War-Ftr Jammu.
73. Role of BSF in 1971 War-BSF ACY.

The BSF operated independently in the Bandipur Sector. Four Battalions and three PGAs placed under command DIG BSF Bandipur were given responsibility to give fire support to the Army units in a wide area from Uri to Gurez.

The 61 Battalion BSF dominated its allotted area of responsibility aggressively through regular patrols. It carried out a brilliant rear-guard action on 22 November 1971 to extricate a BSF Platoon patrolling the area around the FDL Ring Contour, causing heavy causalities to the enemy and destroying several of their bunkers.

In another daring action, one Platoon of the unit under the command of Assistant Commandant Y. S. Bisht infiltrated behind the enemy lines and destroyed an enemy picket through fire assault and returned unharmed.

Two companies of the Battalion were deployed in Gurez Sector during the War. They advanced into Pakistan and captured about four Kilometres of the enemy territory and later established four Posts in the area.

One Company of the Unit under Shri W. S. Elley Assistant Commandant captured "Tota" post of enemy. In another operation under the command of Shri Y. S. Bisht, Assistant Commandant destroyed the Pakistani supplies at the Pakistani post "Dugri".

The commendable performance of the Unit was appreciated by the Chief of the Army Staff. Late Naik Ummed Singh of the Unit was posthumously awarded "Vir Chakra" and Shri W. S. Elley and Shri Y. S. Bisht were awarded the "Sena medal".

It can be emphatically stated that the BSF even though in its infancy performed exceedingly well in the 1971 War both on the eastern and western frontiers. While it lived up to its potential in the actual operation whether they be offensive or defensive, it also played an important role in many other fields which facilitated smooth conduct of operations.

Before the war started, the BSF collected a lot of invaluable and accurate information about the Pakistani troops and their dispositions, which was of enormous value. The BSF personnel had developed intimate knowledge about the borders and therefore, they proved to be of great value to the Army as they helped them familiarise with the area and develop their operational plans.

The BSF overcame the problem of shortage of equipment by improvisation and experimentation. For example, facing shortage of the 3" Mortars, the CENWOSTO of the BSF manufactured them in a very short period.

The BSF also proved its worth by training the Mukti Vahini and softening up the Pakistani Army especially, on the eastern theater, during nine months before the actual onset of the War. This was achieved through fire assaults and several raids in conjunction of the Mukti Vahini.

Shri V.V. Giri, the then President of India appreciated BSF's role during the 1971 War with the following words:

> "The role of the BSF in 1971 War won for it the unstinted admiration of the entire Nation. The BSF forged great camaraderie with the Indian Army, with whom they fought shoulder to shoulder." (*For details, see: https://bsf.gov.in/)

Smt. Indira Gandhi, the then Prime Minister of India paid tribute to the BSF in a letter written to Shri K. F. Rustamji, which is given below:

> "Dear Shri Rustamji,
>
> As the first line of our defence, the Border Security Force had to bear the immediate brunt of the enemy onslaught. The manner in which they faced enemy fire and the support they gave to the Army has played a crucial role in our ultimate success.
>
> Our thoughts and prayers are with the families of the men and the officers who have sacrificed their lives in defence of India and her values.
>
> I should like to express the gratitude of the Government and the people of India to you and to your officers and men.
>
> With kindest regards,
>
> Yours sincerely,
> (Indira Gandhi)"

(*For details, see: https://fsi.mea.gov.in/)

Sacrifice Made by BSF during the 1971 War

The success of the BSF was not without a price. The details of personnel killed, wounded or missing during the 1971 War are given in Table 4.1.

Table 4.1: Details of personnel killed, wounded or missing during the 1971 War

Frontier	Killed	Wounded	Missing	Total
R&G	08	46	07	61
Punjab	50	156	105	311
Jammu	06	17	20	43
Kashmir	06	12	-	18
West Bengal	28	78	01	107
N.E.F.	27	83	-	110
Total	**125**	**392**	**133**	**650**

Table 4.2: BSF Personnel received following decorations during the 1971 War

Decoration	Number
Padma Bhushan	02
Padma Shree	02
Param Vishisth Seva Medal	01
Maha Vir Chakra	01
Ati Vishisth Seva Medal	01
Vir Chakra	11
Sena Medal	46
Vishisth Seva Medal	05
Mention-in dispatches	44
Presidents Police & Fire Services	
Medal for Gallantry	41
Presidents Police & Fire Services	
Medal for distinguished services	09
Police Medal for Meritorious Service	13
DG's Commendations	184

Our Heroes of 1971 War

The following personnel were awarded with Mahavir and Vir Chakras for bravery during the 1971 War:

a) Maha Vir Chakra
   - i) A. C. Wadhwa Ram Krishna, 31 Bn: 10 December 1971 (Posthumous)

b) Vir Chakra
   - i) Lt. Col. O'Connor, NC, 70 BN BSF (IC-1578)
   - ii) DC Joginder Singh (647), 03 BN BSF: 17 December 1971
   - iii) DC Inderjit Singh Uppal, 78 BN (Posthumous)
   - iv) AC Chandan Singh Chandel, BSF (1265): 10 December 1971
   - v) AC Naf Singh Dalal, 40 BN (1616) (Posthumous)
   - vi) AC Lalthawna Lushai, 82 BN: 4 December 1971
   - vii) Sub Inspector Ajit Singh, 21 BN, (66232027)
   - viii) Head Constable Hari Singh, 17 BM (68176022)
   - ix) Head Constable Mohinder (66276037), 27 BN: 3 December 1971 (Posthumous)

x) Naik Chanan Singh (67276037), 27 BN

xi) Naik Umed Singh (68588913), 61 BN: 6 December 1971 (Posthumous)

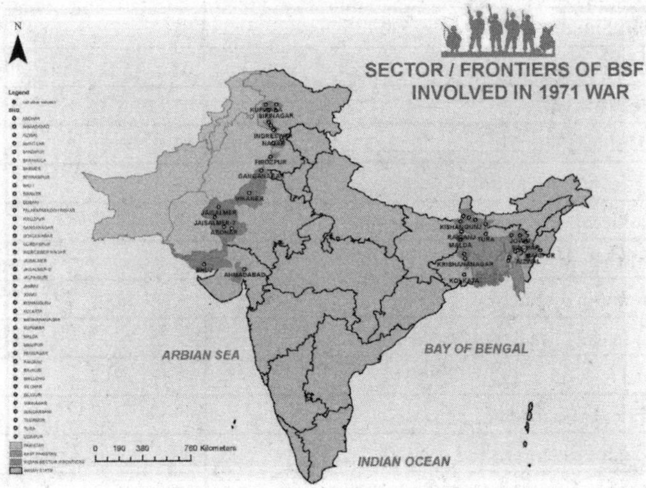

Figure 4.4: Sector/frontiers of BSF involved in 1971 War

BSF and Operation Vijay: Kargil 1999

We are aware of the circumstances leading to the Kargil War in the summer of 1999 and the manner in which the Indian Army and the Air Force succeeded in evicting the Pakistan Army and militants from the area occupied by them. That BSF also played a crucial role in various stages of the Kargil War is however not commonly known. The media played an important role in crafting a narrative that rightly glorified the Army. It is necessary to put the role played by BSF during Kargil War in perspective.

Kargil by the BSF in this War in Perspective

The Kargil heights overlooking the Srinagar-Leh highway are strategically important as their capture by the enemy would severely interfere with logistics and movement of troops to Siachin and make the position of the Indian Army there untenable.

These heights were defended by four regular Battalions of Army and one BSF Battalion. Both the Army and the BSF manned the FDLs along the LC on these heights. The BSF Battalion was holding the Chennigund defended area independently with two companies. The area of responsibility assigned to the brigade being large, there were huge gaps between the FDLs. Some of these gaps and contiguous hill features had properly developed defences.

Most of the high altitude FDLS as a matter of routine were vacated during the winters to be reoccupied during the summers. These positions were occupied by the enemy and used against the Indian troops. Even the Long Range Patrols (LRPs) and the link patrols which were normally sent by the flanking Army Units during the winters to dominate the vacated area were not being sent.

Knowing well about the fact that the Indian troops always vacated these Posts at extremely difficult high altitude, the Pakistani Army and the Jihadi elements supported by them occupied it during the winter of 1998-1999.

The first information about Pakistani intrusion was received by the Indian security forces in early May 1999. Subsequent reconnaissance patrols of the Army were fired upon causing casualties thus confirming the intrusion. The intruders had succeeded in maintaining complete surprise and started interdicting the NH-1A and other targets at will with heavy artillery/mortar shelling immediately after being detected. The extent of intrusion was over a large frontage.

None of the FDLs occupied by the BSF were however vacated in spite of extreme winter and very low oxygen levels. The FDLs occupied by the BSF included Kaksar, Chennigund, Kargil and the highest Post of the Sector i.e., Chorbat La complex (17,000 feet) overlooking the historic Silk Road. Not only was this area not vacated, the Commandant of the 8 BN BSF, Shri S. C. Negi (who also is a mountaineer and has climbed the Mount Everest at the age of 56 Years besides many other peaks), deployed in the area ensured that the troops always were in high morale through frequent visits to FDLs. During these visits Shri Negi also ensured that the defences at the Posts remained well-maintained.

The unit took initiative to further strengthen the defence of Chorbat La by way of occupying another dominating height nearby called "Bravo-1". This is the highest and the most difficult FDL of the Kargil Sector at over 18,000 feet. A small team of 8 to 10 highly committed personnel under Shri Sonam Cherring, Assistant Commandant, were deployed on this post thereby preventing the Pakistani Army from occupying it and thus threatening the defence of the Chorbat La axis. Commandant (Now DIG Retired) S. C. Negi displayed exemplary leadership qualities in ensuring continued occupation of the Defended Area under responsibility of his Unit along with Shri Y. S. Rathore (now Comdt.), Senior BSF officers also regularly visited the troops of the 08 Bn BSF and kept up their morale.

Training company of the unit was sent to the Batalik area and deployed in a pre-reconnoitred area. Around 150 troops of the Unit stranded in Srinagar due to closure of the Zoji La pass were brought forward after partially clearing the pass and deployed for security of administrative bases and culverts/bridges in Batalik on the Indus River.[74] The deployment was completed in face of heavy interdiction by the enemy.

The BSF Battalion HQ, Chennigund became the launching pad for the troops being inducted in the Kaksar area.

Advance party of the 171 Battalion BSF commanded by Shri Sukhbir Singh Yadav, Deputy Commandant arrived in the midst of the battle. These troops of the 171 BN BSF had to be deployed on the FDLs alongside the 08 Bn BSF even without acclimatization to strengthen the defences. Shri Yadav in the process of supervising induction of his troops, succumbed to direct observed artillery fire.

The Unit was ordered to occupy tactically important "Kala Pahar" area which dominated the road connecting Ladakh with Kashmir Valley. This area was heavily mined by Pakistan when they had occupied it during the 1965 War. Shri Surender Singh, Assistant Commandant, of the 08 BSF tasked to occupy the area stepped on one of the scattered mines and lost one of his legs. In recognition of the leadership qualities displayed by him he was awarded with the Parakram Padak.

The Mortar Platoon, of the Unit along with additional Mortars were effectively used to bring down fire on the enemy posts to destroy a number of Petrol, Oil and Lubricant (POL) and ammunition dumps under guidance of Shri Pradip Kumar, Assistant Commandant. Shri Ajit Kumar, Deputy Commandant also effectively directed own Artillery Fire on enemy positions and caused heavy interdiction.

The BSF personnel from the South Indian States were very useful in dissemination of information without threat of breach of security thus enabling quicker dissemination of information. The BSF personnel belonging to Ladakh were also very useful in decoding the enemy transmission after they were deployed at Army Interception Centres. The BSF also provided much needed medical and logistics cover to the Army.

The 153 BN BSF deployed in the Niru area, adjacent to Kargil also did not vacate its FDLs and denied enemy any opportunity to intrude from their area of responsibility.

The Intelligence Branch of the BSF under Shri O. S. Jha Deputy Commandant (G) utilised his excellent network of sources to obtain and process information about enemy activities in the area to facilitate operations by the Army.

The BSF intelligence branch shared as many as five different intelligence reports about increased enemy activities between July and December 1998. The reports pertained to forward shifting of enemy artillery including Air Defence Guns, development of

74. Interview with Shri YS Rathore A. C. (Now Comdt).

new gun positions, vacation/shifting of PoK villages near LC, stoppage of leave of military personnel, deployment of commandos near LC, construction of new tracks and bunkers, heavy stocking of ammunition, frequent visit of senior military officers, heavy presence of militants opposite Kargil, construction of new helipads, etc. These indicators of unprecedented military build-up in the area pointed towards possibility of major operation by the enemy. Frequent sorties by enemy Air Force to Skardu and increased night flying practices were also reported by the BSF Intelligence Branch in December 1998.

However, the comparison with previous years did not indicate any substantial variations, hence the authorities could not interpret the warning signs properly.

Immediately after the detection of intrusions in May 1999, the BSF intelligence sources ascertained the exact nature and extent of intrusion. The BSF intelligence resources were thereafter deployed with the Army authorities in Batalik and Drass areas to detect the presence of intruders if any amongst the locals. They also were deployed to ascertain and keep surveillance over the likely routes of infiltration. The immense contribution of the BSF intelligence effort thus had a vital role in facilitating better conduct of operations to evict the intruders.

The role of BSF in the Kargil War effort was also acknowledged by Ministry of Home Affairs. Further, remarking upon the BSF's human intelligence sources, the National Security Council Secretariat (NSCS) in their report to the Government on Kargil mentioned specifically that they were by far the most superior.[75]

The manifest aim of Pakistan in imposing the Kargil War on India was to cut off the supply routes to Siachen and thereby make the deployment of our troops there untenable. Another Pakistani aim was to take revenge for bifurcation of Bangladesh from Pakistan in 1971. In undertaking this audacious adventure, they forgot to factor in the strong national will of India and the ability of our forces and leaders to take resolute action to evict them.

The BSF made a commendable contribution to the Kargil War effort by holding on to its defended area in spite of extreme weather and terrain conditions. The BSF also made laudable contributions in mobilising its intelligence resources to aid the War effort. These efforts are part of recorded history of the Kargil War, which the general public needs to be made aware of.

---

75. Deshpande, A. ed., (2015). *The First Line of Defence Glorious 50 years of the Border Security Force*. Delhi: Shipra Publications, pp. 127. Available at: http://bsf.nic.in/doc/history/01.pdf

Conclusion

The circumstances of raising of the BSF coupled with its operational philosophy, training, organisational structure, and ethos make it akin to the Indian Army. Though raised as a border guarding force, its troops have displayed their bravery and ability to take on the regular army of the enemy during the 1971 War and the Kargil War. As a force responsible to face the first burnt of the enemy attack, it has displayed remarkable ability to hold on to the defences till the Army gets mobilised. The valour displayed by the BSF personnel during these Wars needs to be highlighted for greater recognition of the Force.

CHAPTER FIVE

Contribution of BSF in Internal Security of India

As discussed in the earlier chapters, the BSF is often called upon to aid the civil authorities in ensuring internal security through anti-insurgency and anti-militancy operations. The BSF also is often called upon to assist the civil administration in conduct of free and fair elections and other duties to restore law and order.

The BSF from its very inception played a crucial role in controlling insurgencies in the North East, Punjab, Jammu and Kashmir besides, being deployed for controlling Gorkhaland agitation in Darjeeling. It is presently involved in fighting the Maoist insurgents in Central India. It has been extensively ensuring smooth conduct of several elections all over India. The BSF also has been assisting civil authorities to control other national conflicts like the Delhi Police Strike of 1967, the Ahmedabad Riots of 1969, the UP PAC Strike of 1973, the Railway strike of 1974, the Bhagalpur riots of 1989 and many such contingencies. The BSF also was deployed to apprehend the notorious sandalwood smuggler Veerappan.

The BSF was the first responder in many disasters for relief works like the Gujarat Earthquake in 2002, the Tsunami in2004, the Kosi floods in 2008, the cyclone Alia in 2009, the Uttarakhand floods in 2013, and the Srinagar floods in 2014.

Contingents of the BSF have been participating in international peace efforts under the aegis of the United Nations.

The BSF has always performed to its best in all the tasks assigned to it and has earned praise from all the stakeholders.

Role of the BSF in Controlling the Insurgency in the North Eastern States

The BSF has been employed in counter insurgency role in the North East from the very beginning. It has displayed exceptional tenacity in operating in inhospitable terrain under difficult circumstances that has received recognition by way of award of several decorations and gallantry medals.

The North East region in India connects with the mainland through a narrow corridor at Siliguri is strategically important, being surrounded by China, Myanmar,

Bhutan and Bangladesh. The seven North Eastern states have witnessed several insurgencies since independence. The causes of insurgency in the North Eastern states can be briefly summarized as follows:

a) Alleged economic and social neglect of the area leading to a feeling of alienation.

b) Lack of economic development in comparison to other parts and resultant lack of employment opportunities.

c) Adversaries of India providing financial and logistics support to the insurgents.

d) The availability of safe havens to the insurgents in the neighbouring countries.

Major operational achievements of the BSF in the North Eastern states are discussed below.

Mizoram

One Battalion of the BSF with Headquarters at Lunglei and three companies of another Battalion located at Masimpur were employed for operations against the Mizo National Army (MNA) and its political wing the Mizo National Front (MNF) from 1962 to 1972. Troops of the BSF earned several gallantry awards during this period in recognition of their gallant action against the Mizo rebels.

In an operation in area Kamzawl, a section of the 84 Battalion BSF charged frontally on the insurgents lying in ambush. The insurgents who had killed a Junior Commissioned Officer (JCO) of the 18 Battallion Assam Rifles and injured another in the ambush heavily outnumbered the BSF troops. However, this did not deter Head Constable Ghan Bahadur Khatri and Head Constable Khum Bahadur Thapa, who led a frontal charge uncaring of the heavy fire brought upon them by the insurgents. The ambush was thus broken, forcing the insurgents to flee leaving behind dead bodies of four of their cadre. The BSF Section was thus able to save valuable lives of soldiers of Assam Rifles. Gallant action of both HC Ghan Bahadur Khatri and HC Khum Bahadur Thapa, was recognised by award of President's Police and Fire Service Medal for gallantry.

Sub Inspector Muktar Singh Khera of the 80 Battalion BSF was awarded the Police Medal for Gallantry in recognition of exemplary leadership and bravery displayed in an operation on 16 January 1972. In spite of being injured, he led his platoon to neutralise a group of armed militants after long strenuous walk of over 12 miles in difficult hilly terrain. Three insurgents were killed in the operation.

Nagaland

One of the agreements reached between Smt. Indira Gandhi and the "Revolutionary Government of Nagaland (RGN)" was the formation of three battalions of BSF to get the RGN cadres absorbed. Additional Battalions of the BSF were thus sanctioned. The first ever recruitment in Nagaland was done and the Naga youth who had given up the path of violence were given preference to raise the 99 Battalion BSF in early 1973 at Kohima. Two more Battalions viz. the 111 and the 112 were also raised. Since the RGN Cadres formed most of the manpower of these units, many officers and men were transferred from other BSF Battalions to ensure proper management of essential logistic and personnel management functions.[76]

The agreement between the Government and the RGN led to the surrender of over 2000 RGN Cadres along with their Arms and Ammunition. The RGN joining the mainstream was a blow to the Naga National Council (NNC) and Federal Government of Nagaland (FGN).

Figure 5.1: Naga undergrounds being inducted in BSF

Successful rehabilitation of the Sema Tribe predominantly recruited to the 111 Battalion encouraged other tribes also to surrender. These formed the manpower of the 112 Battalion BSF.

Ex RGN commanders like Shri Zuheto had a major role in motivating other underground cadres to join the mainstream. The avenues for employment opened for

76. Deshpande, A. ed., (2015). *The First Line of Defence Glorious 50 years of the Border Security Force*. Delhi: Shipra Publications, pp. 78–80. http://bsf.nic.in/doc/history/01.pdf

Naga youth through raising of these Battalions encouraged many others to abandon the path of violence.

The intimate knowledge of these surrendered personnel about tactics, psychology, hideouts of insurgents and knowledge of terrain proved very useful in mounting operations against insurgents leading to virtual elimination of insurgency in Nagaland and restoration of peace in the state. These newly raised units won several gallantry awards in operations against rebels which is a testimony of their heroic deeds.

Shri Zuheto Swu, was awarded the "Kirti Chakra" for his leadership and heroic deeds in capturing of 175 insurgents. Shri Tokhovi Tuku, Assistant Commandant, Inspector Vihoi Sema and Inspector Zekiya Sema, who were all surrendered RGN also were awarded the "Shaurya Chakra" for gallant action in capture of insurgents. Shri Zuheto in spite of grave risk to his life planned and conducted several operations leading to capture of many underground insurgents along with large quantity of arms and ammunition.

Shri B. Sridhar Rao Assistant Commandant commanding a Company at Meluri Post upon receipt of information of movement of insurgents trying to cross over to Myanmar, raided their hideout and successfully captured 21 hostiles alive, along with arms and ammunition. He was awarded the Shaurya Chakra for leadership and bravery displayed.

Besides those mentioned above, these units displayed admirable operational efficiency in preventing any loss to Railway property while deployed in Assam during the Railways strike of 1974 and the student's agitation during May to July 1974. These units earned tremendous goodwill through sensitive handling of potentially violent situations. They also operated proactively to control the situation arising due to clashes between the locals and the Bengalis and ensured early restoration of normalcy. They also ensured smooth conduct of the General Elections in Assam in 1977 and 1980.

Manipur

BSF has played a crucial role in controlling insurgency in Manipur. In fact, two Battalions of the BSF namely the 95 and the 96 were raised by incorporating units of the Manipur Rifles which were deployed on the Indo-Myanmar border till 1997.

The BSF was deployed for counter Insurgency operations again from 1999 onwards and a separate Counter Insurgency Sector was raised to replace the CRPF, which had received several reverses at the hands of insurgents.

Constable Ambar Bahadur was awarded Police medal for gallantry for exemplary bravery in an action on 19 February 1974. He broke an ambush laid by the insurgents by launching a flanking assault on their position which forced them to up stick from their position. He was hit by a bullet on his head during the process and succumbed to his injuries.

A gang of insurgents looted a large cache of weapons and ammunition from a Village Volunteer Force on 25 May 1976 and hid in the house of village headman in the village of Thinghanzang. Shri D. S. Rawat of the 96 Battalion BSF was tasked to raid the hide out. Shri D. S. Rawat planned the operation meticulously to surround the hide out. However, the surprise was broken at the last moment and the raiding party came under heavy fire. The insurgents attempted to break the cordon and a firefight ensued. Constable Kunwar Singh chased one of the militants with fire support from Head Constable Chandra Bahadur. One insurgent fired indiscriminately but was shot dead. Shri D. S. Rawat Deputy Commandant, Head Constable Chandra Bahadur and Constable Kunwar Singh were awarded police Medal for Gallantry for their brave act during the operation.

In 1999, there was an outcry for withdrawing the CRPF from Manipur after an incident in which innocent passengers were allegedly lined up and shot by the CRPF after being downloaded from a bus. The CRPF also had suffered badly at the hands of insurgents. The Government therefore decided to replace the CRPF with the BSF for internal security.

The 117 Battalion BSF was the first Unit to be inducted in December 1999 and was deployed for domination of the Churachandpur Town and surrounding areas. Keeping in view the history of losses suffered by the CRPF in ambushes by insurgents on the Imphal–Churachandpur axis, the Unit adopted the tactics of spreading wide on both sides of road and walk the entire distance from Imphal to Churachandpur. This pushed back the militants away from road and ensured safe passage for the convoy. The Unit adopted variations of this tactic all through its stay at Churachandpur till de-induction for operations against Sandalwood smuggler Veerappan. The tactics ensured that the road connecting Churachandpur to Bishnupur (The area of responsibility allotted to the 117 Bn BSF), where the CRPF had suffered several causalities, remained incident free during tenure of the 117 Battalion at Churachandpur. The Unit dominated the town and surrounding area effectively and prevented militants from carrying out any insurgent activity.

Constables Enduri Ahmed, Satbir Singh and Tilak Chand of the 117 Battalion were awarded the Poilce Medal for Gallantry for the initiative and bravery displayed by them in an operation on the night of 9 June 1999, wherein one UNLF militant was killed and a pistol recovered from him.[77]

77. Authors personal experience.

Shri Vivek Saxena Assistant Commandant and Constable Emamuddin of commando platoon of the 02 Battallion were awarded the Police Medal for Gallantry for gallant action on 23 July 2001 in Sugnu district. Even though injured, they continued to fight the militants and chased them when they tried to escape. Three militants were killed and lot of arms and ammunition was recovered during search of area after completion of operation.

Shri Vivek Saxena AC later was killed during an operation in village Sajik Tampak, where he had launched a search operation on specific information of presence of insurgents. His company came under heavy fire from insurgents numbering about 250 even while they were in the process of cordoning the village. Heavily outnumbered, the officer marshalled his resources for effective retaliation. He moved from one position to another motivating his troops and, in the process, fell to a hail of bullets. He was awarded the Shaurya Chakra posthumously for display of leadership and bravery during the operation.

Assam and Meghalaya

The BSF even when not deployed specifically in counter insurgency role has been involved in actions against them on the borders.

In an action on 13 April 1994, troops of the 88 Battalion BSF deployed on the border in Assam cordoned off the village of Mehargaon in Sonitpur district upon receipt of information of presence of militants. The, militants upon being surrounded opened fire but the troops fought them bravely killing four ULFA militants in the process. Constable Rustam Singh got injured during a combat with the militants but kept fighting till his last breath, was posthumously awarded the President's Police Medal for Gallantry.

On 31 January 2002, a patrol of the 161 Battalion BSF was ambushed by militants in the area of responsibility of Border Out Post Phanda in South Garo Hills of Meghalaya. The Patrol countered the ambush effectively resulting into killing of three militants and injury to another. They also recovered large quantity of Arms and ammunition from the spot. Three Constables lost their lives during the encounter. Constable Prakash Vaishnaw was awarded the Police medal for Gallantry for the bravery shown during the encounter.

Two Battalions of BSF were also deployed to deal with the Gorkhaland problem in Darjeeling, West Bengal that had attained an insurgency like proportions. The BSF successfully assisted the administration in containing violence and facilitating peace process.

Thus, the contribution of the BSF in controlling insurgency and bringing about normalcy in the North East has been immense.

Terrorism in Punjab and the Role of the BSF

Terrorism in Punjab which was aided and abetted by Pakistan with the aim of taking revenge for defeat of 1971, started taking roots from late 1970s. It took the shape of Khalistan movement and became a major separatist movement by 1982. The militancy was at its peak in 1984, when Operation Blue Star took place in June 1984. The Commando group of BSF called "Special Task Force (STF)" played an important role in this operation by carrying out the preliminary operation to clear a Hotel located close to the main entry of "Gurudwara Harmandir Sahab". Five militants holed up in the hotel were killed and two STF Commandos sacrificed their life in the operation and were posthumously awarded the Police Medal for Gallantry for display of exemplary bravery.[78]

The Golden Temple is the most important Sikh shrine and damage caused to it during the Operation Blue Star caused a lot of resentment amongst them. Widespread riots targeting Sikhs after the assassination of Mrs. Indira Gandhi further stoked Punjab insurgency. The BSF was called upon to control the situation and assist the civil administration in restoring normalcy. The BSF was deployed in anti-militancy operations in Punjab in piecemeal manner, since 1984. Some of the Battalions deployed for this purpose operated under overall control of the Punjab Police.

The BSF was soon given independent operational responsibility in many areas keeping in view early successes achieved in eliminating terrorists like Baba Ranjit Singh, who was an "A" Category hard-core terrorist, in an encounter by the 52 Battalion BSF on 24 June 1986 in Batala. Another self-styled General Labh Singh alias Sukha Sipahi was also killed on 12 July 1988 in an encounter with the BSF.

Figure 5.2: Seizures by BSF

78. Authors personal experience.

Strengthening of the Border domination systems, induction of additional Battalions and a new Sector Hq at Gurdaspur in 1987 enhanced the standards of supervision of border guarding operations. These measures proved effective in controlling trans-border movement of terrorists.

The BSF was soon deeply involved in counter insurgency operations in Gurdaspur, riverine Mand area in Kapurthala district and Ferozepur. Many dreaded militants were killed in these operations. The BSF also lost some brave men during these operations including Shri Davinder Singh, a decorated officer of the 1971 War. Many BSF personnel received bravery medals for their role in these operations. The BSF had limited experience of fighting the insurgency in the North East – which was mostly against insurgents operating in the jungle terrain. Having no experience of operating against urban/semi-urban militants/insurgents, it soon learnt the tactics of Khalistani militants and gave a good account of itself by countering them effectively. The BSF carried out several proactive measures to dominate the area allotted to it. The BSF intelligence wing was geared up to provide specific information about militant hideouts to enable raids and cordon and search operations against these hide outs. Surprise was a key element in operations by the BSF as they avoided fixed routine. This coupled with aggressive day and night patrolling-imposed restrictions on movement of militants. The civic action programs undertaken by the BSF during operations in Punjab also had a psychological influence over public who started realising that militancy was hindering the progress of Punjab and leading to avoidable violence. The deployment of the BSF became so large and extensive in Punjab that one frontier was shifted to Gurdaspur to exclusively supervise the BSF Battalions deployed for anti-militancy operations.

The BSF conducted over 150 successful operations against the militants in Punjab during the period of its deployment there. Many of these operations were conducted jointly with the Punjab Police and other security forces. Several dreaded militants were killed or captured during these operations along with the recovery of a huge cache of arms, ammunition and explosives.[79]

The questioning of apprehended militants led to identification of routes adopted by them for infiltration from borders and information about their handlers in Pakistan. This information was gainfully used in plugging the gaps and thus, enhanced the quality of guarding of the borders. This also resulted in the elimination of several terrorists in the process of crossing over to India. Thus, the pressure mounted in the interiors coupled with improved border guarding systems broke the back of militancy in Punjab.

---

79. Gill, K. P. S. (n.d.). Endgame in Punjab: 1988-1993. *Satp.org*. https://www.satp.org/satporgtp/publication/faultlines/volume1/Fault1-kpstext.htm

Certain areas during peak of militancy in 1990-92 were totally dominated by militants, especially in Batala district. The intensive night patrolling in the countryside and roads imposed severe restrictions on movements of militants and thus helped regain control of situation. The BSF also improvised by converting normal vehicles to bullet proof in the BSF workshops. Fabrication and use of bullet proof tractors in the sugarcane fields prevented militants from taking shelter and attacking the security forces from there. This improvisation also prevented causalities to troops.

Figure 5.3: Improvised Bullet proof vehicle fabricated in BSF workshop

The BSF was also assigned the tasks of guarding vital areas and installations in addition to anti-insurgency operations.

An innovative methodology adopted by the BSF to control the Mand area, which was dominated by militants was to form well-trained self-contained teams of the BSF personnel, who moved around this area in garb of militants and collected information about their hideouts and sympathisers. The information collected by them were extremely useful in conducting operations leading to capture and death of several militants in encounters. Farmers were settled in these areas and provided protection. The initiative cleared the area of militants and the BSF received widespread praise including from the Governor of Punjab and the Union Home Minister.

Construction of fence along the Indo-Pakistan border was the final blow to militancy in Punjab. In spite of several successes in the interior against militants, the pressure of militants did not decline due to infiltration from Pakistan through the open border. The fence was therefore conceived to create a formidable obstacle along the border based on study of the US-Mexico and the North-South Korea border. It was erected by the end of 1980s. It was further strengthened with early warning systems and concertina coils and guarded by observation and fire. Construction of fence led to drastic decline in the infiltration giving a body blow to the militancy. Monthly Intelligence Summary of the Punjab Police indicates that the numbers of terrorists crossing over to India came down to mere 15 to 20 per month after the fence came up from a high of about 350 per month at one point of time.

Overall, 107 BSF officers and men sacrificed their life fighting the insurgents in Punjab.

Terrorism in J&K and Role of the BSF

The Kashmir problem has been festering since the independence of India. The situation attained serious proportions since 1989. Pakistan aggrieved by the secession of Bangladesh has adopted a policy of exploiting the fault lines within India to the hilt. They first started with creating instability in Punjab which was controlled through some resolute action by the Security Forces and the political initiatives.

Pakistan simultaneously started instigating local population in J&K and stoking their sense of alienation. Even though local Kashmiris have always helped the Indian security forces against Pakistani raiders whether it was during 1947, 1965 or 1971, Pakistan succeeded in initiating a protracted separatist movement. Pakistan also sent many terrorists into J&K by exploiting gaps along the Line of Control and by giving them moral and financial support besides weapons, ammunition and other logistic support. Pakistan also made an effort to give a religious colour to Kashmir militancy however, it did not succeed. The experience of three wars with India also taught Pakistan a lesson that it cannot take on the Indian Forces directly. Hence, they adopted the policy of "bleeding by thousand cuts"[80] through unconventional war against India.

The uprising in the Kashmir Valley crippled the civil administration. The BSF was deployed in J&K for counter insurgency operations in the late 1980s and to safeguard the integrity of the Indian Union. Initially deployed for security of the Airport and the Raj Bhavan, the BSF was gradually given the responsibility of internal security as well.

80. PTI (2011). Pakistan trying to bleed India through a thousand cuts: Official. *The Economic Times*. https://economictimes.indiatimes.com/news/politics-and-nation/pakistan-trying-to-bleed-india-through-a-thousand-cuts-official/articleshow/10313870.cms

By 1992, the insurgency had gained so much momentum that some localities had become almost like a liberated zone. The BSF thus learnt its first lessons in fighting urban insurgency under circumstances where the population was totally hostile and the sources of information had completely dried. Operating in such hostile environment in the absence of any intelligence was extremely difficult for the BSF and other security forces. Heavily armed militants fired upon security forces from all directions and caused heavy causalities. Later, when the population realised that the foreign militants were inflicting atrocities on them, the intelligence collection improved and the success rate in operations against the militants improved. Some important contributions by the BSF in controlling militancy in Kashmir are detailed below.

Rainawari area located close to the Dal lake in Srinagar was infested by militants of all hues. They occupied the houses vacated by the Pandits in 1990 and carried out their activities from there. The area virtually became a headquarter for the militant groups. It was difficult to approach the area because of Dal lake on one side and several nullahs on the other. With vehicular movement restricted in narrow streets, the troops could only move on foot. In an elaborate operation in August 1991, the area after being cordoned off by the Army was thoroughly searched by the troops of the 69 Bn BSF. The troops were able to clear the area of militants and recovered a huge cache of arms and ammunition and apprehended several militants. The BSF established several posts in the area besides mobile posts on bulletproof bunkers, thus making the movement of militants difficult.[81]

Sopore located 45 km North West of Srinagar was another such area under total control of the militants. The BSF played a major role in clearing this town of militants along with the Army. The militants were flushed out in a prolonged operation and bunkers established at strategic locations for domination. The militants were thereafter unable to re-establish their domination of the town.

The area specific patterns of deployment and absence of any routine in domination pattern adopted by the BSF unsettled the militants and prevented them from causing any damage to the BSF. The entire area of responsibility was divided into identifiable Sectors and Zones and different Units and Subunits were allotted separate areas for operation. The extenuating circumstances like absence of proper accommodation, absence of toilets, unhygienic conditions and long duty hours did not deter them from carrying out their assigned duties with sincerity and dedication. They operated in such a manner that collateral damage to innocent people was avoided.

81. Unit History 69 Battalion BSF and interaction with the then Commandant of the unit Shri Shivaji Singh.

Strategically located bunkers prevented free movement of militants. Located in close vicinity of houses, these facilitated better communication with locals and helped win their confidence. Gradually the people who felt harassed by the militants started giving information about their movement.

During the peak of militancy, the Government of J&K notified the BSF post at Gupkar Road in Srinagar as a police station. Thus, it combined the police powers and tactical capabilities of the Armed Force

The apprehended militants were questioned at what were known as Papa-I and Papa-II. The interrogation of apprehended militants at these institutions by the joint interrogation teams proved very useful in the planning of the operations.

During its deployment in anti-militancy role in J&K, the BSF carried out several successful operations leading to death and capture of several militants and seizure of a large quantity of Arms and Ammunition.

One of the very important operations by the BSF was conducted on 30 August 2003. Rana Tahir Nadeem alias Gazi Baba, who was the Chief Operational Commander of the banned outfit Jamait-e-Islami and the mastermind of the Parliament Attack was killed in a well-coordinated information-based operation processed by the Intelligence branch of the BSF.[82] Knowing well about the frequent change of location by Gazi Baba, the operation was planned and launched at night. Shri N. N. D. Dubey Second in Command who got severely injured in the operation was awarded Kirti Chakra for the valour displayed. Sacrifice of Constable Balbir Singh was recognised by posthumously awarding him the Shaurya Chakra. Shri Binu Chandran Assistant Commandant, Shri C. P. Trivedi, Second in Command, who were seriously wounded in the operation were awarded the President's Police Medal for Gallantry along with Shri K. Shrinivasan, DIG and Constable Rajesh Bhadoria. Police Medal for Gallantry was awarded to Shri Himanshu Gaur, Head Constable (Operator) Hemant Joshi, Manik Chand, Head Constable Kuldeep Singh, Constable Neel Kamal, and Constable Omvir. Large quantity of arms, ammunition and explosive besides communication equipment were recovered during the operation, which broke the back of militancy in the valley.

---

82. Puri, L. (2003). `Gazi Baba' killed in encounter: BSF. *The Hindu*. https://www.thehindu.com/todays-paper/gazi-baba-killed-in-encounter-bsf/article27794563.ece

Figure 5.4: Award of Kirti Chakra to Shri N. N. D. Dubey, 21C

The operation was hailed by all. The Deputy Prime Minister Shri Lal Krishna Advani praised the BSF in the following memorable words

"The success was not accidental but the result of intelligent execution. It was an exemplary achievement on the part of the BSF and the entire credit for the operation goes to BSF." (*For details, see: https://bsf.gov.in/)

The 43 Battalion BSF carried out several successful operations against the militants and eliminated 26 militants and apprehended 47 during its tenure in the Kashmir Valley besides a large cache of arms and ammunition. In an operation on 27 August 2003, the unit acted with alacrity and succeeded in eliminating three dreaded militants who had taken position in the Hotel Greenway - located close to the Chief Minister's residence in Srinagar - after lobbying grenades in the street that injured many. Shri Deshraj, DIG supervising the operation suffered bullet injury in the operation. Five BSF personnel were awarded the Gallantry medals for bravery including one posthumously to Md. Firdosh Khan.[83] Another major achievement of the unit was on 17 November 2004, when they succeeded in eliminating the militants occupying a hill feature located close to the Sher-e-Kashmir stadium, where the then Prime Minister Shri Vajpai was to address a public meeting. The Unit earned five Gallantry medals in this operation. Another seven

83. Battalion History 43 Battalion BSF.

Gallantry medals were awarded to the personnel of the Unit for the gallant action in an operation to clear the Income Tax office building on 7 January 2005 in which two militants were eliminated and all civilians trapped in the building were evacuated.

The contribution of the BSF in fighting militancy in J&K will not be complete without the mention of the achievements of the 171 Battalion BSF. During its tenure in the Valley, the Unit was successful in eliminating 47 hardcore militants and apprehending 35. However, these successes came with a price when the Unit lost its brave Commander Late Shri V. P. Purohit in an operation on 2 August 2001 in Budgam district. Shri Purohit displayed raw courage and led his troops from front till the very end in spite of grievous bullet injury. The late officer was posthumously awarded the Kirti Chakra.

Shri E. N. Ram Mohan, who as the IG BSF Srinagar (Later DG BSF) during the peak of militancy was witness to the heroic deeds of the troops and officers of the force. Excerpts from one of his articles about these deeds reproduced below put the contributions of the BSF and the valour displayed in perspective.[84]

"I was struck by professionalism and confidence of BSF men during difficult situations and particularly the leadership qualities of Officers. These qualities were evident in abundance when I joined the BSF in Kashmir in June 1993. Insurgency was at its peak in Kashmir. There were daily firings on the BSF bunkers. The silence of the night would be shattered a dozen times every night with the staccato sounds of firing from AK-47s and SLRs and sometimes from light machine guns. I marveled at the fortitude of the BSF officers and men living in bunkers in the heart of the town at street corners and road intersections. Troops were living in such difficult conditions and under such constant harassing fire. Once again, I saw bravery and leadership of the officers of the BSF. The force had lost a young officer in an operation just before I had joined. I was reading the Court of Inquiry and I, was struck by the bravery of the officer who was leading the operation. Militants had been located in a house and Assistant Commandant S.P. Azad had surrounded the house with his Commando Platoon. Heavy fire had forced the militants to take cover of the first floor. With fire concentrated on the top floor. Azad led the assault into the house. He entered first and firing from his AK charged up the stairs. A militant, who was positioned near the stairs on the top floor, however saw the officer charging up the stairs and Azad took the burst of the militant's fire and fell and died on the steps. I was to see such frontal acts of bravery repeatedly in the next

84. Deshpande, A. ed., (2015). The First Line of Defence Glorious 50 years of the Border Security Force. Delhi: Shipra Publications, pp. 111–113. http://bsf.nic.in/doc/history/01.pdf.

two years. Assistant Commandant A. K. Ekka was in charge of the Commando Platoon of the 'G' Branch for nearly two years. He got his transfer orders and was relieved. At that time there was an operation in Chanpura, where some Hizbul militants had been surrounded in a government quarter. I was at the spot after we had demolished a wall on one side of the house. Fire was still coming from the house. The commandant was planning to send an assault party into the house. Suddenly, I saw Ekka in uniform with the bullet proof vest. I asked him what he was doing when he had handed over charge. A very shy and quiet officer, he was wishing the ground would swallow him up as he replied that he wanted to go into the house. I took a conscious decision to allow him wondering how I was ever going to get over it if a tragedy took place. He went in with the assault party and they accounted for the two militants holed up inside. I heard somebody say that Ekka was hit. My heart was in my mouth till saw Ekka coming out with a bullet injury on his hand. I can recount many more such instances of courageous acts of officers and men of this Force."

The BSF during the operations against militants always maintained high standards of conduct with the civilians. All efforts were made to avoid collateral damage and human rights violations. Even while keeping a tough posture against the militants, the BSF always retained a human touch. It took to several Civic Action Programmes to win over the masses. These included adoption of schools and provision of furniture, computers, etc. to them, educational counselling for children, promoting national integration by organising tours for local children to other parts of country by using BSF funds, etc. These efforts had a lot of impact in moulding the minds of the people. These also helped in better intelligence collection.

The BSF Intelligence wing has significantly contributed to the successes of the BSF against the militants in the Valley. The information processed by them enabled the BSF to focus on eliminating the leadership of the militants resulting in the lack of coordination amongst militants.

The BSF lost over 1000 of its brave soldiers with over 3700 personnel who were injured during the operations against the militants. The force personnel also earned three Kirti Chakra, one Shaurya Chakra, 74 President's Police Medal for Gallantry and 212 Police Medal for Gallantry.

The BSF was de-inducted from the Kashmir Valley in phases after the Kargil War. The Vohra committee set up after the War recommended that the forces meant for different tasks should be deployed for that particular task. The CRPF which is raised as a force to assist civil administration in internal security and anti-insurgency operations thus was inducted to relieve the BSF which was then deployed for its original task of border guarding. The BSF was finally relieved of the Anti-militancy duties from J&K in 2007.

Left Wing Extremism

Left wing extremism poses a serious threat to India's security. Having started from a nondescript village Naxalbari in North Bengal, it has now spread to a wide geographical area and covers almost the entire Central India. Corruption, an administration far removed from ground realities and extreme poverty add to the grievances of the tribal people who in many areas do not respect the authority of the state.

The BSF was first deployed in the Anti Naxal operations in Chhatisgarh by raising three new Sectors at Raipur, Koraput and Thiruvananthapuram with the task of assisting administration in inculcating sense of security amongst the local population and to ensure that developmental work carries on uninterrupted. The deployment of the BSF over the years has increased to a force strength equivalent of the two BSF frontiers.

Induction of the BSF was resisted strongly by the militants by laying IEDs in conjunction with strong ambushes. These efforts to cause causalities and demoralise the BSF were neutralised by the BSF through adopting varied timings and maintaining surprise of movement. Effective retaliation and counter ambush drills adopted by the BSF made the militants vary of attacking the BSF. Aggressive domination of the area in vicinity of "Company Operating bases (COBs)" by the BSF prevented the militants from close reconnaissance and resorting to another of their favourite methodology of fire assaults on Posts.

Figure 5.5: BSF Patrolling on Motorcycle

After initial acclimatisation with terrain and operational environment the battle-hardened troops of BSF achieved effective domination of the area and put the militants on defensive. The evidence of success of the BSF lies in the fact that its personnel have been awarded a number of gallantry awards with minimum causalities.

The tactical and battle craft training that the BSF troops receive has proved very useful in operating against the Maoist militants. Some important successes against the militants and their inability to snatch weapons from the BSF personnel firmly established the morale and physical ascendency of the BSF over them.

A patrol of the 200 Battalion BSF upon being ambushed by militants on 29 August 2010 in Durgkondal area of Chhattisgarh immediately retaliated effectively which forced militants to keep their heads down thus preventing aimed fire at troops. Simultaneous encircling movement by troops unsettled the militants forcing them to flee without achieving their aim. Head Constable Pramod Kumar Singh, Constable Arup Rakshit, Constable Bheema Shankar and Constable Tejendra Singh even though grievously injured, displayed exemplary bravery and presence of mind during the operation and kept the militants at bay. Their sacrifice was recognised by posthumous award of the Police Medal for Gallantry. Huge quantities of explosives and other materials were recovered.

Inspector Gaurav Godbole of the 161 Battalion BSF, even though, injured in first burst of fire from militants, displayed exemplary presence of mind to take his vehicle out of the killing zone of an ambush sprung by a group of 60-70 militants, upon his convoy of three vehicles near Pottangi on highway Koraput-Vishakhapatnam on 26 August 2013. The ambush accompanied with an IED blast completely destroyed the second vehicle of the convoy. Even though only 15 in number, the troops responded to the bravery of their commander and took positions on a dominating height nearby enabling the troops in the second vehicle to extricate injured personnel from the vehicle destroyed by IED. The heavy retaliation forced the militants to flee from the site without achieving their aim of looting weapons from injured persons. Inspector Gaurav Godbole and Head Constable Sunil Kumar were awarded the President's Police Medal for Gallantry. Their dauntless courage and camaraderie ensured that lives of two injured persons were saved and militants were forced to flee. Large quantity of explosive was also recovered from the ambush site.

Establishment of the COBs in remote areas has imposed severe restriction on the movement of militants. Emphasis on maintaining data of villages, analysis of crime pattern and modus operandi of the militants has helped in improving the domination pattern. It has also improved the flow of operational intelligence. This strategy frustrated the militants to an extent that they attempted assaults on some of these remote posts to deter BSF.

In one such attack on the night of 2 April 2012, they launched a massive fire assault on the COB Udanpur of the 41 Battalion BSF in Chhattisgarh. The militants involved in the assault were more than 200 in numbers. The young Company Commander Arun Dhyani Dy Commandant having foreseen such an eventuality had invested his time in strengthening defences of the COB, moved from Bunker to Bunker motivating his troops and ensuring that they exercised proper fire control. The militants before launching the assault had cut of electricity supply to the COB. The troops put the Night Vision devices available to good use in detecting the movement of militants. The militants were forced to retreat after an intense firefight of three hours. The militants could not cause any causalities to the BSF personnel. Large quantity of arms, ammunition and empty cases were recovered from the site after the operation. The grit and determination displayed by Shri Dhyani and his troops demoralised the militants and asserted the moral ascendency of the BSF.[85] Leadership qualities and bravery displayed by Shri Dhyani Deputy Commandant and bravery displayed by Constable Kamlesh Singh and Constable Satyavir singh was recognised by awarding the Police Medal for Gallantry.

The BSF also suffered some losses in these areas. One major loss was that of Comdt Jeevan Ram Khaswan of the 107 Battalion BSF along with his 2 I/C Rajesh Sharan and three other personnel who lost their lives in an IED blast on 10 February 2012 in Malkangiri.

The focus of the BSF on strategy of winning hearts and minds alongside aggressive domination paid lot of dividends. The strategy involved identifying the difficulties of the tribal people located in remote areas and assist in their alleviation through the Government and, if feasible from the budget allotted for Security Related Expenditure (SRE).[86] Establishment of Posts in remote areas helped improve communications as the roads and tracks were required to be built to connect these areas. Extensive public contact programme undertaken by the BSF resulted in better understanding of the reasons for presence of the BSF in these areas and the harm that militants were causing to the interests of people. Holding regular medical camps and distribution of free medicines not only helped mould the public opinion but and was also a useful method of obtaining information. Once the people realised that the BSF was there for good

85. Interaction of author with Shri Arun Dhyani Dy Commandant and Battalion History of 41 Battalion BSF.
86. Ministry of Home Affairs (2015). Security related expenditure. *Pib.gov.in.* https://pib.gov.in/newsite/PrintRelease.aspx?relid=124274

of people, they started opening up and information about militants started trickling in, thus facilitating better coordination for operations. Thus, the BSF has managed to project a better image of the Government in these areas.

In conclusion, this can be said with authority that the BSF besides its prime role of guarding the borders is also proficient in anti-militancy operations. That the BSF is often called upon to perform these tasks is a tribute to its operational philosophy and ethos. The junior leaders and troops have displayed exemplary courage and leadership qualities even in face of grave danger to their lives in these operations. This also is a reflection on the high standards of training, motivation and sense of camaraderie among troops and junior leaders.

Contribution in Controlling Other National and International Conflicts

The BSF is also often called up for performing duties to aid the civil authorities for restoration of the law and order and to ensure smooth conduct of elections at various levels. Some major events in which the BSF was deployed to restore law and order are discussed below.

Delhi Police Strike, 1967

The first major assistance for restoration of the law and order the force was called upon to perform within two years of its raising was to control the Delhi Police Strike in 1967. The Delhi Police had gone on strike on 13 April 1967 in protest against the termination of service of some of the police personnel on grounds of indiscipline. The police personnel gathered in large numbers around North Avenue and tried to break into the residence of the Home Minister. Senior Delhi Police officers panicked and fearing backlash, wanted the BSF to operate without weapons and use sticks instead. This was outrightly rejected by the BSF commanders and the BSF prepared for action against striking policemen and encircled them. Finding the BSF troops advancing with bayonets fixed, the striking Policemen raised their hands and surrendered. The operation was over in just 21 minutes. The action of the BSF came in for a lot of praise from the then Home Minister Shri Y. B. Chavan.

Ahmedabad Riots, 1969

Serious communal riots broke out in Ahmedabad in September 1969 and the BSF was called upon to control the situation. As during the Delhi Police strike, the Gujarat State Police officers initially wanted the BSF to operate with sticks and deploy in penny pockets. However, they were informed that the BSF as an armed Force could be deployed only with weapons and not below a section level as per instruction of the Government.

Figure 5.6: Ahmedabad Riots-BSF to rescue of people

As the situation went beyond control, the BSF companies which were kept in reserve were deployed in the city area. The deployment pattern ensured that the troops were in mutual support and dominated the lanes and the by lanes by establishing pickets and patrols. The troops were ordered to exercise restraint and use force only as a "right to private defence".

Judicious use of force in accordance with necessities of the situation, complete sense of impartiality was the USP of the BSF in this sensitive assignment. These helped creating a sense of confidence and faith in the abilities of the force amongst population of Ahmedabad. The human face of the BSF was on display in the relief camps organised and managed by the BSF. The work of the BSF was so highly appreciated that the state police requested the BSF to train three of its Armed Battalions and Units to face up to such contingencies.[87]

UP PAC Strike

Uttar Pradesh Armed Police went on strike in 1973[88] and the BSF was called in to disarm them. As per the initial plan both the BSF and the Army were to be deployed to handle the situation together. However later, the Army and the BSF were tasked to operate separately to disarm different UP Provincial Armed Constabulary (PAC) Units. While

87. Rajgopal, P.V. (2013). The British, the Bandits and the Bordermen: From the Diaries and Articles of K. F. Rustamji. New Delhi: Wisdom Tree Publishers.
88. Chishti, S. (2018). In light of Hashimpura, recalling PAC, UP's controversial armed police force. *The Indian Express*. https://indianexpress.com/article/explained/in-light-of-hashimpura-recalling-pac-ups-controversial-armed-police-force-5430170/

the Army had to resort to use of fire injuring several personnel, the BSF accomplished the task peacefully with great tact and negotiating skills displayed by its officers. The BSF came in for wholesome praise from all quarter for the action.

Railway Strike, 1974

The railwaymen went on strike in 1974[89] to air their long pending grievances leading to breakdown of communications and transportation of goods including food grain and fuel throughout the country. In spite of the Government declaring the strike illegal, the railwaymen did not return to work and continued with their strike. The BSF was called upon to ensure that the "wheels" kept moving. They were assigned the tasks of: (a). Escorting the trains and guarding the cabins; (b). Protection of the railway lines and vital installations; (c). Patrolling in the big railway colonies at important places; and, (d). Protection and escorting the willing workers.

Figure 5.7: Patrolling by BSF to secure Railway a station

The BSF which was mainly deployed in Bihar, Uttar Pradesh and West Bengal did a good work in controlling the striking workers at Patna, Danapura, Mughalsarai and other places and preventing them from interfering with those who did not want to be part of the strike. They also ensured safe work environment for the willing workers. The BSF also patrolled the railways colonies and ensured security for the families of the loyal workers. The BSF communication personnel were utilised to ensure that the communication system of the Railways remained functional.

89. Sherlock, S. (2001). *The Indian railways strike of 1974: a study of power and organised labour*. New Delhi: Rupa.

The BSF performed its duties with thorough dedication and that made a favourable impression on the General public and also on the authorities.

Bhagalpur Riots

The BSF was inducted in Bhagalpur to control the October 1989 communal riots, when the situation had gone beyond control and a lot of bloodbath had already taken place. The civil administration and Police were in total disarray, it was a ghastly site when the BSF reached Bhagalpur. There were large hordes of people moving threateningly towards Muslim dominated areas. The BSF had no time to assess the situation and immediately carried out Flag Marches in the town to put fear amongst the criminals and deployed troops at sensitive places to prevent the rampaging mobs from causing harm to minorities.

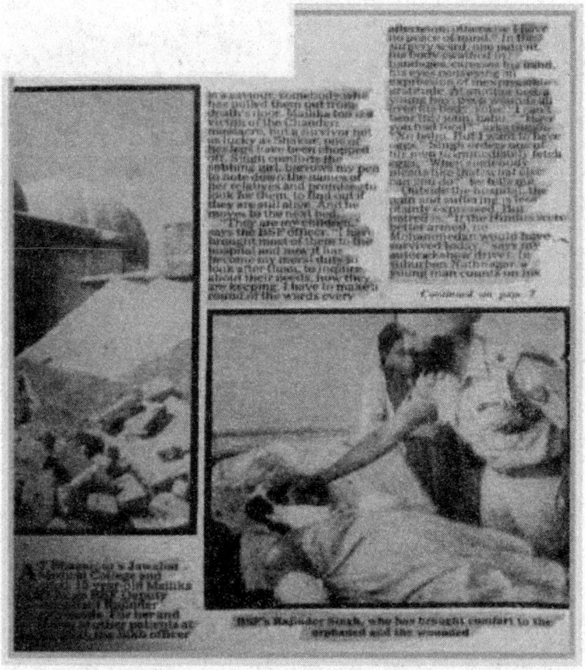

BSF's Rajinder Singh, who has brought comfort to the orphaned and the wounded

Figure 5.8: BSF Personnel taking care of wounded in riots

The BSF established relief camps and looked after those rendered homeless. They also looked after the injured and ensured their evacuation to hospitals after first aid in the relief camps. The local church helped out when feeding thousands in the relief camps became difficult. The BSF also helped out in tracing the missing besides tracing and burying those thrown in the nearby River Ganges.

The humane face of the BSF endeared them to the grateful victims of riots and the BSF came in for lavish praise from locals as well as the authorities. The local and national dailies were effusive in praise of the role played by the BSF in controlling these riots.

Besides above, the BSF has been involved in several other cases in aid to civil authorities like the operations to apprehend the Sandalwood smuggler Veerappan, where its performance was recognised by way of an award of Rs. 40 lakhs by the Karnataka Government.

BSF and Elections

The BSF since its inception has been called upon to ensure free and fair conduct of elections. Earlier the deployment of the BSF was restricted for elections for Parliament and State legislatures. However, seeing the impartial conduct of the BSF in these duties, it is now being called upon for security even for elections to the Panchayats and other lower representative bodies. In recent years, it has been involved in the Panchayat elections in West Bengal, and Jammu and Kashmir. The BSF has also been entrusted to ensure smooth conduct of elections to Tripura Tribal Council in Tripura state for last several years.

Conclusion

In conclusion, it is apparent that the BSF has made very useful contributions to the internal security of the country, be it fighting the militants or, the insurgents or, in assisting the civil authorities to uphold law and order or, at the time of elections. The public admires the force because of its professional conduct, impartial behaviour and humane approach.

However, the inability of civil authorities to comprehend the operational ethos of the force sometimes lead to problems. Implication of the BSF being an armed force is not clear to them. They therefore expect and want the BSF to operate with sticks. They do not realise that the BSF is not trained to operate in this manner. The civil authorities also do not understand that the BSF troops operate in subunits with the smallest being a section strength. They therefore often want the BSF troops to deploy in ones and twos. Misunderstandings are thus created when the Police and the civil authorities are informed that the BSF cannot operate in the manner suggested by them. Therefore, there is a requirement for better understanding of the BSF operational philosophy by the civil Police and other authorities.

Other issues that the BSF faces during their deployment to aid the civil authority is the lack of familiarisation with the area. Therefore, it is essential that Police representatives familiar with the area are associated with the subunits going out for the operations. The presence of the civil police representative also, is essential because the BSF does not have the powers to search the premises in the areas where the Armed Forces Special Powers (AFSPA)[90] is not promulgated.

Disaster Response

As has been discussed in earlier chapters the BSF is often called upon to assist the civil authorities in alleviating the situation arising due to natural disasters. The BSF played a stellar role in calamities like the Odisha super cyclone in 1999, the Gujarat Earthquake in 2001, and the Tsunami in 2004. As first responder, the BSF has been involved in rescue of victims and providing them with medical assistance. The BSF water wing was thickly involved in rescue and relief during the Tsunami of 2004.

In 2005, the Government raised a National Disaster Response Force (NDRF) and two BSF Battalions were converted to exclusively perform the role of Disaster Management. These were placed at Kolkata and Guwahati. Subsequently, one more Battalion was converted to disaster management Battalion in 2010 and was located at Patna. These Battalions performed yeomen's services during the Odisha floods in 2007, the Kosi floods in Bihar in 2008, the Cyclone Alia in May 2009, the Uttarakhand floods 2013 and the Srinagar floods of 2014. The BSF water wing and air wing is also very often requisitioned for rescue and relief operations during these operations.

Besides above, the BSF with its pan India presence and resources at its disposal often comes to the help of people residing in remote border areas during local disasters.

Contribution of the BSF to United Nations Peace Keeping Efforts

For the last three decades, the BSF has regularly been contributing troops to the UN Peacekeeping missions. Since the first contingent was sent to Kampuchea, other United Nations Police (UNPOLs) contingents have been deployed in strife-torn areas like Namibia, Mozambique, Cambodia, Angola, Bosnia and Herzegovina, Sudan, Liberia, South Sudan, Cyprus and Haiti. The Formed Police units (FPU) of the BSF are presently employed in Haiti and Congo.[91]

Shri Kunwar Virender, Deputy Commandant, laid down his life in the line of duty for the UN while deployed in Namibia. Shri Satish Chandra Menon, DC, BSF who

---

90. The Hindu Net Desk (2018). What is AFSPA, and where is it in force? *The Hindu*. https://www.thehindu.com/news/national/what-is-afspa-and-where-is-it-in-force/article23648102.ece
91. *Border Security Force*. (n.d.). Border Security Force UN Mission. http://bsf.nic.in/en/un.html

laid down his life in Congo on 2003, and HC Khetpal Singh in 2007 were awarded the Dag Hammarskjold medal posthumously for their valuable contribution in UN Peacekeeping operations.

Besides UN Peace Commission, the BSF also provides security to the Indian High Commission at Colombo in Sri Lanka under the control of the Ministry of External Affairs.

The BSF is thus employed for a wide variety of roles besides its primary role of guarding the Indo-Pakistan and the Indo-Bangladesh Border. That it has been performing these tasks successfully is a tribute to its training, ethos and leadership provided especially by the junior leaders.

CHAPTER SIX

Security Challenges on the Eastern and Western Borders

The operational environment on eastern and western borders varies drastically from each other. The terrain, demographic profile and crime patterns pose different challenges hence, strategy for managing/guarding these borders will also vary from each other. The border guarding systems in place on the western borders, especially on border in Jammu and LC is totally militaristic, whereas more cooperative practices are adopted on the eastern borders.

Eastern Borders

India's 4096 km long border with Bangladesh poses major challenges as it is not aligned to any geographical feature. Further the border is zigzag with several turns making it difficult to identify unless marked by pillars. One fourth of the border being riverine poses different challenge

Border Domination

The population density is very high in Bengal and even higher in Bangladesh. Large number of people live on far side of the fence right up-to the International Boundary, commonly referred to as the Zero Line. Many of the villages and small towns are located on both sides of International Border with only a street separating them.

Figure 6.1: A Border Pillar located inside the courtyard of a house

The border is thus porous with people having relations on both the sides. Similarity of culture, language and physical appearance on both the sides makes it extremely easy for intruders to merge with the locals. Identification of illegal immigrants becomes further difficult due to easy availability of identity papers. Further, it is logistically difficult to ensure continuous presence of the troops at every place.

Almost one fourth of the Indo-Bangladesh Border being riverine, poses its own challenges because it is not amenable to construction of an obstacle facilitating exploitation of these areas by intruders. The water wing of the BSF dominates these riverine borders. The BSF thus has to come up with sound border guarding practices to prevent exploitation of these borders. The repair and maintenance process of boats and ships also needs to be simplified to ensure that most of them remain operational at all times which is not the case at present.

The typical geography and demography of the borders along Bangladesh and the area of responsibility of each "Border Out Post (BOP)" being large, requires that the BSF must integrate technology in border guarding. This will ensure continuous surveillance of the entire area besides reducing the physical and mental stress on the troops and provide the much-needed rest and relief to them. Additionally, effective utilisation of intelligence resources is important in order to collect and disseminate actionable information in appropriate time frame.

The fencing is prone to being breached and exploited by criminals. The organisation therefore needs to come up with design of a fence which is difficult to breach. Obstacle value of the Fence should also be augmented with help of subsidiary obstacles and early warning devices.

The commanders also have to deal with the negative impact of fence on the troops as they have psychologically started treating the fence as border. Most of the border domination operations are presently being conducted on the home side of the fence, especially at night, thus practically leaving the area ahead of the fence free to exploitation by criminals and smugglers. The farmers working in their fields ahead of the fence and those living in the villages along Zero Line also feel unsafe in absence of any protection. This also prevents the troops from proper familiarisation with the area along the international border and its exact alignment thus increasing chances of encroachment by Bangladeshi farmers. In fact, proper study of the Strip Maps (Cadastral Maps of border area) has led to recovery of land encroached by the Bangladeshis.

The mind-set of the troops and the commanders therefore has to change from "fence is to be protected" to "sanctity of the international boundary is to be ensured". This is possible only through more effective domination of area ahead of the fence, both during day and night. Presence of patrols during day will inculcate confidence amongst villagers residing ahead of the fence or cultivating their fields. Domination of area during night will also prevent criminals from approaching the fence and contacting their counterpart thus preventing smuggling and other crimes.

Land Acquisition

One of the major challenges faced by the BSF on the eastern borders is the acquisition of land for the BOPs and the Fence. Firstly, the process of acquisition of land even for such security related purpose is extremely lengthy and tedious. Secondly, scarcity of available land because of heavy population density is a major cause of this problem. Land being the only source of income for people, they are unwilling to part with it even when large compensation is offered. The government therefore has to work out attractive compensation package to persuade the villagers to part with their land. This could include appropriate monetary compensation apart from providing them with an alternative means of income through gainful employment.

Acquisition of Land for BOPs will enable deployment of troops centrally in their Area of Responsibility (AOR), thus facilitating proper domination. Completion of fence in remaining patches will hinder the border criminals in their activities. It will also enhance the quality of border domination, especially when the fence is flood lit. Commanders must therefore liaise with the respective State Governments and other civil authorities to expedite the process of acquisition. Coordination also is necessary to ensure continuous supply of electricity for flood lights.

Illegal Migration

Illegal migration from Bangladesh is a major challenge on Indo-Bangladesh borders. Heavy density of population in Bangladesh and consequent fragmentation of land holdings, coupled with frequent inundation of large portions of the country every year has resulted in agricultural activities becoming uneconomical. Employment opportunities in Bangladesh being limited due to low level of industrialisation and limited opportunities in service sector, Bangladeshis find migrating to India an attractive proposition to look for better opportunities.

Above push factors coupled with pull factors i.e., better performing economy, more employment opportunities, easy availability of identity documents and porous borders lead to migration of Bangladeshi nationals to India illegally by exploiting gaps in the fence and through riverine border.

Heavy influx of illegal migrants is said to have led to the transformation of demography of the bordering states enabling Bangladeshi illegal migrants to become major influence in the polity of these states. The influx also has put heavy burden on the resources of India leading to agitations like that in Assam during the 1980s. Various estimates put the number of illegal Bangladeshi migrants in India to about 20 million. In fact, a large number of illegal migrants have settled in metro towns also, where they have almost monopolised the unskilled domestic help market.

The influx has ebbed to a large extent as a result of strengthening of border guarding infrastructure and fence. However, it has not stopped totally. The challenge for the BSF is to identify the routes exploited by illegal migrants for infiltration and ensure that adequate measures are taken to block them. The commanders must also understand that the process of identification of such routes is a continuous one as the illegal migrants keep changing routes depending on the standard of vigil in a particular area.

Intelligence resources must be deployed to gather information about the middlemen or touts, who facilitate illegal migration. The BSF must also coordinate with the civil authorities to ensure that the illegal migrants living in the border area are identified and deported at the earliest. Coordination with the jail authorities is also important to ensure timely deportation of those illegal migrants who have completed their sentence.

An important measure in this context is to co-ordinate with the civilian authorities and the Police to identify those persons, who are involved in preparing and supplying fake identity documents to these illegal migrants. Our intelligence effort should also focus on this aspect. We must also coordinate with the Police and other civil authorities to take strict action against such collaborators and antinationals.

The influx of Rohingyas from Myanmar through Bangladesh is a problem of recent origin. There are about 8,00,000 Rohingya Muslim minorities in Rakhine (Arkan) state of Western Myanmar bordering Bangladesh. Due to recent violence against them in Myanmar a large number of these minorities have taken refuge in Bangladesh. Many of them also try to cross over to India and about 40,000 have succeeded in doing so and reach the interiors of India. The BSF has to intercept them at the border in the same manner as they do with other illegal migrants. A large number of them have been apprehended on the borders.

Cattle Smuggling

One major challenge that the BSF faces on the border with Bangladesh relates to cattle smuggling and their perceived inability to prevent it. The BSF also receives most brickbats for alleged excesses committed by its troops against cattle smugglers.

Cattle originates from Rajasthan, Punjab, Haryana, Madhya Pradesh, UP, Bihar, and Jharkhand. Travelling unhindered through the breadth of Northern India it reaches "Cattle Haats" in West Bengal, Assam, Myanmar and Tripura by road and train.

As per Government instructions the "Cattle Haats" should be located beyond eight kilometres of the border. However, at most places these are located very close to the borders which facilitate cattle smugglers to purchase them from these Haats and send it across to Bangladesh.

Cattle smuggling to Bangladesh mostly occurs from area which is unfenced or riverine border. All wings of the Bangladesh Government actively facilitate this illegal trade. In fact, Bangladesh refers to the criminals involved in this activity as "Cattle Traders". Each cattle crossing into Bangladesh is said to be registered at the Border Out Post (BOP) of Bangladesh Border Guards where an entry tax is levied before it is allowed to go in.

Figure 6.2: Cattle seized by BSF on a BOP

Cattle smuggling to Bangladesh is estimate to be about $ 500 million worth annually. Every night, the troop detachments of three or four are faced with hundreds of armed cattle smugglers pushing thousands of cattle through the river into Bangladesh. These contrabandists mostly use sharp-edged weapons and firearms that are country-made to attack troops. Where the border is fenced, the smugglers cut the fence to carry out the smuggling.

Troops trying to prevent cattle smugglers, being heavily outnumbered, face lethal attacks. In the process several cases of serious injury and lynching of troops have occurred. Death or injury to a cattle smuggler on border especially, if they happen to be Bangladeshi national leads to lot of adverse attention in Bangladeshi media, causing public outrage and adverse publicity for the Bangladesh Government. The BSF is projected as a trigger happy force in Bangladesh media. Human right groups too are quick to decry use of force and several cases alleging violation of human rights are filed against them.

Less Lethal Strategy

Use of "less lethal strategy" has been put into effect after signing of the "Comprehensive Border Management Plan" in 2011. This has created its own set of challenges for troops and Commanders. The strategy involves use of Pump Action Guns (PAG), Stun Grenades, Chilly Grenades, etc. to deter the criminals. The aim of the strategy is to temporarily incapacitate the targeted offenders and minimize fatalities or permanent injuries. Detailed SOP have also been issued in this regard in which, inter alia, it has also been stated that these weapons should be used in self-defence only, and not as an assault weapon to inflict casualties on trans-border criminals. The criminals knowing well that the restrictions on use of firearms have been imposed have become emboldened and do not hesitate in surroundings and attacking troops. The troops also have become reluctant to the use of firearms for fear of enquiries. Resultantly, casualties to the troops have increased.

The challenge before the commanders therefore is to prevent cattle smuggling without compromising the safety and security of the troops and at the same time, reduce causalities to criminals. The troops have to be trained to exercise their right to private defence in the face of danger to their self or their colleagues while ensuring the "use of minimum force". Senior commanders need to ensure that the troops having acted in good faith are not subjected to undue pressure. Commanders must realise that complete ban on the use of firearms is not practical. Decision regarding the use of force has to be left to the troops on ground. Lower functionaries, who operate in small detachments thus have to be trained and encouraged to exercise initiative and take real-time decisions without waiting for instructions from the higher headquarters.

Human Rights Issues

Besides implementing the less lethal strategy, the commanders must ensure that the troops are well aware of the Human Rights Issues. The human rights group are very active on the eastern borders and are always on the lookout for lapses on the part of the BSF. The use of less lethal strategy and understanding importance of the use of minimum force will drastically reduce the chances of human rights violations.

Some human rights violations also occur because of improper conduct by troops. There have been instances when troops have misbehaved with ladies which not only brings bad name to the force but also reflects badly on the standard of discipline of the individual and the unit concerned. The troops sometimes also use excessive force with criminals after having apprehended them, sometimes leading even to deaths. All such cases must be dealt with sternly after an impartial enquiry and guilty should be awarded appropriate punishment. This is essential to enhance faith of locals in the BSF.

Controlling Smuggling

The terrain and the porous border make the Indo-Bangladesh border prone to smuggling of several contraband items like Drugs Fake Indian Currency Notes (FICN), Gold, etc. besides cattle smuggling.

India has been dealing with the menace of drug trafficking for long. India's proximity to two of the world's highest illegal opium growing zones along with some of its external and internal factors contribute to making India a transit, a source and a profitable destination for drugs. Bangladesh is used as a transit for smuggling drugs into India. Though there are no authentic studies to point out number of people hooked to opium and the number of people consuming host of other easily available drugs including opium, phensedyl and poppy husk, synthetic drugs and other pharmaceutical drugs, which are easily available in the chemist shops. The smuggling of drugs in the Eastern Theatre and their increasing consumption has become a menace.

In the recent past, smuggling of a party drug by name "Yaba" into India from Myanmar and Bangladesh has started and increased manifold in a short period. Some quantities of this drug were initially seized from the Border along Mizoram. However, it is now also being seized from borders along Tripura and other areas in large quantities.[92] The value of seizures of this drug had exponentially risen to almost Rs. 10 crores in 2018 from meager Rs. 60 lakhs in 2017.

The smuggling of the FICN from across the Indo-BD border has always been a concern for the Indian law enforcement agencies. High degree of porosity in the border and inhabitation right up to the Zero Line at many places provide favourable ground for the FICN operatives along the Indo-BD border. The portion of the border along Malda district in West Bengal is particularly notorious for smuggling of Fake Indian Currency Notes (FICN).

---

92. *Press Trust of India* (2019). Smugglers in Tripura switching from cannabis to Yaba: BSF. https://www.business-standard.com/article/pti-stories/smugglers-in-tripura-switching-from-cannabis-to-yaba-bsf-119112900328_1.html

There is a ban on consumption of alcohol in Bangladesh. This makes it an attractive item for smuggling to Bangladesh from India. A cough syrup by the name "Phensedyl" with comparatively large alcohol content is used as a replacement for alcohol in Bangladesh. It is seized in large quantities by both the BGB and the BSF all along the border. Modus operandi is to procure and keep large stocks of this syrup in pharmacies close to the border and smuggle it across by throwing it from over the fence to be collected by Bangladeshis from there.

The BSF requires concentrating on preventing smuggling of the above items both from India and Bangladesh. The Coordinated Border Management Plan (CBMP) signed (in 2011)[93] between DGs of both border guarding forces provides for joint identification and periodic review of sensitive areas prone to smuggling. This exercise should be carried out regularly and deployment pattern varied accordingly. Variation in deployment pattern refers to the operational activities like patrols or, ambushes only. The timing. Duration and periodicity of these operations must be varied regularly to maintain surprise. It does not imply that we have to change the locations of BOPs, etc.

Such crimes can further be controlled by proper coordination with civilian authorities viz. Police, Customs, Narcotics Control Bureau, etc. and coordinating intelligence collection efforts by the BSF as the leading intelligence agency at the borders.

Challenge therefore is to ensure that troops dominate the area ahead of the fence properly besides the area on own side both during day and night.

Integration of Border Population

The relations between BSF and border population on these borders is generally adversarial. This is because general thinking of the BSF personnel is that everyone amongst the border population is a trans-border criminal or smuggler. On the other hand, many amongst border population think of the BSF as a hindrance to their efforts to earn livelihood. For the border population, smuggling is a way of life, not a crime.

The BSF must realise that *raison d etre* for the existence of the BSF is because of the borders and the border population. The principal role of the BSF is to inculcate a sense of security amongst the people living in the border area. Therefore, the border population is the most important stake holder on the borders.

Winning the confidence of the border population is therefore extremely important to facilitate better border domination. This is possible through good behavior of the troops with them, especially with the women. The BSF must institutionalise the system

93. Haroon Habib (2011). Bangladesh, India ink border deal. *The Hindu*. https://www.thehindu.com/news/national/bangladesh-india-ink-border-deal/article2308225.ece

of interaction with the border population at different levels to address grievances relating to their daily activities caused due to restrictions placed on them for move across the fence. The troops manning the fence gates should be adequately equipped with soft skills to deal with them politely. Regular domination of area ahead of fence as discussed above will also boost their confidence and create a favourable mind-set amongst them about the BSF.

The border population sometimes resorts to agitations against the restrictions that have to be perforce placed on them for movement in border areas. The BSF in such cases must deal with them patiently and explain the necessity of those restrictions and assuage their feelings. Regular interaction with the border population at all levels and especially at the level of the BOP and the Company is essential to keep the communication channels open. The entire border security infrastructure has been created to incorporate the salient role of bringing a sense of security to the border population and their grievances must be heard and viable solutions found. Proper communication will also reduce the instances of human rights violations.

Initiative such as conducting skill development programs for them from own resources or by utilising the Civic Action Funds (CAP) would go a long way in not only creating cordial atmosphere but also reduce crime by equipping them with appropriate skills to take up an honest living. The CAP funds are directly allotted to the BSF Units on borders. These can be effectively used for the welfare of the border population by enhancing the infrastructure existing in border areas.

It should be an endeavour of the BSF Units to identify the needs of the border population and utilise the funds accordingly. For example, the funds have been effectively used for providing computers to the schools and skilling the children in their usage. The funds have also been gainfully utilised in training the youth in tailoring, motor driving and motor mechanic, etc. The youth who are exposed to the functioning of the BSF through these skill development programmes will be like ambassadors of the BSF spreading word about good deeds. These steps will yield to better cooperation with the local people.

BSF has the potential to play a vital role in the government's implementation of the Border Area Development Programme (BADP). Deployment of the BSF in far-flung remote areas can be utilised not only for the identification of difficulties and needs of population living there and plan for infrastructure to be created, but also to ensure proper implementation of various works under this program. Ten percent of the funds directly allotted to the BSF for security related works should be judiciously utilised for the benefit of both the BSF and the border population.

Proper Documentation and Maintenance of Records

A large number of documents have been prescribed to be maintained at the BOPs. Many of them duplicate the data. The BSF needs to look into these from two levels. Firstly, there is a need to rationalize the list of documents to avoid duplication. Secondly, there is a need to sensitise the BOP and Company Commanders about the necessity of keeping the records updated, especially those pertaining to operations and Crime Data. With introduction of online connectivity and GIS, etc., the data bank should be readily available to commanders at higher levels for comparison and analysis.

Personnel at the BOP and the Company level must be able to prepare proper FIRs and other related documents for reporting cases to the Police and the Customs. They should also regularly follow up these cases with appropriate authorities. Improper framing of the FIR and absence of follow up mechanism leads to either closing of the case or acquittal of criminals. The leaders need to rectify this anomalous situation. This can be achieved through proper training - on the job and in the BOP. Regular follow up with the Police and the Customs in processing these cases will go a long way in deterring the miscreants and prevent them from taking advantage of the weakness of system.

Cooperation Amongst Various Agencies

Cooperation amongst different agencies operating on the borders is essential to achieve the common goal of providing a secure environment to the border population. Besides, effective coordination at ground, an institutional arrangement under an appropriate authority will be more effective in achieving this aim. A mechanism like "Border Protection Grid" in bordering states under the overall supervision of a State Level Standing Committee can achieve this purpose.

BSF works in close coordination with Customs, Railways, state police and other agencies. The force is tasked to ensure security of one of most sensitive trains across the world "Samjhauta Express" the symbol of peace between India and Pakistan which has often been targeted by terrorists to escalate tensions between the nuclear power nations. BSF troopers are vested with the task of escorting the train from Zero line to Attari railway station, where it undertakes practiced drill once informed by railway authorities about the train's arrival, which includes deployment of troops at all sensitive positions and then proceeds for opening gate. Once the train enters India, the joint team of railway and customs officers initiate security checks. BSF troops mounted on horseback and foot mount vigil during the initial checking process, which takes about an hour and is then escorted to Attari railway station for completion of immigration and other formalities. The BSF also ensures security to Thar Express starting from Bhagat ki Kothi

(Rajasthan, India) to Karachi and Maitree Express from Kolkata (West Bengal, India) to Dhaka Cantt (Dhaka, Bangladesh).

Figure 6.3: BSF escorting Samjhauta Express returning to India from Zero line[94]

BSF is also tasked to ensure security of ICP (Integrated Check Post, where customs and immigration formalities are done besides ensuring prevention of anti-national activities that includes seizures of contrabands and FICN).

Border Haats

The aim of the "Border Haats" is to facilitate trade of local produce. This will involve a lot of interaction amongst the civilians of both the countries and thus, may facilitate interaction amongst the criminal elements as well.

The task of the BSF therefore will involve regulating the entry and exit of the locals to these Haats and ensure that only the authorized persons enter India after conclusion of proceedings at the Haats. The BSF will also have to ensure that contraband is not traded at the Haats. Extensive liaison will have to be carried out with the Police, the Customs and also, with the BGB of Bangladesh. This will have to be ensured at the four existing Haats functional at Kalaichar, Balat, Srinagar and Kamlasagar and all future such Haats - six of which will be established in near future (including four at Bholaganj, Nalikata (Ghumaghat), Shibari and Ryngkua in Meghalaya and two at Palbasti (Rangana) and Kamalpur in Tripura. In addition to above, proposal of 62 more border Haats along the Indo-Bangladesh border is pending with the MHA/Commence Ministry.

94. Photo credit - https://www.thehindu.com/news/national/Help-us-export-more-to-Pakistan-says-Punjab/article17308367.ece

Coastal Police Stations

Sunderban is the largest inter-tidal area (approx. 26,000 sq kms) formed by meeting of the great river system Ganga and Bahramputra with the Bay of Bengal along the Indo-BD Border. Sixty percent of the Sunderban falls in Bangladesh and forty percent in India. It is the only mangrove Tiger land in the world, famous for its flora and fauna.

Coordination with the coastal Police Stations, 11 of which are functional (total sanctioned 14) in these areas will be essential to prevent the overlap of operational area with the BOPs/Floating BOPs of the BSF located in this area.

Population up to International Border, Across the Fence, Religious and Linguistic Affinity and Widespread Poverty

Figure 6.4: Border Pillar located at the edge of a house

One major problem that the BSF faces on the eastern borders is in regard to dominating the villages located ahead of the fence. At many places, the border cuts across villages and even houses.[95] People residing in these villages have unrestricted access to Bangladesh as it is not possible to deploy troops permanently there. The state

95. T. T. Bureau (2015). *Living on the edge. Telegraphindia.com*. https://www.telegraphindia.com/7-days/living-on-the-edge/cid/1313943

governments are finding it extremely difficult to relocate these villages in depth area. Reasons are firstly, non-availability of land to relocate them in depth area and secondly, the residents are not willing to leave their ancestral homes even if offered better location in the interiors. Even though permanent solution lies in shifting these villages to depth area however, this not being feasible in the near future, the BSF needs to deploy its sources to gather intelligence and keep a check over the activities, besides regularly patrolling the area and showing our presence.

The above-mentioned aspects coupled with the religious, linguistic and cultural affinity makes it difficult to distinguish between the Indian and the Bangladeshi nationals. Moreover, easy availability of forged identity documents complicates the issue.

Widespread poverty in the border areas must be addressed urgently by the government to wean away the population from crime. This can be done through effective implementation of the BADP schemes as discussed above.

Integrated Check Post (ICP)

Border Management in the Indian context too is gradually evolving from being a restrictive function to an enabling one which facilitates easy transit of personnel and goods across physical borders.

The proposals of setting up the Integrated Check Posts (ICP) were first mooted in 2003 with a view to locate all elements required to facilitate the process of transit of goods and persons at one place. Since a lot of infrastructure was required to be created for this purpose, Land Ports Authority of India came up in January 2004 to supervise the land acquisition for these ICPs and their construction, management and maintenance. These are to be set up along the borders with different countries and would consist of the Customs, Immigration and other regulatory agencies within one facility.

A total of 13 ICPs have been sanctioned by the MHA and responsibility for providing security to the eight ICPs located along the Indo-Pakistan and Indo-BD border is with the BSF. Three already functional ICPs along the Indo-Pakistan and the Indo-BD border are at Attari (Punjab), Petrapole (West Bengal) and Agartala (Tripura).

The BSF in order to ensure security at these ICPs has to coordinate with the agencies operating from there. The BSF personnel deployed at these ICPs should be aware of the processes adopted by these agencies and facilitate their work. It is also imperative that these agencies are made aware of the capabilities and constraints of the BSF. It will be the responsibility of the local formation and the Unit Commanders to ensure this.

The Intelligence Branch of the BSF will have a vital role to play here. Information collected by them will be extremely useful in preventing any security breach.

Western Borders

The BSF is manning 2289.6 kms of the IB besides, being positioned on the LC with Pakistan under the Army Operational Control. The BSF thus is deployed in the toughest and the most inhospitable terrain ranging from the marshy lands of the Rann of Kutch to the deserts of Rajasthan, from the snow bound mountainous areas of Kashmir to the dense jungles of the North East. The BSF deployment in remote and inhospitable areas is a great strain on human endurance and psyche. It is to the credit of the border men that they continue to perform their task with the great zeal and vigour, in spite of severe hardships. The wide diversity of terrain, demography and operational environment pose security challenges, which differ widely according to the area as discussed below.

Kashmir Frontier

Deployment on Line of Control

The LC passes through difficult underdeveloped terrain with few means of communications. The high-altitude snow-clad mountains, where troops are deployed pose great physical and psychological challenges to troops and commanders alike. Various aspects are discussed below.

Figure 6.5: An FDL on the Line of Control

Deployment on the LC is in sub-unit strength on the Forward Defended Localities the operational command of different sub-units, units or even formations of the Army. The deployment therefore is scattered with no centralised control of the Unit Commandant.

The first challenge therefore is to integrate operational philosophy with that of the Army through training, both at the foundation level and also at the time of induction. High level of coordination is necessary at all levels for this purpose. The role of Sectors and Frontier is basically restricted to administrative support as all operational control rests with the Army. The troops have to be well versed in the "operations of war" likely in the LC scenario.

The unit commanders have to manage the supply chain properly to ensure adequate availability of rations, ammunition and equipment at FDLs. This is especially important during winters for which advanced winter stocking is a major exercise in itself.

Isolation and effect of high altitudes is often the cause of depression and other physical ailments amongst troops. Hence, psychological management of the troops through regular visits by commanders, doctors and if need be through counselling by specialists is necessary. Regulation of troop movement during winters due to threat of avalanches is essential. Cease fire violations are a norm in the LC environment and therefore, it is essential to ensure that the troops are not exposed to unprovoked enemy fire. Management of leave of troops also attains importance because of restrictions imposed by the Army.

Deployment in Anti Militancy Operations

The Kashmir valley is at the heart of Jammu and Kashmir and is known worldwide for its scenic beauty. The population is largely Muslim with a fair sprinkling of Hindus in the urban area. The Kashmir Valley is surrounded by high mountains, where the density of population is very less. The BSF is often deployed to fight militancy in the state of J&K by separatists which controlled by their handlers in Pakistan resulting in unrest in the Valley.

Misguided youth often resorts to stone pelting and other antinational activities. Militants also resort to attacking the security forces by ambushing them and IED/Grenade attacks. Stone pelting is often resorted to incite the SFs to retaliate and draw attention of world community over alleged human rights excesses/violations on the Kashmiris.

"Detailed instructions vide ARMY HQ LETTER NO.12795/SD 5 dt 31/1/76 about command and control of BSF, Police and other Paramilitary Forces while deployed on LC. Extract at **Appendix 'H'**. The instructions need to be updated in view of several developments having taken place in the interregnum."

Troops have to be well-versed to counter the tactics adopted by the militants and their sympathisers. Training in use of proportionate force will reduce human rights violations. Intelligence branch has a major role to play in the success of operations in the Valley. Coordination with other intelligence agencies operating in the Valley will improve effectiveness. Coordination with the Police and the other state authorities is also crucial for quick disposal of the cases pertaining to actions against militants and also, those filed against force personnel.

Civic action to win over the hearts and minds of the population is important in anti-militancy scenario. Funds allotted for this purpose should be properly utilised. Troops also must project a positive image through proper and courteous behaviour with the civilians.

Jammu Frontier

LC as it descends down the Pir Panjal Ranges in the NW circuits around the Poonch and Rajouri to join the demarcated border in Chhamb. The demarcated border and the LC areas differ from each other in terrain and demography. The population in Poonch/ Rajouri area is predominantly Muslim, the area is underdeveloped and has only limited means of communication.

On the LC portion, the BSF is deployed under the Army Operational Control on the FDLs and challenges as discussed above under the Kashmir frontier, are applicable here too.

Along Jammu, about 200 kms of the International border is considered disputed by Pakistan. The border is yet to be demarcated. Presently, it has been demarcated by the old pillars constructed to delineate the boundary between the kingdom of Jammu & Kashmir and Punjab. This is a cause of many disputes between the two country's border guarding forces. Pakistanis object to any kind of work being done by India close to the border siting its disputed status and resort to unprovoked firing to prevent such work including developmental work undertaken by BSF or even civil authorities. The BSF is compelled to retaliate and civilians become the unintended sufferers.

The inimical Pakistani policies have converted the borders into live ones, with daily firing of small arms and even high trajectory weapons sometimes. Border guarding is further made difficult by the changed profile of the border crossers, who are either militants or are carrying costly drugs. Such smugglers are willing to fight their way through, unlike the border criminals and smugglers of the past.

Causalities to civilians, their cattle and adverse effect on the daily routine of the border population due to firing are matters of grave concern. While some monetary compensation is given for the loss of life or injury, it is the psychological effect on the minds of young children which leaves a long-lasting scar. This often leads to unpleasant situations on the borders with the civilians blaming the BSF for the situation. The commanders need to assuage their feelings and explain the situation to them through repeated interactions. The nation also needs to resolve this issue once and for all with Pakistan so that the border population can lead a peaceful life.

This border is also strategically important as the national highway connecting Jammu with the rest of the country is parallel to the border at a distance of less than 10 kms in most of the places. The importance is also due to several strategically important military and civilian establishments located within close vicinity.

Initial attempts to fence the border in the last decade of 20th century had met with strong resistance from Pakistan and led to repeated cease fire violations. However, the fencing could be completed in most of the area, except where it is not feasible due to riverine stretches, after informal cease fire came into effect in the beginning of 2003 and lasting till 2014.

The unfenced riverine patches are highly vulnerable to infiltration by Pakistan based militants and the ANEs who repeatedly try to infiltrate into India with support from Pakistan Rangers and the Army, who resort to repeated ceasefire violations to divert attention of troops to facilitate the militants. Pakistan security forces also often resort to sniper firing to inflict losses/injuries to the BSF personnel.

Land Ahead of Fence

Cultivable land ahead of the fence requires farmers to go across to cultivate it. Security considerations require that the farmers and their implements be searched both when they are going and coming back through the fence gate. This movement of farmers is regulated through the gates in the fencing. The BSF also has to provide security to the farmers working ahead of the fence. Proper SOPs for Gate Management have been framed and are being followed. The problem of search of women going across the fence has to a large extent been resolved after recruitment and deployment of women constables.

The cultivation across the fence, however is severely hampered due to frequent firing leading the population to agitate. The commanders and local troops have to deal with the situation with empathy and patience. They also will be required to coordinate with the counterpart to facilitate cultivation.

Wild Elephant Grass

Thick growth of elephant grass (*sarkanda*), especially in the riverine areas provide excellent place for the infiltrators to hide and smugglers to conceal their consignments.

Instances of tunnels being dug through these areas from Pakistan have come to notice. It is therefore important to patrol these areas regularly. Wild grass is also amenable to catching fire. Sometimes, when the wind direction is favourable to them, the Pakistanis deliberately set it on fire leading to fire spreading to Indian side and destroying the crop. It may therefore be prudent to cut this wild grass and destroy it. This will, besides saving the crops, also facilitate better domination of the area.

Weather

The weather in these areas is extreme, with temperatures soaring over 45 degrees Celsius during the summers and going below Zero degree Celsius during the winters. High humidity during summers and rainy season saps energy and adds to the difficulties faced by troops in performing their duties. Dense fog and biting cold during the winters add to difficulty of operations at night and most part of the day.

Located in the foothills of the Himalayas, the current in the rivers is very high. The river bed also becomes very wide during the rainy season. This leads to washing away of the fence. The heavy current also has the capacity of uprooting the surveillance devices placed in the riverine area and as a result, these have to be uninstalled during this period, thus causing difficulties in surveillance of these areas.

Type of Crimes

The area is prone to infiltration by the militants, who find several strategically important targets in nearby area. Easy approach towards both the Kashmir Valley and Punjab makes the area vulnerable to exploitation by the militants. As discussed above, the Pakistani Army and the Rangers actively support and facilitate these attempts by the militants.

Other crimes include drug and weapons smuggling. Comparative ease of infiltration vis-a-vis adjoining Punjab and easy dispersal avenues makes this border quite vulnerable to these crimes.

Punjab Frontier

The land of five rivers is a flat, fertile and highly developed land in the Indian sub-continent. The boundary is de-jure and demarcated. The border area has fair density of population, who are mainly involved in agriculture. The rail and road communications are well-developed on either side and the whole area has an extensive network of canals. There are no geographical barriers except the rivers. On India's side, the Sikhs form the majority and on Pakistan's side, the Muslims form a majority; however, the dialect and customs are historically similar. The population on either side is industrious, adventurous and nationalistic.

Peculiar Features

The area is open, plain and flat country with no natural divides except the rivers, which have vast tracts of elephant grass along their banks. There exists a highly developed rail and road communication interspersed with a network of canals.

The population density is fairly high and is mainly dependent on agriculture. They are industrious and economically well-off. The language, customs and culture on both the sides of the border is similar even though they follow different religions.

Boundary line is de-jure and demarcated and area is cultivated up to the extremes of the boundary line. Border on India's side has been fenced strongly. Many amongst population are involved in trans-border crimes like smuggling of narcotics.

The border fence needs to be dominated round the clock entailing heavy manpower requirements. High elephant grass and tall crops in close vicinity of boundary line provide cover and safe routes to criminals.

Fencing has led to drastic reduction in trans-border crime. It has also compelled the border crossers to change their modus operandi. They now use methods like conceal and clear, throwing over the fence and also dig tunnels to smuggle their contraband.

Figure 6.6: A border Patrol along fence

The operational and administrative challenges prevailing in Punjab; therefore, are similar to that of Jammu except, for the fact that the border along Punjab being duly demarcated on the ground is not a cause of any dispute. There has been no instance of firing on the border.

A joint retreat ceremony is held every day at Atari/Wagah check post. A suicide bombing had taken place on the Pakistani side of the border on 2 November 2014 during the ceremony, killing 60 and injuring 100 Pakistanis. The BSF also needs to take necessary steps to prevent any such incident occurring on own side of the border at Atari and also, at other places like Hussainiwala and Sadqi, where such retreat ceremonies are also held even though at a much lower scale.

Atari has started functioning as an ICP and therefore, the challenges of operating there as discussed above under Bangladesh, are applicable here too.

As explained earlier, the State Governments are required to utilise the BADP funds in the border blocks starting from the villages located closer to the border. The utilisation of funds for schemes in the villages located farther from the border has to be done in the later stages. The BSF representative in the State Level Committee for this purpose has to highlight this to ensure implementation in letter and spirit.

Smuggling of Heroin through the border along Punjab is a major challenge with several hundred kilograms being seized by the BSF and other agencies every year. In earlier times, Afghanistan's poppy fields were a major source of drugs that move into India.

The Taliban are hugely responsible for the trade as they patronage poppy cultivation which is a major money generator for them. According to United Nations Office on Drugs and Crime, vast areas in Afghanistan is ustilised for poppy cultivation, which keeps increasing every year leading to a spike in production.[96] Smuggling of Narcotics through the borders of India is therefore unlikely to slacken despite the unceasing efforts made by the border authorities of the concerned states to suppress the drug dealers and peddlers.

The BSF must remain alert to prevent this and the Intelligence branch of the BSF should closely coordinate with other intelligence agencies to obtain and disseminate real time information to the troops to enable them to take measures to intercept any such attempt.

As in Jammu, wide riverine gaps on the Punjab border make fencing unfeasible in those stretches. More than 40 such unfenced gaps are proposed to be covered by the "Comprehensive Integrated Border Management System (CIBMS)"[97] which are presently on trial at many places on the western and eastern Borders. The system must

96. Kshitij Bhargava (2018). The Chitta economy: How the business of drugs works in Punjab. *The Economic Times*. https://economictimes.indiatimes.com/news/et-explains/the-chitta-economy-how-the-business-of-drugs-works-in-punjab/articleshow/65634397.cms?from=mdr
97. Prabhjote Gill (2019). India is going to use sensors to protect its borders where it can't put up fences. *Business Insider*. https://www.businessinsider.in/india-border-security-with-bangladesh-pakistan/articleshow/68285991.cms

be tested in wide variety of terrain and weather conditions viz. humid, fog, rains and storms, etc. for effectiveness before introducing them on a wider scale. Another step required is to construct embankments to not only prevent change of course of rivers, but also to provide a stable platform for installing CIBMS on these. The BSF leaders will be required to coordinate with river and flood control authorities to ensure this.

Rajasthan and Gujarat Frontiers

The Rajasthan and Gujarat region has generally open, flat, under-developed terrain, which is sparsely populated. The great Thar and Rann are wastelands. However, the availability of network of canals has converted the northern districts of Rajasthan into fertile cultivable lands and these have thus become almost identical to the adjoining areas of Punjab. To its south is the semi-arid terrain and the great Thar Desert. The lack of vegetation, phenomenon of shifting sand dunes in the Thar desert has allowed only marginal development and the area continues to be uninhabited or sparsely populated. The cultivable lands of north and semi-desert area have fairly high density of population and people are economically well-off. Migrant farmers from Punjab and hinterlands with a mix of Hindus and Sikhs comprise the population in North and the Hindu majority gets pronounced as one moves southwards towards the semi-arid terrain and the Thar desert. Water being scarce poses problem of providing fresh drinking water to the BOPs.

The Gujarat border fall mainly in the Rann of Kuchh area. The Rann is a salty wasteland, flat and firm when dry and quaggy when wet. The Great Rann lies in the southern part, which is devoid of habitation, however the northern fringe adjoining the "Thar" is thinly populated. The area is undeveloped and communications are limited especially during wet season. There is also a great scarcity of potable water in the Rann. The demographic pattern is a mix of Hindus and Muslims. "Bets" are small high grounds in the Rann. These Bets are populated and are visible from a distance. These are therefore good navigational aids for the border criminals.

The area across Rajasthan and Gujarat in Pakistan is generally fertile, with good vegetation except for areas in immediate vicinity of the Thar and the Rann. The population in Pakistan in border area is mainly Muslims with sprinkling of Hindus in selected pockets. The population on both sides is industrious, adventures and have similarities in dialects and customs.

The area consists of vast barren and open terrain with little or no vegetation. High intensity winds and storms blow from the south-west to north-east direction for most part of the year and restrict visibility. Very high temperature during summers make moving out extremely difficult, however nights are cooler.

Figure 6.7: Fencing in Rajasthan

High shifting sand dunes have knuckles in the north-east direction and gradual slops in the south-west direction. Flat salty waste of the Rann turns quaggy when wet. There is lack of prominent landmarks making navigation difficult for patrols. Underdeveloped terrain and acute shortage of potable water create administrative difficulties.

The boundary is de-jure and properly demarcated except for 99 kms in the southernmost tip adjoining the Arabian Sea in the Sir Creek area. The entire land border along Rajasthan and Gujarat has been fenced.

Effects on Operations

Physical domination is difficult due to vastness and inadequate means of communications. The Unit Headquarters being located in depth are far away from BOPs. This coupled with limited means of communication, lack of water resource and restricted cross-country movement cause lot of logistic problems. Hostile weather also takes a toll of men and machines.

Low visibility due to dust storms prevent observation and domination of the area and enables criminals, to move safely. Historical similarities of population and their adventurous attitude promote trans-border crimes, particularly smuggling.

The construction of fence has led to reduction in border crimes to a large extent. However, shifting sand dunes degrade the obstacle value of fence as it gets buried under sand or gets damaged extensively. Operational and administrative difficulties get compounded in the Rann during the wet season due to extreme harshness of weather and quaggy conditions.

Boundary dispute and un-demarcated stretches of boundary in Sir Creek in Gujarat are potential areas of conflict. The Sir Creek dispute covers approximately 99 kms long segment of the IB from Sir Top to Sir Mouth. The dispute is on the interpretation of the maritime boundary line that is between Kutch and Sindh. Prior to independence, the provincial region was under the Bombay Presidency of British India. In 1947, post-Sindh joined Pakistan and Kutch joined India and thus, the dispute over the interpretation of the boundary in the area.

Water wing of the BSF dominates the creek area using Floating BOPs and other patrol boats. All-terrain vehicles have also been inducted in the area thus improving the standards of domination.

A recurrent problem encountered in this area is that fishermen of both countries deliberately or otherwise stray into the territory of other country. This happens partly because of difficulty in identifying the boundaries and partly as a deliberate act for bigger catch of fish. Hopefully with likelihood of Sir Creek dispute being settled in near future this problem will end.

Conclusion

The BSF with its widespread deployment all along the eastern and western borders has to face up to operational environment, terrain and demography, which vastly differs from area to area. Each area has its own peculiar challenges and the commanders have the responsibility to analyse these and prepare operational strategy most suitable for that area. The periodic changeover of troops also necessitates frequent reorientation and adaptation to changed operational environment. The commanders therefore have to be flexible in their approach. Each situation is different and same yardsticks cannot be applied to all of them.

The commanders have to realise that borders are dynamic places. The emphasis in over 50 years of existence of the BSF has gradually changed from the Border Guarding to the Border Management. The necessity therefore is to convert the borders from "barriers" to "bridges". All round cooperation – with counterpart, with other stakeholder agencies of India and neighbouring countries, and most importantly with border population is the future challenge for an effective management of borders. Challenge also is to reorient the thinking process of border-man to think of border population as an ally in the effort to provide a safe environment on borders

Modernisation and extensive use of technology is a necessity to ensure adequate rest and relief to troops, which face severe fatigue due to long hours of duty. The changing nature of crime and tactics adopted by the border criminals also necessitates enhanced reliance on technology.

In order to achieve this, it is essential that the BSF raises a perspective planning cell tasked with responsibility to analyse future trends in various aspects of border management.

CHAPTER SEVEN

Recommendations

"Change is the only constant" is a common saying. Same is true for the borders too. The operational environment at the borders is dynamic and vastly different from 1965, when the BSF was raised. The environment further keeps changing with changing nature of border crime and relations with the neighbouring country. The level of available infrastructure development and the employment opportunities that are present in the border areas also effect the environment.

The BSF was raised in view of the necessity to have a well-trained force readily available to tackle minor skirmishes and bring about uniformity in our dealings with the counterpart. The force therefore was required to be trained and equipped in a militaristic manner. The initial requirement was exclusively to guard the border against infiltration and trans-border crime. The concept of border guarding having evolved to border management necessitates changes in operational philosophy, equipment and human resources management practices adopted by the force.

A glance at Rule 15 of the BSF Rules 1969, which describes the role of the BSF would be essential. The Roles ascribed are as under:

a) Promote a sense of security among the people living in the border areas;

b) Prevent trans-border crimes, unauthorised entry into or exit from the territory of India; and,

c) Prevent smuggling and any other illegal activity. (*For details, see:https://www.mha.gov.in/sites/default/files/bsfAct&Rules_2.pdf)

Therefore, just as Comdt. N. S. Jamwal in his paper "Border Management: Dilemma of Guarding the India-Bangladesh Border" (2004) discussing the many dimensions of India-Bangladesh border management mentions, it must be reiterated that one of the most imperative task of the BSF is to inculcate a sense of security amongst the border population. This role should therefore be given top priority over the other two by the organization while planning deployment and operations.

This has also been emphasised by the group of ministers appointed to go into aspects of the Kargil conflict in their report, wherein they have recommended that a more comprehensive system of border management needs to be put in place in order to integrate the border population with the mainstream. The border guarding forces including the BSF thus have to modify their operational philosophy accordingly.

The situation along borders is dynamic. The situation along the Indo-Pakistan borders cannot remain perpetually hostile. Further, the nature of crime on the eastern borders will also change in due course. There ultimately has to be peace and tranquility to ensure stabile life for the border population. This is visible in so far as the borders from Punjab southwards are concerned. The only problem along these borders is the crime related to smuggling of Drugs etc. This crime pattern is likely to continue in future too. The border management system, therefore have to be modernised by extensive use of technology and doing away with present manpower intensive systems. Electronic surveillance of the borders with appropriately placed Quick Reaction Teams (QRTs) to intercept the criminals can be one solution.

Similarly, with development slowly reaching the border areas both on the Bangladesh and the India side, it will reduce dependence of the border population on crime as more employment opportunities will be available. Thus, border guarding methodology will need to modify accordingly. The BSF should be prepared to face these challenges.

Operational

Line of Control (LC)

Besides being responsible for guarding the Indo-Pakistan and the Indo-Bangladesh border, many units of the BSF are also deployed on the Line of Control (LC) in Kashmir, under the Army Operational Control.

Deployment of the BSF on LC is in small sub-units under different units of the Indian Army. Peace at the LC remains fragile and frequent cease fire violations by Pakistan in their attempt to facilitate infiltration of the militants keep occurring. The LC passes through high mountains not connected by roads and tracks. Some of the Forward Defended Localities (FDLs) remain cut off during winters due to heavy snow and fear of avalanches. The area along the LC is sparsely populated specially in the high reaches.

Mixed deployment with the Army poses a challenge for proper integration of troops for required tasks. The Army has its own drills for conduct of operations and the BSF has to adapt to these drills for smooth integration and success. This necessitates thorough pre-induction training, both in order to understand the drills and also for proper acclimatisation.

Another challenge that the BSF faces due to mixed deployment is of command and control. The troops being under operational command of the Army, face some administrative difficulties, especially for leave, etc. The BSF Commanders therefore, need to properly coordinate with their Army authorities in resolving these issues.

One major challenge on the LC is of survival in hostile terrain and weather conditions. The border man has to remain physically fit and mentally robust to be able to survive through long periods of isolation. Lack of oxygen at high altitudes may at times lead to some ailments having long term effect. It is therefore extremely important to properly acclimatise before deployment. Effect of adverse weather conditions also leads to decreased physical capacity. Non-availability of fresh vegetables and fruits in high altitude and difficulty of movement during winters necessitates advanced storage of packaged food consumption of which over long periods leads to loss of appetite. Prolonged deployment in high altitude, long periods of isolation due to difficulty of movement especially during winters in few cases may cause severe depression and psychological problems.

The challenge before commanders therefore is to ensure high morale of troops through constant interaction and rotating them at regular intervals to avoid any of the adverse effects discussed above.

The BSF will continue to operate on the LC in case of a war. Since the BSF will be fighting shoulder-to-shoulder along with the Army, the commanders will have to ensure war preparedness of the force. Proper familiarisation with the role the BSF is expected to perform, ensuring that they are properly equipped and logistically self-reliant to perform that role are the challenges that the BSF commanders have to face and resolve in coordination with Army.

What If LC Is Recognised as International Border?

It is unlikely that the operational environment on the LC will change anytime soon. Regular exchange of fire and attempts by the adversary to infiltrate the militants are likely to continue and the Army will remain operationally responsible for the LC. However, in the eventuality of the LC being converted to an International Border sometimes in the future, the BSF must have a plan to take over the responsibility of manning these borders. The plan will have to include aspects of raising additional manpower for the task, deciding on a deployment pattern, procuring equipment and weapons, etc. Planning for ensuring smooth supply chain will be extremely important because unlike the plain borders, the terrain poses a major challenge. The BSF will have to plan on lines of the systems presently adopted by the Army for this purpose.

Indo-Pakistan and Indo-Bangladesh Border

These were open borders till early 1990s. Militancy in Punjab and continued support to it from Pakistan necessitated creating an obstacle system. Thus, the border with Pakistan was fenced. The fence had a major role in containing border crime and cutting of the logistics that sustained militancy in Punjab. The success of fence along Punjab border influenced the decision to fence the border along Rajasthan and Gujarat as well.

The fence was also constructed along the Indo-Bangladesh border in late 1990s and early in the decade that followed. This has controlled the border crimes to an extent. However, almost one-fourth of the Indo-Bangladesh border being riverine is not amenable to fencing.

Fence and Related Issues

The fence and emphasis of commanders that it must not be breached has created a mental barrier amongst the troops. They now consider guarding of the fence to be the end-all of guarding the border thus leaving the 150 Yards strip of land falling on far side of the fence generally unpatrolled, especially at night. This situation is exploited by criminals as they hide their consignment in this area for later clearance by farmers, who are in league with them. The BSF therefore, needs to ensure that this area is patrolled more frequently both during the day and at night. This also is necessary to inculcate confidence amongst the farmers working in their fields across the fence. Going ahead of the fence on a regular basis will ensure that encroachment in our territory does not take place. This will also prevent criminals from adopting the "conceal and clear" modus operandi as described above.

The fence has restricted the movement of those farmers whose land falls on the far side of the fence necessitating installation of gates at regular distances. These gates have to be manned continuously to ensure easy access of farmers to their fields. Women folk also need to go across the fence quiet often and they can be searched only by women. Therefore, there is requirement of women at the gates. Till recently, this was being done by obtaining the services of ladies from nearby villages. However, with the induction of the Women Constables in the BSF, the task is now being performed by them. The increased interaction with civilians at the gates necessitates that our troops be fairly conversant with the local language and endowed with soft skills. These aspects should therefore, be included in their training at different levels.

The fence has been lit with help of floodlights. This entails heavy expenditure. There also is requirement of backup generators to cater for power cut or failure of grid. Besides above, the diffused light from the flood lights enables the criminals to locate position of our patrols and ambushes. The leaders therefore need to think of a more economical alternative. They may experiment with a sensor-based system, which will switch on the lights as soon as intruders reach within a reasonable distance where patrol or, a QRT can intercept them. Besides, being economical it will ensure surprise by concealing locations of the patrols and ambushes. The leaders should also explore the possibility of installing solar power for flood lights.

Illegal Migration

As brought out in earlier chapters, illegal migration to India from Indo-Bangladesh border is a major problem. There are various factors for this phenomenon. Firstly, the population density is much heavier on the Indo-Bangladesh side and huge population resides on the far side of the fence right up-to Zero Line. Many of the villages and small towns are located on both sides of the border with only a street separating them. The border is porous and people have relatives on both sides of the border. Similarity of language and physical appearance of locals makes it extremely easy for intruders to merge with the population. It becomes further difficult to identify them because of easy availability of identity papers. Secondly, it is logistically difficult to ensure continuous presence of troops at these places.

This problem of illegal migration from the eastern borders has to be tackled at many levels.

At the level of the BSF the commanders have to ensure strengthening of border guarding systems, effective domination of riverine gaps, frequent variation of the operational pattern, effective deployment of intelligence resources, completion of remaining fencing and its regular repair and maintenance besides ensuring hundred percent flood lighting of the fence. The commanders also must coordinate with the Police and other authorities to ensure that illegal migrants are not able to get fake identity papers.

At the level of the government, some kind of identification system for residents of the border villages can be devised. The BSF at its own level can introduce biometric/ finger identification system for people residing beyond the fence and crossing the fence gates for work. The Unit deployed at Siliguri had done this experiment with great amount of success during 2013-14[98]. This is recommended to be replicated and institutionalised.

Induction of Modern Technology

On India's western border, security mechanism employs long border fence with illuminated flood lights. The effectiveness of technical equipment is hindered by lack of stress on familiarising on the manpower with these equipment. Thus, there is lack of

---

98. Biometric scan. (1 December 2014). *The Telegraph Online*. https://www.telegraphindia.com/states/west-bengal/biometric-scan/cid/291347

compatibility between man using the equipment and the equipment itself. Effectiveness of equipment is further curtailed by the lack of proper repair and maintenance facility. Another factor further compounding the problem is the lack of technical expertise of supervisory staff. Due to these factors, even the already available technological resources are put to only limited use. In such a scenario, operational and cost-effectiveness of technology-intensive solutions like the "Comprehensive Integrated Border Management Solution (CIBMS) has to be assessed carefully. It is for the same reason that integration of surveillance systems like the Battle Field Surveillance Radar (BFSR) Thermal Imagers and the Long Range Recce and Observation system (LOROS), etc. have not been very effective and have failed to address the problem of stress on troops and border guarding systems remain manpower intensive.

Troops generally are hesitant to use the available surveillance devices, because of lack of training in their use. Secondly, the fear of inquiries in case of damage, etc. to these costly equipment makes them hesitant to use them. In absence of adequate field trials in varying terrain conditions, the devices do not succeed everywhere. This happens because the end user feedback is not taken into consideration. The procurement of these devices should be done after taking ground conditions into consideration. This will imply procuring different types of devices for different areas. For example, the underwater cameras installed as part of trials under the CIBMS will get washed away in heavy current during the monsoons.

Technology and border practices implemented in Israel and the US are often advocated for implementation on the Indian borders. Israeli borders are well-suited for advanced technology because of very small geographical size, highly literate and technology savvy population and compulsory military service, etc. Hence, comparison with Indian scenario is not appropriate. On the other hand, there are many similarities in the security scenario prevailing along the western borders of India and the southern borders of America. Indian authorities can closely examine recent US border technological practices, its drawbacks and experiences so that, appropriate lessons can be drawn to its advantage. India must take note of the initiatives taken by the US authorities to secure their borders during the last one and a half decade. They have been trying to explore and make use of economically feasible and cost-effective methods to bring improvements to their border security. India also needs to similarly focus on the indigenous solutions which are economical and user-friendly.

Any surveillance system being considered for introduction, therefore, must be subjected to rigorous field trials before being procured for extensive use. Feedback from end user i.e. the Jawan on ground is extremely important before introduction.

It must be ensured that the technology introduced is simple to use and suitable for the terrain, where it is deployed. For example, "Aerostat" may be useful in areas like Rajasthan and Gujarat, where border areas are sparsely populated. These may however not succeed in Punjab or on the eastern borders, where the population density and movement along the border being heavy both during the day and at night, makes it difficult to distinguish between an intruder and a genuine farm worker. Similarly, equipment like the BFSR does not enable a Jawan to distinguish between the movement of humans or other types of movements. Hence, these technologies are not successful in border surveillance, especially in the densely populated area.

The challenge therefore, is to identify correct technology that augments effectiveness of existing border guarding infrastructure, surveillance, infrastructure detection and communication technologies as well as physical structures and ensure their optimal utilisation to improve border security. The challenge therefore, is to identify devices which besides being economical facilitate better surveillance and reduce pressure on manpower thereby ensuring proper rest and relief.

The devices introduced should be able to survey large areas, which can be monitored from a centrally located Post enabling a Quick Reaction Team (QRT) located there to react in appropriate time frame to intercept and counter any threat. This will entail ensuring quick mobility and therefore, a network of lateral and axial roads in border area close to the fence must be developed. Such surveillance devices should also be linked with the Company and other superior Hqrs. in order to facilitate proper monitoring and supervision of operations. This will also facilitate quick redeployment of resources wherever required

Another challenge before the leaders is to ensure that troops are capable of confidently using the available surveillance devices in order to enhance quality of vigil on the borders. It must therefore be ensured that they are properly familiarised with these devices through adequate training/practice during their professional training and hands on practice whenever new technology is introduced. It would be much better if training and maintenance aspects are built in the tenders, while procuring these devices. Commanders must dispel the fear of inquiries that inhibits troops from optimal utilisation of these devices.

The end users on many occasions come up with innovative solutions to problems. Border men similarly are capable of coming up with solutions which can enhance quality of surveillance. This talent available in the force must be harnessed. BSF authorities have been encouraging technological innovation through annual competitions, however, these mostly remain an academic exercise. Solutions suggested during these competitions must be patented, be produced on a mass scale and used on ground to enhance border domination after field trials. This will, besides enhancing quality of border guarding also result in saving of financial resources.

In brief, the challenge before Commanders is to enhance quality of border guarding through seamless surveillance by way of induction of new technology and optimum use of available resources. This will result in ensuring proper rest and relief to troops and thus, reduce their stress.

The organization must have a roadmap for modernization only then the funds - which are aplenty- can be utilised gainfully. In spite of several suggestions at different points of time and many false starts, the BSF still does not have a perspective planning cell, which should be tasked to visualise future trends and make recommendations for modernisation. Modernisation should be need based rather than being vendor driven. Vendors hard sell their equipment but the organisation must make proper assessment of utility of a particular equipment after extensive field trials. The decision makers must have adequate knowledge of ground realities to be able to assess utility of an equipment for a particular terrain and operational environment. The BSF must avoid tendency of adopting "one size fit" solutions because, an equipment which is suitable for one particular area may not be suitable in the other. This will, besides ensuring proper utilisation of equipment also ensure prudent utilisation of scarce resources. Modernisation should also extend to modernising the man behind the machine through adequate training in handling the equipment.

Domination of Riverine Areas

The area of Sir Creek in Kutch of Gujarat towards the south of the Indo-Pakistan border is riverine. This border is still disputed hence not demarcated. The fishermen on both the sides often stray into the area belonging to each other and are apprehended by counterpart border guarding force. The challenge therefore is to ensure that fishermen of both the sides do not stray or even if they stray, they are retrieved at the earliest. This will require effective coordination with the Pakistan rangers.

For border guarding to be effective, the troops need to be properly trained in water craftsmanship besides being trained for normal border guarding operations. Floating BOPs and Speed Boats are deployed to patrol the area. All-terrain vehicles have also been inducted about a decade ago. Evolving drills for domination of the area is a challenge because permanent troops are not earmarked for this area.[99]

99. Jha, S. (2020). India-Pak tension keeps BSF busy at Sir Creek estuary. *Deccan Herald.* https://www.deccanherald.com/national/west/india-pak-tension-keeps-bsf-busy-at-sir-creek-estuary-790944.html

Proper training of troops for effective domination of the area whenever they are inducted in this area needs a lot of attention. Besides water craftsmanship, the troops also need to be properly trained in navigation because of the lack of identifiable landmarks in riverine areas.

Training of troops can be properly organized through coordination with the Coast guard and the Indian Navy and utilising their expertise in this field. The BSF will have to eventually establish its own training facility after attaining adequate domain knowledge.

Further, it is extremely important to properly coordinate with the Coast Guards and the Indian Navy to ensure operational synergy for optimum results. This will also ensure that there is no overlap in operations by different agencies.

There are large stretches of riverine borders in the east including 153 Kms in the Bay of Bengal and in Assam, where a large portion of the border passes through the mighty Brahmaputra River. Besides these, there are several smaller riverine stretches in the east. About one-fourth of the Indo-Bangladesh border falls in riverine category and cannot be fenced. Guarding these riverine stretches poses a major challenge to the BSF. Lack of obstacle and lighting makes it difficult to guard these riverine stretches especially during the night. Fishing activity in the rivers crisscrossing the border also adds to the problem because it facilitates easy contact between the criminals of both the countries enabling them to coordinate their criminal activities. Deployment of the BSF being limited, activities of everyone cannot be kept under watch. Technological solutions will therefore have to be sought to prevent these criminal acts.

Cattle Smuggling on the Eastern Borders

As discussed earlier in the book, the crime pattern varies drastically between the eastern and the western borders. While drugs and weapon smuggling are major threats on the Indo-Pakistan borders, it is cattle smuggling, which is a major crime on the Indo-Bangladesh border.

Cattle smuggling cartels transport cattle all the way from the western and northern parts of the country and smuggle it across to Bangladesh mostly through the riverine stretches. Criminals armed with sharp edged weapons operate in large strength, heavily outnumbering the troops. As discussed above, domination of riverine stretches under these circumstances poses major challenge. And commanders need to work out drills to counter this problem especially since it leads to causalities to both the troops and the criminals.

Bangladesh meat and leather industry being heavily dependent on cattle coming from India, authorities there treat the activity as trade and the criminals involved in the activity as cattle traders. Therefore, causalities to criminals if they happen to be

Bangladeshi causes lot of strain in the relation with Bangladesh. Some measures like use of less lethal weapons have been taken to overcome the problem. However, these measures have imposed a cost in form of increased causalities to the BSF troops. The challenge before the BSF authorities therefore is to prevent cattle smuggling, while at the same time ensuring minimum causalities to the troops and the criminals. Less lethal weapons like "Pump Action Guns" and "Chili Grenades" are now being used however; troops have to be trained to use them more effectively so that fatalities are avoided. The focus has to be on apprehending the criminals so that their linkages can be established.

The force must also coordinate with authorities of different states to prevent flow of cattle to the border areas. Measures are also required to coordinate with state authorities to shift the cattle Haats located very close to the border in contravention of policy. The force is likely to grapple with the problem of cattle smuggling for a long time in absence of any clear-cut government policy on the matter.

Widespread unemployment, lack of viable economic opportunities and lure of heavy profit through cattle smuggling lead many residents to indulge in this illegal activity. Infrastructure development in the border area and providing employment opportunities to residents therefore, assumes lot of importance.

At the Government level, the states have to be sensitized about the problem and asked to take measures to prevent cattle from being transported to bordering states in contravention of the norms laid down by animal rights activists.

Cease Fire Violations (CFV) on the Line of Control and the Border in Jammu

One major problem on the western border is the frequent violation of the cease fire along the LC and the 200 km stretch of border in Jammu. Pakistan resorts to firing mostly to cover movement of infiltrators, who may be carrying consignment of weapons and/or drugs. Almost war like operational environment therefore necessitates an emphasis on developing drills and SOPs for effective retaliation, while at the same time ensuring that the sanctity of the LC is not violated. It must be ensured that the troops inducted in this area undergo rigorous pre-induction training before taking over the operational responsibilities.

Frequent violations of cease fire can cause lot of difficulties to the border population disrupting their daily life and farming activity.[100] This has negative economic and psychological ramifications besides being a threat to the human and cattle lives.

100. PTI (2020). 2019 recorded highest ever ceasefire violations by Pakistan in Jammu and Kashmir in last 16 years. *The Economic Times*. https://economictimes.indiatimes.com/news/defence/2019-recorded-highest-ever-ceasefire-violations-by-pakistan-in-jammu-and-kashmir-in-last-16-years/articleshow/73100346.cms

The local population sometimes adopts an agitational approach, if the BSF does not retaliate. Retaliation to satisfy public ego is extremely problematic and the commanders must not succumb to that pressure. They should interact more frequently with the population and explain the advantages of exercising restraint. They should also explain to the population that retaliating at our own place and time of choosing may yield better results rather than retaliating in a mechanical manner.

The senior commanders also must educate our own troops that retaliation must never be a panic reaction and not retaliating immediately is not an act of cowardice. Exercising effective fire control is essential for ensuring peace and tranquility for benefit of both the local population and the Border Guarding Force.

Retaliation whenever undertaken should be after proper analysis of situation by commanders either by visiting the spot or assessing it through asking relevant questions from those on spot. This will also enable the troops deployed on nearby posts to take measures to avoid any damage or casualty to them and collateral damage to the civilians working or staying in nearby areas. This will also allow the commanders to fetch up the reinforcements needed if any. In other words, it has to be ensured that the Unit Commanders and troops do not become trigger happy.

Motivation of the Troops should not be based on anti-Pakistan rhetoric. They should be trained to logically analyse a situation after proper assessment. Unnecessary aggression must not be displayed while carrying out normal border guarding duties. However, the patrols and ambushes must always remain alert for any eventuality. This will bring temperatures down, reduce tension and lead to normalisation of situation.

Any work being undertaken in the vicinity, especially if it even remotely can be interpreted as a defence work is recommended to be undertaken after duly informing the counterpart. Such acts of confidence building will reduce tension and meet long-term objective of enhancing trust between the counterparts.

The local commanders must open the channels of communications. They should as soon as possible try to contact the counterpart through a flag meeting and control the situation by arriving at an amicable solution to a developing situation. The Company Commanders and Battalion Commanders will therefore have to be delegated adequate authority to call for such flag meetings.

More channels of communication should be opened on the lines existing along the Bangladesh border. Presently, only one Sector of the BSF in Jammu is nominated as a nodal point for communication with Pakistan. Incidents happening anywhere along the wide frontage can be discussed with the counterpart only through this channel. It would be much easier if the Unit Commanders or, at least all the Sector Commanders are allowed to contact in case of exigencies. This will help de-escalate situation much more quickly because the local commanders are much better aware of the developing situation. They being located close to the place of incident, can also visit the spot in a realistic time frame and exercise their personal influence to de-escalate the situation.

Besides above, the BSF is also expected to assuage the difficulties of border population by providing them shelter, food, etc. during prolonged episodes of cease fire violations. As discussed above, opening channels for effective communications with counterpart in order to minimise such the CFVs and de-escalate situation are essential.

Introducing Unpredictability in Operations

The borders along Punjab and Rajasthan are prone to smuggling of drugs and weapons. These borders are well fortified with fence and lighting. However, the armed criminals try to exploit gaps after studying the domination pattern, which over the years has developed a certain amount of predictability. The criminals have analysed the domination pattern and evolved ways to breach it.

Thus, the challenge is to ensure surprise by adopting unpredictable patterns of domination, extensive use of surveillance devices to facilitate economy in use of manpower as discussed above and deploying intelligence resources to obtain prior information about likely crimes. These measures will enhance efficiency of troops and provide more rest and relief.

Border Protection Grid

Proper coordination between the BSF, Police and other security agencies operating on the border and the Intelligence agencies is essential in order to achieve synergy in border guarding. A step has been taken in this direction by designating the BSF as the Lead Intelligence agency for borders manned by it with limited role of coordinating intelligence effort. However, there is need for coordination in other fields too.

Various agencies responsible for different functions related to controlling crimes along the border appear to operate in silos resulting sometimes into clashes and misunderstanding. There also is an overlap and interdependence in the functioning of these agencies. For example, the BSF apprehends criminals, lodges FIR and hands them over to Police for further prosecution. However, necessary feedback from the Police as well institutionalised follow-up mechanism to ascertain disposal of these cases does not exist. Similar is the case with the disposal of contraband seized and handed over to customs or illegal entrants apprehended and handed over to the Police for further disposal.

An institutionalised border protection grid will enable the representatives of each agency to meet at pre-decided frequency and coordinate their activities in each bordering state. A common communication grid can be created to enable these agencies to share actionable information on real time basis. This Border Protection Grid can function under the supervision of the State Level Standing Committee.

War Time Role

One of the most important reasons for raising the BSF was the inability of the State Armed Police Forces to face even minor skirmishes. The policy makers therefore had conceived of a force capable of facing the first brunt of enemy attack and hold the enemy back till the Army could be deployed. Several BSF Battalions are earmarked for deployment under the Army operational control for war effort. It is therefore essential for the Commanders to ensure that the troops are familiar with their war time role. Besides the Force Headquarters at Delhi, who have to identify the particular Battalions for war time role and coordinate with the Army Hqrs., the Frontier and Sector Hq. have important role of liaison with respective formation Hqrs. to ensure that troops and units familiarise adequately with their war time deployment and tasks. The BSF Units must actively participate in the war games and exercises conducted by the Army. This will enable easy integration with the Army. Physical recce of the proposed area of deployment will familiarise troops with the terrain, threats and likely contingencies in the task to be performed.

Mine laying is an area where our commanders need to focus. The Army expects the BSF to provide troops for laying protective mines, where BSF deployed. Preparation for this task is therefore necessary during peacetime too. Every Unit must have at least one platoon of trained manpower for this purpose. Training for war time role also needs to be focused on, both at the training institutions as well as in the respective theatres.

India and Pakistan are both nuclear powers and the possibility of the use of these weapons in an all-out war between the two countries cannot be ruled out. Leaders therefore have to train troops for this eventuality. Necessary equipment to minimise the effect of the NBC fallout will also have to be procured. Troops will also have to be trained to use these technologies. The buildings and Bunkers constructed on the borders will also have to be NBC protected.

Proper coordination at all levels with the Army authorities is the key to keeping our troops battle ready.

Internal Security

The report of the Group of Ministers set up after the Kargil War, realising the ill effects of frequent withdrawal of the border guarding forces from the borders recommends:

"Border Guarding Forces need to be distinguished from other CPMF and the Central Police Organisations because of their distinctive functions. It is imperative that the Border Guarding Forces are not deployed in the States to deal with internal disturbances, law and order duties and counter insurgency operations. Withdrawal of Border Guarding Forces, for such duties limits their capabilities to guard the borders effectively. While there may be exceptional circumstances where it may be necessary to utilize the services of Border Guarding Forces for performing law and order/ counterinsurgency duties, as a rule, these forces should not be withdrawn from the borders.[101]" Yet it often becomes imperative for the BSF to be deployed in Aid to Civil authorities because of various contingencies like seriousness of internal threat, lack of available forces, etc. The tasks mainly include operating in militancy and insurgency prone areas and assisting in smooth conduct of elections, etc.

Tasks may sometimes include assisting civil authorities in maintaining "Law and Order" especially in cases of riots, etc. when the situation goes beyond the control of the Civil Police.

The force needs to be prepared for these tasks through adequate training. The Force and Frontier Headquarters need to be proactive in anticipating the prevalent situation in the country and plan for contingencies. Proper coordination with concerned state authorities is essential to ensure adequate preparation for the tasks. Coordination for operational intelligence about the area of deployment is also extremely important.

Disaster management is another area where the BSF is required to assist the Civil Administration. The BSF has dedicated Battalions located at central places for this task. Besides this, the BSF may be called upon by the local authorities to assist in rescue and recovery during disasters like floods, fire accidents, building collapse etc. in areas close to their deployment. Such assistance should be provided liberally as the BSF possesses the wherewithal for this.

---

101. Report of the Group of Ministers on National Security. (2000). [online] VIF, New Dehi: GoI, p.62. Available at: https://www.vifindia.org/sites/default/files/GoM%20 Report%20on%20National%20Security.pdf

Figure 7.1: BSF providing rations to flood effected on borders

The elections being very frequent nowadays, all units must be ready to move for such duties at a very short notice. Commanders must prepare and keep an election kit containing all instructions related to elections ready. At supervisory levels, the commanders must prepare the SOPs for ensuring an effective domination in the absence of withdrawn troops and also, for various contingencies that may arise during the elections.

Troops face a lot of administrative difficulties while moving for internal security duties and elections. Transport and accommodation at the place of deployment are the most critical problems faced by the troops. The challenge for commanders is to anticipate and properly coordinate with the railway and state authorities to alleviate these problems.

Training for all the above aspects must continue to be part of the curriculum.

Managing Thinned Out Borders

One of the critical problems is non-availability of reserves. The entire force is committed on the border or in the internal security. None of the reserve units is available for rotation. Even the training companies are often not available thus interrupting the company collective training routine, which was the norm in the past.

The problem is further accentuated with frequent withdrawal of troops from the borders for election related deployment. This thinning out from borders further burdens the remaining troops, which are already overstretched. Thinning out from the borders is a serious compromise with national security as the ability to maintain similar levels of vigil is compromised leading to increased infiltration and trans-border crime.

The report of Group of Minister's set up after Kargil War states, "The repeated withdrawal, in large numbers, of para-military forces from border guarding duties for internal security and counter insurgency duties has led to a neglect of the borders. These forces have also been unable to perform optimally due to cannibalization of battalions and even companies."[102]

The thinned-out borders pose a major challenge, which can be overcome only by adopting modern border guarding practices through extensive introduction of technology thereby reducing dependence on manpower besides focusing on enhancing intelligence collection abilities.

The frontier, Sector and Unit commanders must prepare contingency plans for quick redeployment of troops to ensure that the Companies/Units required to go far such duties are relieved promptly without any adverse impact on domination of borders.

Intelligence

Prior information about crime and criminals enables troops to take preemptive actions. Therefore, the BSF must focus on collection and dissemination of actionable intelligence in an appropriate time frame. Strengthening of Intelligence wing of the BSF and the introduction of technology therefore is extremely important.

The report of Group of Ministers referred above states, "Lack of institutionalized arrangements for sharing and coordination of intelligence at various levels and particularly at the field level, is a primary weakness in proper management of borders. The present tendency on the part of each agency to guard its turf, even at the cost of compromising national security interests, needs to be deprecated and put down sternly."

The Government has accordingly taken a decision to designate the border guarding forces as the "Lead Intelligence Agencies (LIA)" of respective borders as per the recommendation from the Group of Ministers (GoM) report.

Synergising efforts of various intelligence agencies operating in the border areas for better security is therefore the responsibility of the BSF. While formal measures like periodic meetings of agencies have been implemented, it is important to interact at informal levels to develop a rapport in order to achieve better results. The responsibility

102. Report of the Group of Ministers on National Security. (2000). *VIF*. New Delhi: GoI, p. 60. https://www.vifindia.org/sites/default/files/GoM%20Report%20on%20National%20Security.pdf

of the LIA entails proper coordination to ensure economy of effort and cross verification of information.

Some assets have to be deployed to collect information about issues effecting the national security. However, major effort must be oriented towards collecting and disseminating real time information about border crimes and criminals.

Criminals and their accomplices are resorting to extensive use of Internet and mobile telephones to coordinate their nefarious activities. The intelligence branch therefore, needs to adapt to technology in a big way to keep proper surveillance over the activities of criminals. Follow-up on interceptions and seized mobile phones must be meticulous for better results.

Training of Intelligence personnel is extremely important. Most of the intelligence personnel cannot distinguish between information and intelligence. They should be trained to properly analyse information to draw a bigger picture and convert it into actionable intelligence.

Importance of "human int" cannot be undermined even in this day of extensive use of technology. Therefore, the intelligence branch must raise high quality sources in border areas. The model practiced by "Shashastra Seema Bal (SSB)" should be studied properly for its suitability to the BSF environment. The SSB before being tasked to guard the border was an agency tasked to train the residents of the North East in resisting the occupation army in case of capture of that area. The civilians were also trained to collect information about the enemy. The SSB personnel who operated in civil clothes literally merged themselves with the local population to collect information. The practicability of adopting this model should be studied properly

Intelligence sharing with the counterpart is also important in order to control crime and ensure a secure environment on borders. Subsequent to signing of the Comprehensive Border Management Plan between the BSF and the "Border Guards Bangladesh (BGB)" systems for exchange of information about border crimes have been put in place. Similar initiative is required on the western borders with the Pakistan Rangers. However, keeping in view the relations with Pakistan, this may take some more time.

Preventing Moral Degradation Amongst Troops

An important concern for commanders is ensuring integrity amongst troops. Even though the instances of corruption amongst the BSF personnel are far less than other organisations, yet we cannot afford to be complacent. Rampant cattle smuggling along the eastern borders, isolated deployment and lure of easy money are temptations leading to involvement of troops. In most cases, involvement is at individual levels. However, some instances of organised connivance have also come to notice which is serious cause of concern. The vigilance and Intelligence branches need to keep a close watch to prevent such activities. Vigilance staff should be trained in collecting actionable information and use of technical devices through which incriminating evidence can be recorded and linkages established. Any person indulging in wrongful activities must be dealt with strictly under the law to convey an unambiguous message to others.

Cooperation with Counterpart BGF

The border guarding forces of neighbouring countries have common interest of keeping the borders secure and ensure safe environment for border residents to enable them to carry out their daily routine peacefully. The counterpart border guarding forces must therefore operate in close cooperation with each other.

While cooperation and understanding with the Bangladesh Border guards at all levels is of high standard, the same cannot be said about cooperation with the Pakistan rangers.

On the Indo-Bangladesh border, a well-established system of periodic meetings at different levels to resolve issues of mutual concern has been put in place. System of Coordinated patrolling of the borders has been found to be extremely useful in preventing crimes. Periodic review of the areas that are vulnerable for different types of crimes i.e. vulnerability mapping is carried out. In addition to the "The Guide Lines for Border Guarding Forces, 1975," the "Coordinated Border Management Plan" has been signed between the BSF and the BGB in 2011, thus ensuring enhanced cooperation between them. The ISD facilities have been made available up-to the level of a Unit Commander enabling them to immediately contact counterpart in contingencies and resolve issues.

However, a lot needs to be done on the Indo-Pakistan Borders in order to enhance the level of cooperation with the Pakistani Rangers. The guidelines for border guarding forces agreed in late 1950s and early 1960s stand superseded after the 1971 war. Fresh guidelines are required to be framed considering all aspects.

Frequent violation of ceasefire also results in mutual distrust and minimal interaction between the two border guarding forces. Even the formal structured meetings are not held regularly. These are even otherwise restricted at the Sector level or above. The biennial conferences between the DG BSF and the DG Pakistan Rangers is also held only sporadically because of ambiguous policy about bilateral talks at any level with Pakistan.

System for regular meetings at the level of the Unit Commander with the Wing Commander of the Pakistan Rangers needs to be restored. Such meetings are requisitioned only for specific purpose in a contingency. A system similar to one practiced on borders with Bangladesh needs to be put in place. The possibility of installing direct telephonic links with the BGB should also be examined.

Integration of Border Population

Earlier, the common perception was that the scope of border management is restricted only to border guarding by preventing trans-border crimes and smuggling. However, Border Management has now acquired a much wider scope. Border management now focuses on integrating border population with the mainstream. This implies development of the border area by improving infrastructure and providing employment opportunities. The scope of Border management now extends to facilitating formal cross-border movement of persons and goods.

Development of the borders therefore has a wider context and a lot of trans-border and inter-agency cooperation has become essential. Troops have to function in close cooperation with other agencies both of India and counterpart operating on the Integrated Check Posts (ICP) and the Land Custom Stations (LCS). The troops therefore need to be familiar with functioning of these agencies.

Border Area Development Programme

The Department of Border Management, Ministry of Home Affairs has been implementing the Border Area Development Programme (BADP) through the State Governments as part of a comprehensive approach to Border Management. The programme aims to meet the special development needs of the people living in remote and inaccessible areas situated near the international border and to saturate the border areas with the essential infrastructure through convergence of Central/State/BADP/Local schemes and participatory approach.

The BADP was initiated in the border areas of the western region during the Seventh Five Year Plan period for ensuring balanced development of the border areas through the development of infrastructure and promotion of a sense of security among the border population.

The programme now covers 394 border blocks of 111 border districts in 16 States and 2 Union Territories which includes 167 border blocks in 55 districts of 8 North

East States (including Sikkim), located along the international land border. The States covered are Arunachal Pradesh, Assam, Bihar, Gujarat, Himachal Pradesh, Jammu & Kashmir, Manipur, Meghalaya, Mizoram, Nagaland, Punjab, Rajasthan, Sikkim, Tripura, Uttar Pradesh, Uttarakhand and West Bengal. Under this programme priority is given to the areas closer to the border.

The BADP is an important intervention of the Central Government to bring about development of border areas by supplementing the State Plan Funds to bridge the gaps in socio-economic infrastructure on one hand and improving the security environment in border areas on the other. (*For details, see: https://www.mha.gov.in/)

With its widespread deployment, the BSF is the sole visible representative of Government in remote areas. The BSF therefore should be co-opted to identify needs of the border population and help prepare relevant schemes for their benefit. The BSF may also have to provide its services to supervise the implementation of schemes and ensuring quality of work. The BSF can assist Government in ensuring that the schemes made are integrated in overall development plan and not standalone schemes.

Civic Action Programme

Besides the BADP, some funds are directly allotted to the BSF for the "Civic Action Programme (CAP)". These funds are not meant as an overlap of the BADP efforts for improvement of the infrastructure. The BSF should utilise these funds for those schemes, which enhances the skills of the border population and make them employable.

These funds may also be utilised in encouraging the border village communities in setting up skill enhancement centres for tailoring, computer education centres, etc. Computers, books and sports equipment can also be provided to enhance the skills.

Some Civic Action can also be done through available resources without any financial implications. For example, qualified personnel can be deputed to schools/ madrasas located in border area for providing career counselling, providing computer education, conducting periodic sports activities, etc. troops can also be utilised to provide coaching to youth of border area and prepare them with necessary physical and knowledge skills for employment in forces.

Local commanders can also liaise with NGOs operating in the area to utilize funds available with them for making improvements in the quality of life of the villagers. For example, services of NGOs like "Smile India foundation" for correcting "Cleft Lip condition" and "Artificial limb Manufacturing Company (ALMANCO)" to provide assistive aids to physically challenged persons in border areas has potential to create a lot of goodwill.

Facilitating Trade and Transit

Border management is increasingly being viewed as a function, which facilitates trans-border movement of persons and goods from authorised transit points. Large number of "Land Custom Stations (LCS)" and "Integrated Check Posts (ICP)" have been sanctioned along the borders. The BSF will be closely associated with the functioning of these establishments because security implications.

The ICPs and LCS are operated by multiple agencies working in close coordination with each other. These include the Customs, the Immigration, and the Police. The BSF will be responsible to ensure security at these places to prevent entry of unauthorized person or goods into India.

The BSF will have to work in close coordination with these agencies and therefore, the commanders will have to ensure that the troops deployed at these places are familiar with the procedures to prevent delay in clearance of goods and persons.

Similar coordination will be required with agencies of counterpart deployed on their LCS/ICP.

Special emphasis has to be given to intelligence collection and coordination with counterpart so as to intercept suspects and contraband at the border itself.

We must strive to have smart border management practices which will involve intra agency cooperation within the country as also with the agencies of neighbouring country to facilitate smooth border crossings for both men and material. Therefore, facilities should be co-located in both the countries and the facilities within the country should preferably be sequentially located in one building to facilitate seamless procedure. More importantly, a common data base should be created for use by all agencies and also by the two neighbouring countries. Thus, having SMART borders is a multidisciplinary concept, which involves multiple agencies and departments. In Europe, the access control technology even though developed in private sector is operated by government agencies and involves data management, travel management, biometric access and surveillance. In India as well, we need to transform from physical manning to comprehensive electronic surveillance and proactive approach.

Training

The training system of the BSF should aim at preparing the leaders of the force as confident ambassadors of India, when interacting with the counterpart border guarding forces. It should endow them with capability to comprehend wider national security concerns and role of border guarding forces in achieving these. The leaders have to liaise extensively with the civil administration and other stakeholders in achieving the common goal of providing safe environment at the borders. Extensive liaison is also required with the Army authorities in order to comprehend and carry out the war time role.

Commanders must therefore, be suitably equipped with the knowledge of the functioning and hierarchy of these stakeholders, besides in-depth knowledge of capabilities and limitations of our own organization. Training inputs must enable leaders to project a good image of the force. Importance of soft skills due to increasing interaction with the border population must also be given due emphasis.

The troops must be well-equipped with the skills and attitudes to carry out the tasks while ensuring economy of efforts i.e., with minimum casualties to the troops. They should be able to inspire confidence amongst the border population that they are at the borders for the welfare and protection of the border population. The border population should feel confident of approaching the BSF in times of need.

The force needs to evolve an unambiguous training policy to achieve the above aims and objectives. Multifarious roles that BSF requires to perform implies that a proper balance has to be ensured in imparting skills amongst the troops relating to all these aspects. The training curriculum therefore must assign proportionate importance to different aspects of the BSF functioning. This must be ensured at all the stages of the training and for all levels.

The purpose of the basic training is to bring about attitudinal changes and inculcate skills necessary for performing basic function. These will vary for different levels in the hierarchy. Identification of training needs of each level is therefore important to design curriculum according to those specific needs.

Several training programme, which do not appear to have any correlation with the role expected to be performed, are prescribed at various levels. The training programmes should be devised only after identifying performance gaps and working out the training needs for different levels.

At the junior most level, a constable is required to be proficient in handling his weapon, carrying out proper observation (with or without surveillance devices) in order to distinguish between patterns and learn drills to be followed during border guarding, operations of war and internal security. Training curriculum for them should be designed accordingly. The curriculum at the induction level must include inputs to change their attitude from a civilian to a uniformed force person.

At higher levels, inputs related to leadership, man management, administration, documentation for various activities - both operational and administrative, coordination with different agencies operating on borders, aspects of diplomacy in dealing with counterpart, etc. are more relevant. For officers/leaders, awareness about strategic issues having implication on the border security is important. The curriculum at different stages in the hierarchy must cater to these needs.

Sporadic intake and repeated withdrawal of troops for the internal security and election duties has totally disturbed the well-structured training system of the force.

Irregular intake has resulted in periodic overburdening and under utilisation of the training capacity. Over burdening leads to adverse trainer-trainee ratio, thus, diluting the levels of supervision of the training. This adversely effects the operational efficiency leading to causalities.

Repeated withdrawal of troops from the borders for various duties hinders availability of training companies for collective training as these get deployed for duties, thus depriving troops of the much-needed refresher training and break from the routine. The leaders, therefore, have to devise ways of ensuring a refresher training of the troops without interfering with the normal operational duties. Various systems like training at the platoon level or the "On Job Training," etc. can be thought of.

The content of collective training program also needs to be reviewed and redesigned to suit the local requirements. The annual firing "Range Course" also, needs to be studied in view of the fact that more emphasis is now on less lethal methodology. The use of minimum force being the guiding principle in border duties, especially on the eastern borders, the commanders also need to have a relook at the concept of "*ek goli ek dushman*". More emphasis is required on the night firing as most of the firing incidents take place at night.

Training in use of technical surveillance devices at the basic induction level and also, whenever new devices are introduced is extremely important for better efficiency.

The intake at various levels will continue to vary depending upon the vacancies caused due to wastage. In eventuality of over recruitment, the training institutes need to evolve mechanism to ensure proper trainer-trainee ratio through staggering of training events and/or getting additional instructors attached/posted.

Training for soft skills is increasingly becoming important because of enhanced interaction with the border population at the fence gates and large-scale involvement in the internal security and election duties. These must therefore, be included in curriculum at all levels.

The existing Faculty of Studies (FOS) must be strengthened and manned by personnel mentally equipped to carry out research in the field of operations and other related aspects of the functioning of the BSF. It should have adequate resources and discretion to organise and participate in various seminars and discussions in order to evolve and refine training methodology and Border Management Practices.

The FOS should also focus on developing literature specifically for operational role of the BSF. Literature relating to other aspects viz. personnel management policies specific to the BSF requirements also should be prepared. Periodic "Training Need Analysis" to upgrade the training contents and modules must also be undertaken by it.

Personnel Management

Personnel management in a fighting force like the BSF remains a critical area. The challenge is to find the right kind of people to join the force and keep them motivated enough to retain them.

While several persons are willing to join the force for employment, it has to be ensured that they have appropriate psychological orientation for the difficult operational and administrative environment they will be faced with. While a lot of emphasis is placed on physical fitness, there is no psychological assessment of the candidates. It is high time to initiate these so that only mentally strong persons join the force. This will help curbing the rising instances of indiscipline and connivance. This will also reduce attrition in the force, which is presently very high.

One important aspect of personnel management is to provide adequate opportunities for career growth to an individual. The task of the commanders in BSF is made difficult by the narrow the pyramidal organisational structure. Therefore, alternative solutions like assured career progression have to be extended more liberally to provide financial succour in absence of growth opportunities. The commanders must also ensure that the case of the BSF for various benefits is properly projected to the statutory bodies like the Pay Commission.

Another challenge is to ensure proper administration and living conditions at the BOPs on the borders. There were lot of deficiencies ab initio and situation has further exacerbated with a rapid expansion of the force. The Commanders have got their task cut out to convince the authorities and persuade them to adequately compensate the troops for tough working conditions faced by them in remote areas away from their families. The commanders must also ensure that there is parity of pay and allowances, wherever the BSF is deployed alongside the Army on the FDLs. Presently, there is a lot of difference which is a cause of resentment amongst the troops. The authorities must also be convinced to alter the status of the BSF from a civilian force to an Armed Force for the purpose of allowances and pension benefits.

Leadership issue is another important matter to be looked into seriously. Most BSF officers retire at middle levels because of lack of opportunities, thereby wasting the domain knowledge and expertise gained by them. The supervisory and policy level leadership lacking insight of operational philosophy, ethos of the force and the environment in which the BSF operates is found lacking in formulating policies suited to the organisation. The policies must suit the requirement of the BSF and not skewed towards policing. Therefore, it is essential that policy level positions are occupied by those officers who have grown from ground level.

Force is now recruiting women in different ranks. Their intake is planned to rise to 15% as per the government policy, which is a large number.[103] So far, the number was very small, hence they were being given light duties. However, with increase in their numbers they will be required to perform all duties that are expected of their male counterpart.

Induction of women also raises few more issues. They have been in the force for about ten years now. They are now getting married and raising families. They are therefore required to be extended facilities like Crèche, maternity leave, child care leave, etc. They may therefore not be available for duties for long periods. Secondly, proper facilities have to be ensured for women personnel at all establishments keeping their physiological needs in view. These have come up at some places, however more is required to be done in this regard. Thirdly, with the induction of women, the "Nirbhaya Committee" stipulations have to be implemented. There male counterpart also have to be sensitized about gender related issues.

The issue of rest and relief discussed earlier in the chapter needs to be addressed seriously through induction of surveillance devices and effective use of intelligence inputs.

Another issue that the commanders need to take up with the authorities has implications both for operations and personal management. This relates to abolishing the additional company introduced as part of a BSF Unit in the early 2000. Some additional staff has been authorised to Units in order to provide administrative support to this additional company, but that is not adequate. Secondly, it has put heavy operational and administrative burden on the Unit Commandant as it has increased the already

---

103. Press Information Bureau (2016). Union Home Minister inaugurates 7th National Conference on Women in Police. *Pib.gov.in*. https://pib.gov.in/newsite/PrintRelease.aspx?relid=134233

stretched span of control of a Unit by at least 20%. This has severe negative implication on the quality and quantity of supervision exercised by the Commandant.

In order to ensure operational efficiency, it is imperative that this additional company should be abolished and original organisation of six companies in a Unit restored. The released companies should be put together to raise additional Units. This can be achieved with minimum financial implications because the number of BOPs and infrastructure for them is already authorised. Few command elements, support company elements and higher supervisory headquarters will only be additionally required.

The move will also enhance career avenues for personnel as the units raised by pooling these companies and additional supervisory headquarters raised will enhance promotional avenues.

Logistics

The BSF has a well-structured system of procurement of weapons, equipment and stores. However, the equipping policy needs a relook.

As discussed above in this chapter, the procurement of surveillance devices has to take the ground realities into account. The procurement also must be done only after extended field trials and obtaining feedback from ground operatives. Simply copying solutions adopted in the USA or in Israel may not be advisable because the operational conditions and financial abilities differ drastically. We need indigenous solutions. We also need to encourage the BSF personnel to come out with innovative ideas for research and implementation if found suitable.

Authorisation and procurement of weapon systems is another area for commanders to focus upon. The tendency to equip the force with high calibre weapons must be avoided and only those weapons should be procured, which are of practical use. For example, rocket launchers and grenade launchers have been authorised. However, manpower has not been authorised for these weapon systems. These weapons are of no use during normal border guarding operations anywhere except perhaps on the LC and on the Jammu Border, where also these can be used only with the permission of the Army Authorities. These are also not effective in the type of terrain where the BSF operates for the anti-maoist operations. Even if used, there is a danger of heavy collateral damage. Additional authorisation without corresponding manpower enhancement creates the problem of care and maintenance of these weapons. Further procurement of such weapons therefore should be restricted for sectors and units deployed in these areas.

Time is also ripe to evaluate whether artillery is required to be retained in the BSF? Firstly, the number of artillery units being limited, they cannot provide effective fire support to entire BSF. Secondly, during normal times the artillery fire can be opened only upon specific orders of competent Army authority even in the LC environment. Thirdly, during war the BSF will be integrated with the Army and therefore, artillery fire support will be inherently available to the BSF. Even the existing artillery units will be placed under the Army command. Therefore, there is no rationale for retaining the artillery in the BSF. The manpower released by disbanding the artillery can be utilised to enhance the strength of the training institutions and supervisory headquarters, where the authorisation of manpower is less.

The authorisation of 80 mm mortar and mortar platoons is also recommended to be reviewed. The manpower authorised to mortar platoon is being utilised for normal border guarding duties. Resultantly, there is no emphasis on training for mortars and it is undertaken only at the time of annual competitions. Further, war deployment of the BSF will be staggered and the fire cover will be provided by the respective Army formation/ unit under whose command the unit/companies are deployed. Moreover, mortars will be brigaded during hostilities and hence, will be utilised only under the orders of the Army authorities. It may therefore be worthwhile to authorise mortars as sector stores to be utilised wherever the need arises. Centralisation of mortars will also pave the way for better training on these weapons. The manpower augmented at the Sector headquarters in this manner will be useful for their operational and administrative requirements for which they are so far dependent on manpower attached from the Units.

The system of procurement of clothing and equipment should also be decentralised at appropriate level. This will expedite the procurement. Further, there is a need to take a relook at the system recently adopted wherein troops are given cash in lieu of clothing authorised to them. This has led to the problem of difference in quality and shade, etc. of these items.

Perspective Planning Cell

The BSF is in dire need of having its own think tank in shape of a perspective planning cell which should be tasked with analysing and projecting future requirements of the force in various fields of activity including operations, personnel management, training and logistics requirements, etc. A beginning has been made in form of the Institute of Border Management Studies (IBMAS) through local resources. Requirement is to regularize it by obtaining proper government sanction.

Department of Border Management

As recommended by the group of Ministers after the Kargil War, a Department of Border Management has been established under the Ministry of Home Affairs, this Department should be strengthened by staffing it with practitioners from the border guarding forces and other agencies responsible for different aspects of border management, instead of bureaucrats, who lack perspective due to inadequate exposure to the borders. Practitioners will be more suited for policy-making relating to the borders.

Conclusion

Border management is constantly evolving. It is no longer confined to guarding borders, which tends to treat the borders as barriers, the systems are evolving towards cooperative management and converting borders into bridges. This is a paradigm shift and poses many challenges for the organisation. The BSF will have to keep evolving its operational philosophy according to changing operational environment. The commanders need to remain alive to the dynamic environment and ensure readiness of the organisation for all future challenges.

Appendix and Annexure

Chapter 1 (Appendix A)

सत्यमेव जयते

Ministry of External Affairs
Government of India

India & Bangladesh

Executive Summary

Attempts have been made to arrive at a comprehensive settlement of the land boundary between india and bangladesh (the erstwhile East pakistan) since 1947. The Nehru-Noon agreement of 1958 and the agreement concerning the demarcation of the land boundary between india and bangladesh and related matters of 1974 (referred to as 1974 lba) sought to find a solution to the complex nature of the border demarcation involved. however, three outstanding issues pertaining to an un-demarcated land boundary of approximately 6.1 km, exchange of enclaves and adverse possessions remained unsettled.

The protocol (referred to as the 2011 protocol) to the 1974 lba, signed on 6th September 2011 during the visit of the prime minister to bangladesh, paves the way for a settlement of the outstanding land boundary issues between the two countries. This historic agreement will contribute to a stable and peaceful boundary and create an environment conducive to enhanced bilateral cooperation. it will result in better management and coordination of the border and strengthen our ability to deal with smuggling, illegal activities and other trans-border crimes.

In building this agreement, the two sides (india and bangladesh) have taken into account the situation on the ground and the wishes of the people residing in the areas involved. as such, the 2011 protocol does not envisage the displacement of populations and ensures that all areas of economic activity relevant to the homestead have been preserved. The 2011 protocol has been prepared with the full support and concurrence of the State governments concerned (assam, meghalaya, tripura and west bengal).

In planning the agreement, an elaborate process of consultation with people in the areas involved was carried out, including through the visit of an india–bangladesh delegation to some of the enclaves and adverse possessions in may, 2007. The feedback received indicated that the people residing in the areas involved did not want to leave their land and would rather remain in the country where they had lived all their lives. The views of the concerned State governments in favour of realigning the boundary to maintain status quo in respect of territories in adverse possession were also taken into account. although this was contrary to the 1974 lba, which stipulated the exchange of territories in adverse possession, both sides decided that to avoid large scale uprooting and displacement of populations against their wishes, it would be necessary to preserve the status quo and retain the adverse possessions as would be determined through joint surveys. The 2011 protocol accordingly departs from the 1974 lba in seeking to maintain the status quo of adverse possessions instead of exchange of territories in deference to the wishes of the people to remain in their land.

The 2011 protocol will result in a fixed demarcated boundary in all the un-demarcated segments, exchange of 111 indian enclaves in bangladesh with 51 bangladesh enclaves in india and a resolution of all adversely possessed areas.

In the exchange of enclaves, india will transfer 111 enclaves with a total area of 17,160.63 acres to bangladesh, while bangladesh would transfer 51 enclaves with an area of 7,110.02 acres to india. While on paper, the exchange of enclaves between india and bangladesh may seem like a loss of indian land to bangladesh, the actual scenario is quite different as the enclaves are located deep inside the territory of both countries and there has been no physical access to them from either country. in reality, the exchange of enclaves denotes only a notional exchange of land as the protocol converts a de facto reality into a de jure situation.

The inhabitants in the enclaves could not enjoy full legal rights as citizens of either india or bangladesh and infrastructure facilities such as electricity, schools and health services were deficient. further, due to lack of access to these areas by the law and order enforcing agencies and weak property rights, certain enclaves became hot beds of criminal activities. a number of parliament questions, representations from members of parliament, inhabitants of the enclaves, NgOs and political parties received over the years have urged government to carry out an expeditious exchange of enclaves. in the implementation of the 2011 protocol, the exchange of enclaves will have fulfilled a major humanitarian need to mitigate the hardships that the residents of the enclaves have had to endure for over six decades on account of the lack of basic amenities and facilities that would normally be expected from citizenship of a State.

In respect of adverse possessions, india will receive 2777.038 acres of land and will transfer 2267.682 acres of land to bangladesh through implementation of the

2011 protocol. as in the case of enclaves, however, the reality is that the area to be transferred was already in the possession of bangladesh and the handing over of this area to bangladesh is merely a procedural acceptance of the de facto situation on the ground. Similarly, areas in adverse possession of india in bangladesh will now be formally transferred to india with the implementation of the 2011 protocol. more important, the 2011 protocol will allow people living in the adversely possessed areas to remain in the land to which they have deep-rooted ties, sentimental and religious attachments.

No constitutional amendment is envisaged for resolution of un-demarcated sectors under the 2011 protocol as this is within the competence of the Executive wing of the government. However, exchange of enclaves and the drawing of boundaries to maintain statusquoofadversepossessionsinvolvingtransferanddejurecontrolofterritoriesrequires a constitutional amendment. Article 368oftheconstitutionstatesthat"anamendment of this constitution may be initiated only by the introduction of a bill for the purpose in either house of parliament, and when the bill is passed in each house by a majority of that house and by a majority of not less than two-thirds of the members of that house present and voting, it shall be presented to the president who shall give his assent to the bill and thereupon the constitution shall stand amended in accordance with the terms of the bill."

A settled boundary is an essential prerequisite for effective cross-border cooperation. it reduces friction, helps neighbours consolidate mutually beneficial exchanges and promotes confidence in building better relations. The 2011 protocol will ensure that the india-bangladesh boundary is permanently settled with no more differences in interpretation, regardless of the government in power. This also helps on issues of security concern, including security cooperation and denial of sanctuary to elements inimical to india.

Ratification of the 2011 protocol would represent a historic step culminating in the resolution of the long pending land boundary issues between india and bangladesh. The agreement has been widely welcomed by the people of both countries, particularly in the areas involved. its implementation will allow india and bangladesh to focus on unlocking the full potential for mutually beneficial bilateral cooperation through enhanced security, trade, transit and development.

****

Note on Land Boundary Agreement

India and bangladesh signed a protocol (referred to as the 2011 protocol) to the agreement concerning the demarcation of the land boundary between india and bangladesh and related matters, during the visit of prime minister dr manmohan Singh to dhaka, on September 6, 2011. The protocol, along with the agreement between india and bangladesh concerning the demarcation of the land boundary between india and bangladesh and related matters (referred to as 1974 lba), signed on may 16, 1974, has facilitated the resolution of the long pending land boundary issues between the two countries. The 2011 protocol addresses the unresolved issues pertaining to the un-demarcated land boundary of approximately 6.1 km; exchange of enclaves; and adverse possessions. maps indicating location of un-demarcated segments and adverse possessions (annexure i) and Enclaves in india and bangladesh (annexure ii) are attached.

2. Background

a) after the partition of india in 1947, the radcliffe line became the border between india and East pakistan and following the liberation of bangladesh in 1971, the same line became the border between india and bangladesh. Although the demarcation of the border between india and the then pakistan had started soon after the partition, progress was slower than expected, due in part to the difficulties in determining precisely where the border ran. Even though some of these boundary disputes were sought to be settled by the Nehru-Noon agreement of 1958, subsequent hostilities between the two countries left the task unaccomplished. Even after the creation of bangladesh, the boundary dispute between the two countries inherited the legacy of history and fractured politics.

b) both countries were able to conclude the land boundary agreement in 1974, soon after the independence of bangladesh, to find a solution to the complex nature of border demarcation. The agreement has been implemented in its entirety, except for three outstanding issues pertaining to (i) undemarcated land boundary of approximately 6.1 km in three sectors viz. daikhata-56 (west bengal), muhuri river-belonia (tripura) and lathitila-dumabari (assam); (ii) exchange of enclaves; and (iii) adverse possessions. although the agreement was not ratified by india, its implementation, except for the issues mentioned above, represents significant progress, given the fact that both the countries share an approximately 4,096.7 km long land boundary. in respect of dahagram and angarporta enclaves of bangladesh, article 1(14) of the 1974 lba provides for access to these enclaves by leasing in perpetuity an area of 178 metres x 85 metres near tin bigha. This was implemented through letters of Exchange on October 7, 1982 between the then foreign minister of india and the then foreign minister of bangladesh and on march 26, 1992 between the foreign Secretary of india and the additional foreign Secretary of bangladesh.

c) during the visit of prime minister Sheikh has in a of bangladesh to india in January 2010, india and bangladesh expressed the desire to reach a final resolution to the long-standing problem and agreed to comprehensively address all outstanding boundary issues keeping in view the spirit of the 1974 land boundary agreement. Subsequently, detailed negotiations, joint visits to the concerned areas and land surveys were undertaken, resulting in the protocol concluded in September 2011.

d) in finalising the 2011 protocol, the situation on the ground and wishes of the people residing in the areas involved were taken into account and the written consent of the concerned State governments was obtained.

3. documents

A summary of the documents relevant to the boundary demarcation issue between india and bangladesh is given below:

a) agreement between the government of the republic of india and government of the people's republic of bangladesh concerning the demarcation of the land boundary between india and bangladesh and related matters, may 16, 1974 (annexure –iii):

The agreement provided meticulous guidelines for an early and amicable delineation of the hitherto un-demarcated portions of the boundary in 13 sectors as well as for an expeditious resolution of related matters like the exchange of the enclaves and adverse possessions. The two governments also agreed to give people citizenship rights of the State they were staying in, pending which status quo was to be maintained. any dispute on account of interpretation or implementation of this agreement was to be settled peacefully through mutual consultations.

b) terms of lease in perpetuity of tin bigha - area, October 7, 1982 and implementing tin bigha lease, 26 march, 1992 (annexure –iv):

in terms of clause 14 of article 1 of the agreement between the government of republic of india and the government of the people's republic of bangladesh concerning the demarcation of the land boundary between india and bangladesh and related matters, signed in New delhi on 16th of may 1974, india agreed to lease in perpetuity to bangladesh, an area of 178 m x 85 m, or approximately 3.74

acres to connect these two enclaves with panbari mouza of mainland bangladesh at a token price of bd taka 1 per annum which has since been waived off. The stipulated lease in perpetuity finally came into effect on June 26, 1992, with the Exchange of letters. The lease connected the bangladesh enclaves of dahagram and angarpota and mainland bangladesh at alternate hours during the daylight period. Twenty-four hour access for bangladesh nationals through tin bigha to the enclaves was acceded to during the prime minister's visit to bangladesh in September 2011, thus fulfilling a long standing request of bangladesh.

c) The protocol (2011 protocol) to the agreement between government of india and bangladesh concerning the demarcation of land boundary between india and bangladesh and related matters (annexure–v):

   The 2011 protocol was signed on September 06, 2011, between the External affairs minister of india and the foreign minister of bangladesh in the presence of the prime ministers of the two countries to address long pending land boundary issues between india and bangladesh. The protocol forms an integral part of the lba 1974 and is subject to exchange of instruments of ratification by the governments of india and bangladesh.

4. difficulties in resolution of the land Boundary dispute

(a) Berubari dispute:

i) In the standard model of geopolitics, international borders are clearly delineated, one-dimensional lines that absolutely separate sovereign states. in practice, however, borders are often contested and sometimes indistinct - and few are as fraught as the boundary separating india from bangladesh. The berubari dispute was one such, arising from an omission in the written text of the radcliffe award and erroneous depiction on the map annexed therewith. radcliffe had divided the district of Jalpaiguri between india and pakistan by awarding some thanas to one country and others to the other country. The boundary line was determined on the basis of the boundaries of the thanas. In describing this boundary, radcliffe omitted to mention one thana, Thana boda. berubari union No. 12 lies within Jalpaiguri Thana, which was awarded to india. however, the omission of the Thana boda and the erroneous depiction on the map referred to above enabled pakistan to claim that a part of berubari belonged to it.

ii) The dispute was resolved by the Nehru-Noon agreement of 1958 whereby, inter alia, half of berubari union No. 12 was to be given to pakistan and the other half adjacent to india was to be retained by india. To implement this agreement, the constitution 9th amendment act and acquired territories (merger) act were adopted in 1960.

This legislation was challenged in the courts by a series of writ petitions, which prevented the implementation of the agreement. The Supreme court decision on march 29, 1971, finally cleared the way for the implementation of the agreement. This, however, could not be done because of the pakistani army crackdown in East pakistan and the subsequent events which led to the emergence of bangladesh as an independent country. Following the independence of bangladesh, the lba 1974 was signed to address the issues of border demarcations.

(b) enclaves:

i) The hasty partition of the subcontinent was flawed in several respects which left unresolved the fate of hundreds of 'enclaves' of both the countries. There are 111 indian enclaves in bangladesh (17,160.63 acres) and 51 bangladesh enclaves in india (7,110.02 acres). The indian enclaves in bangladesh are located in four districts-panchagarh, lalmonirhat, kurigram and Nilphamari. all of bangladesh's enclaves lie in west bengal's kochbehar district.

ii) The lba 1974 agreement enabled bangladesh to retain the dahagram and angarpota enclaves; india retained berubari, which was contiguous. article 1(12) of lba 1974 states that enclaves should be exchanged. further article 3 stipulates that when areas are transferred, the people in these areas shall be given the right of staying on where they are, as nationals of the State to which the areas are transferred. while the lba of 1974 has stated that the territory has to be exchanged, it had not specified any administrative procedures with respect to the people living in such territories till the exchange process was completed. india was keen to exchange enclaves in accordance with the lba. There were, however, procedural issues that first needed to be addressed, including the determination of the number of people living in enclaves in both sides.

(c) adverse possessions:

i) The adverse possessions have been a bone of contention between successive governments in india and bangladesh and had impeded the final resolution of the boundary issue. unlike enclaves, there was no jointly compiled and accepted list of adversely possessed territories or lands (except in South berubari in west bengal). The situation had been compounded by changes in the course of rivers and even encroachments, over the decades.

ii) it also became difficult to implement article 2 of the 1974 lba, which states that the two countries are expected to exchange the territories in adverse possessions in already demarcated areas after signing boundary strip maps by plenipotentiaries. people living in the adverse possessions are technically in occupation and possession of land beyond the boundary pillars, but are administered by the laws of the country of which they are citizens and they enjoy all legal rights, including right to vote. They have deep-rooted ties to their land which goes back decades and are categorically unwilling to be uprooted. Many local communities had sentimental or religious attachments to the land in which they lived. it thus became extremely difficult to implement the terms of lba 1974 as it meant having to uproot people from the land in which they had lived and developed sentimental and religious attachments to.

5. Justification

a) un-demarcated Segments: Though the issue of the un-demarcated land boundary was addressed in the 1974 lba, it could not be implemented due to differences of perception in the interpretation of the lba and in view of the ground realities. The lack of clarity on the boundary between the two countries caused tensions and disrupted the lives of people living in these areas.

b) Enclaves: The inhabitants in the enclaves could not enjoy full legal rights as citizens of either country and infrastructure facilities such as electricity, schools and health services were deficient. further, due to lack of access to these areas by the law and order enforcing agencies and weak property rights, certain enclaves became the hot bed of criminal activities. a number of parliament questions and representations were received from members of parliament, inhabitants of the enclaves, NgO's and political parties urging that the exchange of enclaves be expedited.

c) Adverse possessions:

   i) despite the limited nature of dispute on the border, the non-settlement of adverse possessions has led to tension between the border guarding forces of the two countries. muktapur, pyrdiwah and Naljuri along the meghalaya-bangladesh border had witnessed firing incidents in the recent past. in dumabari area (assam) firing took place between the two security agencies as early as in 1962 and again in 1965. In muhuri river area (tripura), 10 incidents of firing were reported between bSf and bgb, the last reported in 1999. in boroibari (assam), in a firing incident in 2001, 16 bSf personnel were killed.

Thus, the adverse possession areas have been flashpoints between india and bangladesh exacerbating the tensions along the border and between the two neighbouring States. The issue got further complicated with the increasing population pressure in bangladesh, use of bangladesh soil for anti-india terrorist activities, and refuge for terrorists, militants and criminals. all of this necessitated the need for an early settlement of the outstanding land boundary issues between india and bangladesh.

ii) during the joint visit of an india-bangladesh delegation in may, 2007 to the adverse possession in South berubari, the people residing there expressed an unusually strong view that they would not accept an exchange of adverse possessions.

iii) The government of west bengal in 2002 had suggested that the boundary be realigned with the line of actual possession, thus converting de facto control into de jure control. Similarly, the government of meghalaya was also reluctant to give up the territories in adverse possession and had requested that status quo be maintained along the adverse possessions.

6. efforts towards a comprehensive package solution

a) it was evident that a comprehensive resolution of the boundary issue was necessary at the earliest in the larger interest of the country's security, furtherance of bilateral relations and regional stability and prosperity.

b) in resolving the issue of enclaves, a list of the enclaves, along with maps was jointly reconciled, signed and exchanged in april 1997.

c) keeping in mind the objective of seeking a viable solution, india and bangladesh established the Joint boundary working group (Jbwg) in 2001 to address the outstanding land boundary issues, namely, the border dispute comprising 6.1 km of an un-demarcated stretch, enclaves and adverse possessions. The Jbwg met four times over the last ten years. The mandate given to the Jbwg was to evolve a comprehensive package proposal to resolve all pending issues pertaining to the boundary dispute.

d) during the 4th meeting of the Jbwg, india and bangladesh agreed to take into account the situation on the ground and the wishes of the people residing in the areas involved in trying to find an expeditious solution to all outstanding issues. The two sides also decided to jointly survey the adverse possessions to come to a final determination about its status based on ground realities.

e) a headcount was conducted jointly by both sides from 14- 17 July, 2011 according to which the total population in the enclaves was determined to be around 51,549 (37,334 in indian enclaves within bangladesh and 14,215 in bangladesh enclaves within india).

f) The concerned State governments were closely associated with the process of determination of adverse possessions. land records were scrutinized, the wishes of the people in possession of the lands were ascertained and land survey and index maps of the adversely held areas prepared by State government surveyors. Similarly, the joint surveys of the boundary demarcation in the three un-demarcated segments were carried out by the State Survey departments in their respective areas of the boundary with bangladesh. There was close coordination between the central and State authorities.

g) In building this agreement, the two sides have taken into account the situation on the ground and the wishes of the people residing in the areas involved. as such, the protocol does not envisage the dislocation of populations and ensures that all areas of economic activity relevant to the homestead are preserved

h) A comprehensive package proposal was evolved to settle the outstanding boundary issues, in consultation with the bangladesh side. This resulted in the signing of the 2011 protocol.

7. Implications

a) in the exchange of enclaves, a de facto reality gets converted to a de jure situation. The areas in respect of enclaves that would be acquired by india and transferred to bangladesh are placed at annexure vi & annexure vii, respectively. 111 indian enclaves with a total area of 17,160.63 acres in bangladesh are to be transferred to bangladesh, while 51 bangladesh enclaves with an area of 7,110.02 acres in india are to be transferred to india. while on paper, the exchange of enclaves between india and bangladesh may seem like a loss of indian land to bangladesh, the actual scenario on the ground is quite different. These enclaves are located deep inside bangladesh and there has hardly been any direct access to them from india since 1947. Similarly, bangladesh has had minimal, if any, access to its enclaves located deep inside india. in effect, the exchange of enclaves denotes only a notional exchange of land.

b) a joint headcount conducted from 14-17 July, 2011 determined the total population in the enclaves to be around 51,549 (37,334 in indian enclaves within bangladesh and 14,215 in bangladesh enclaves within india). in respect of enclaves, the 1974 lba states that the people in these areas shall be given the right of staying where they are as nationals of the State to which the areas are transferred. feedback from a visit jointly undertaken by an india–bangladesh delegation to some of the enclaves and adverse possessions in may 2007 revealed that the people residing in indian enclaves in bangladesh and bangladesh enclaves in india did not want to leave their land and would rather be in the country where they had lived all their lives. movement of people, if any, is therefore expected to be at a minimum level.

c) in respect of adverse possessions, it must be noted that in reality the transferred area has already been in possession of bangladesh and the handing over of these areas to bangladesh is merely a procedural formal acceptance of a de facto reality on the ground. The same applies to indian adverse possessions within bangladesh that would be transferred to the indian union in implementation of the 2011 protocol. in the implementation of the protocol, india will receive 2777.038 acres of land and transfer 2267.682 acres of land to bangladesh. adverse possession areas that would be acquired by india and transferred to bangladesh are placed at annexure viii & annexure ix respectively.

d) The 2011 protocol provides for redrawing of boundaries to maintain the status quo of adverse possessions and has dealt with them on an 'as is where is' basis by converting de facto control into de jure recognition. people living in the adverse possessions are technically in occupation and possession of land beyond the boundary pillars, but are administered by the laws of the country of which they are citizens and where they enjoy all legal rights, including the right to vote. They have deep-rooted ties to their land which goes back decades and are categorically unwilling to be uprooted. many local communities have sentimental or religious attachments to the land in which they live. Over time, it became extremely difficult to implement the terms of 1974 lba as it meant uprooting people living in the adverse possessions from the land in which they had lived all their lives and to which they had developed sentimental and religious attachments. a joint visit by an india–bangladesh delegation to some of the enclaves and adverse possessions undertaken in may 2007 revealed that the people residing in the areas involved did not want to leave their land and would rather be in the country where they had lived all their lives. Some of the concerned State governments also had views on the issue.

These and other inputs from the people involved made it evident to both sides that retention of status quo of adverse possessions seemed the only option. in any democracy, the will of the people must remain significant, and the 2011 protocol has accorded highest priority to it - every effort has been made to preserve all areas of economic activity relevant to the homestead and to prevent dislocation of people living in the border areas. both india and bangladesh agreed to maintain the status quo in addressing the issue of adverse possessions instead of exchanging them as called for in the lba, 1974.

e) The demarcation of un-demarcated boundary in the three pending segments has followed ground realities, created a fixed boundary and resolved a problem that has eluded solution for decades. The boundary strip maps would have to be jointly prepared and signed by the plenipotentiaries of the two countries to implement the understanding reached in the protocol.

f) Signing of the Strip maps pertaining to adverse possessions would set the stage for exchange of land of the adverse possessions as well as exchange of land records and enclaves between the two sides.

g) The implications pertaining to the concerned State governments are given below with regard to adverse possessions and demarcation of boundary:

    i) west bengal: South berubari, with a population of 15,000, is a sensitive area because of a temple regarded as one of 51 Shakti peeths in the indian subcontinent and an important pilgrimage spot for hindus. The boundary in this sector has been drawn keeping in mind this sentiment and the agreement reached in the joint demarcation conducted in 1998 as a result of which South berubari will be retained in india. in other areas too, such as bousmari, old records, actual position on the ground and the people's wishes were kept in mind while determining the extent of adverse possessions. with regard to demarcation of daikhata 56, natural/geographical boundary in this region has been made the international boundary between the two countries, which is a normal practice in the demarcation of international boundary.

    ii) meghalaya: The state government's views on adverse possessions were accommodated through verification of actual position on the ground and wishes of the people. as a result of the joint survey in pyrdiwah, the adverse possession has been recognized on the indian side by bangladesh. in muktapur/dibir hawor area, the protocol facilitates the visit of indian nationals to kali mandir, drawing of water and exercise of fishing rights from the water body of muktapur has been accepted. in other areas too, the homesteads and economic activities of indian citizens has been protected.

iii) tripura: as agreed in the protocol, the boundary shall be drawn along the course of Sonaraichhera river as per ground realities. with regard to demarcation of the muhuri river/belonia Sector, keeping in mind the ground realities as well as wishes of the people, the boundary in this sector has been finalised according to the local demand; the cremation ground area has been allotted to the indian side and boundary has become a fixed boundary. further, the protocol has provisions of raising embankments by both the sides to stabilize the course of the river. to india's advantage, fencing on zero line has also been agreed. government of tripura, while agreeing to the demarcation in this sector, has conveyed that compensation for the loss of private land may be provided on account of demarcation.

iv) assam: The interests of tea and pan planters have been protected while finalizing the border between india and bangladesh in this sector. with regard to demarcation of the lathitilla and dumabari sector, the line drawn by radcliff and actual position on the ground has been followed.

8. Advantages

The major features of the 2011 protocol regarding the india- bangladesh boundary are also its advantages. These are as follows:

- as the protocol is the outcome of bilateral negotiations, it is mutually acceptable and durable and paves the way for settlement of the long pending land boundary issues;
- it takes into consideration the situation on the ground and the wishes of the people;
- it takes into account the views of the concerned State governments and has their written consent;
- The exchange of enclaves will mitigate major humanitarian problems as the residents in the enclaves and others on their behalf had often complained of the absence of basic amenities and facilities;
- The settlement of adverse possessions will lead to tranquillity and peace along the border;
- The protocol provides for a comprehensive package solution involving "give and take" on both sides;
- it represents a permanent solution to a decades old issue;

- The newly demarcated boundaries are a fixed boundary, thereby adding to certainty regarding the future;
- a settled boundary reduces friction, helps neighbours consolidate mutually beneficial exchanges and promotes confidence in building better relations.
- it paves the way for closer engagement and mutually beneficial relations between india and bangladesh and the region;
- This also helps on issues of strategic concern, including security cooperation and denial of sanctuary to elements inimical to india.
- while land will be exchanged, the protocol does not envisage the displacement of populations;
- The protocol ensures that the india-bangladesh boundary is permanently settled and there should be no more differences in interpretation, regardless of the government in power.

9. Constitutional amendment

No constitutional amendment is required for a resolution of the un-demarcated segments of the land boundary by an agreement as this is within the competence of the Executive wing of government. however, the issue of exchange of enclaves and redrawing of boundaries to maintain status quo in areas of adverse possessions involves the transfer of territories from one State to another and therefore requires a constitutional amendment. article 368 states that "an amendment of this constitution may be initiated only by the introduction of a bill for the purpose in either house of parliament, and when the bill is passed in each house by a majority of that house and by a majority of not less than two-thirds of the members of that house present and voting, it shall be presented to the president who shall give his assent to the bill and thereupon the constitution shall stand amended in accordance with the terms of the bill".

10. Conclusion

The effective management of our borders is the first essential step to creating a defined and peaceful boundary that will provide a stable and tranquil environment for cross-border cooperation with bangladesh. The protocol to the 1974 land boundary agreement, signed on 6 September 2011 by the foreign ministers of india and bangladesh in the presence of the prime ministers, paves the way for a settlement of the long pending land boundary issues between the two countries. This includes demarcation of the remaining un-demarcated areas, territories under adverse possession and exchange of enclaves. in building this historic agreement, the government has received the full support and concurrence of the State governments concerned. in implementing the agreement, people living in the border areas will not be dislocated.

The ratification of the protocol to the 1974 land boundary agreement would be a historic step culminating in the demarcation of the land boundary between india and bangladesh, a task that has remained unresolved for decades, and not replicated elsewhere along our borders in recent times. both sides have arrived at this agreement in a spirit of friendship, mutual understanding and a desire to put these issues behind us. The agreement has been welcomed by the people of both countries and will lead to easier management of the international border by the border guarding forces. The implementation of the 2011 protocol and 1974 lba will lead to the india-bangladesh boundary becoming stable and peaceful. it will ensure that people living along the border live in peace, amity and harmony. This will enable both countries to focus on other bilateral issues, including development of mutually beneficial cooperation and pave the way to realization of a common destiny through enhanced cooperation, growth and development of both nations.

****

Annexure - I

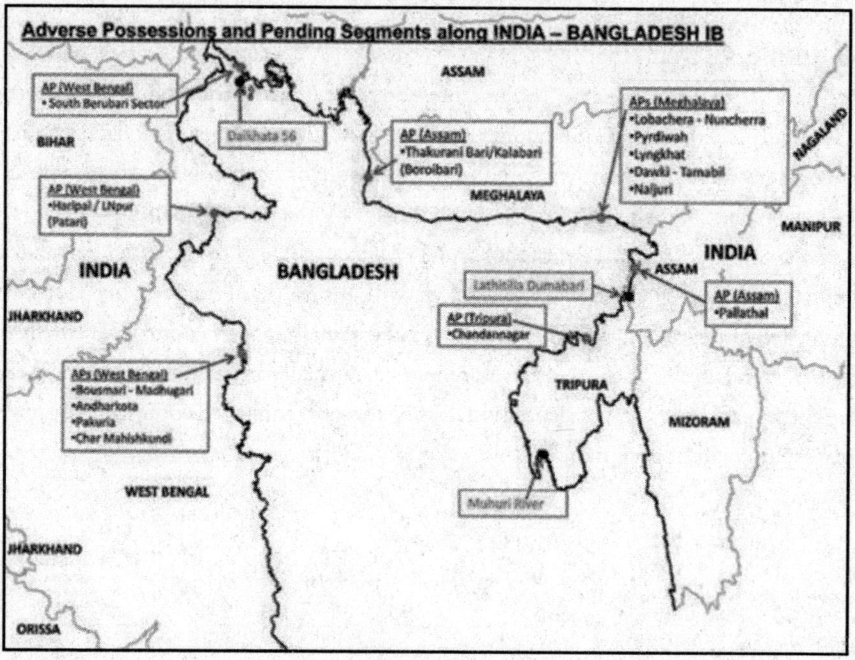

Adverse Possessions and Pending Segments along INDIA – BANGLADESH IB
AP (West Bengal)
• South Berubari Sector
Dalkhata 56
ASSAM
AP (Assam)
•Thakurani Bari/Kalabari (Boroibari)
APs (Meghalaya)
•Lobachera - Nuncherra
•Pyrdiwah
•Lyngkhat
•Dawki - Tamabil
•Naljuri
NAGALAND
BIHAR
AP (West Bengal)
•Haripal / LNpur (Patari)
MEGHALAYA
MANIPUR
INDIA
BANGLADESH
ASSAM
INDIA
Lathitilla Dumabari
AP (Assam)
•Pallathal
JHARKHAND
AP (Tripura)
•Chandannagar
APs (West Bengal)
•Bousmari - Madhugari
•Andharkota
•Pakuria
•Char Mahishkundi
TRIPURA
MIZORAM
WEST BENGAL
Muhuri River
JHARKHAND
ORISSA

Annexure - II

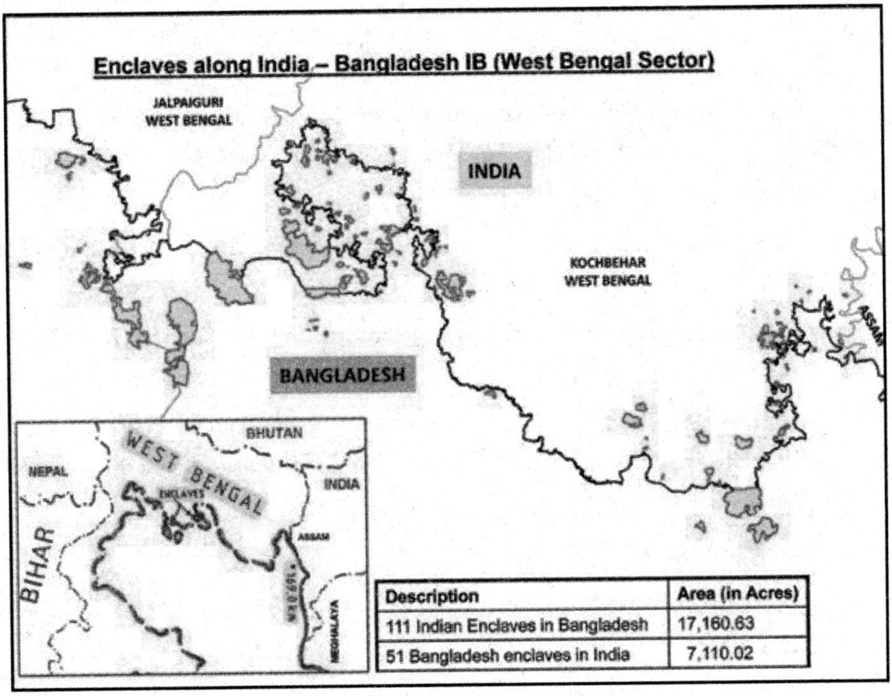

Description	Area (in Acres)
111 Indian Enclaves in Bangladesh	17,160.63
51 Bangladesh enclaves in India	7,110.02

Annexure - III

Agreement

Between the Government of the republic of India and the Government of the People's republic of Bangladesh concerning the demarcation of the land boundary between India and Bangladesh and related matters.

The Government of the Republic of India and the Government of the People's Republic of Bangladesh.

Bearing in mind the friendly relations existing between the two countries.

Desiring to define more accurately at certain points and to complete the demarcation of the land boundary between India and Bangladesh,

Have agreed as follows:-

Article 1

The land boundary between India and Bangladesh in the areas mentioned below shall be demarcated in the following manner:

1. **Mizoram-Bangladesh Sector**

   Demarcation should be completed on the basis of the latest pre-partition notifications and records.

2. **Tripura-Sylhet Sector**

   Demarcation which is already in progress in this area on the agreed basis, should be completed as early as possible.

3. **Bhagalpur Railway Line**

   The boundary should be demarcated at a distance of 75 feet parallel to the toe of the railway embankment towards the east.

....2/-

4. **Sibpur–Gaurangala Sector**

   The boundary should be demarcated in continuation of the process started in 1951-52 on the basis of the District Settlement Maps of 1915-1918.

5. **Mahuri River (Belonia) Sector**

   The Boundary in this area should be demarcated along the mid-stream of the course of Muhuri River at the time of demarcation. This boundary will be a fixed boundary. The two Governments should raise embankment on their respective sides with a view to stabilising the river in its present course.

6. **Remaining portion of the Tripura-Noakhali/Comilla sector**

   The demarcation in this sector should be completed on the basis of Chakla-Roshnabad Estate Maps of 1892-1894 and the District Settlement Maps of 1915-1918 for areas not cowered by the Chakla-Roshnabad Maps.

7. **Fenny River**

   The boundary should be demarcation along the mid-stream of the course at the time of demarcation of that branch of the Fenny River indicated as the Fenny River on Survey of India Map Sheet No.79 M/15 Ist Edition 1935, till it joins the stream shown as Asalong C on the said Map. From that point on, downstream, the boundary should be demarcated along the mid-stream of the course of the Fenny River at the time of demarcation of the boundary. The boundary in this sector will be a fixed boundary.

....3/-

8. **Rest of Tripura-Chittagong Hill Tract Sector**

The boundary will follow the mid-stream of that branch of the Fenny River, referred to in para 7 above, upto Grid reference 009779 (map sheet as in para 7 above) from where the boundary will follow the mid-stream of the eastern-most tributary. From the source of this tributary, the boundary will run along the shortest distance to the mid-stream of the stream marked Bayan Asalong, on the map referred to above, and thence will run generally northwards along the mid-stream of this river till it reaches its sources on the ridge (indicated by grid reference 046810 on the map referred to above). From there it will run along the crest of this ridge upto Bhogoban Trig Station. From Bhogoban Trig Station upto the tri-junction of the Bangladesh-Assam-Tripura boundary (Khan Talang Trig Station), the boundary will run along the watershed of the river systems of the two countries. In case of any difference between the map and the ground, the ground shall prevail. The boundary will be a fixed boundary in this sector.

9. **Beanibazar-Karimganj Sector**

The undemarcated portion of the boundary west of Umapati village should be demarcated in accordance with the agreed basis of demarcation, leaving Umapati village in India.

10. **Hakar Khal**

The boundary should be demarcated in accordance with the Nehru-noon Agreement of September, 1958,

....4/-

treating Hakar khal as a geographical feature distinet from the Ichhamati River. The boundary will be a fixed boundary.

11. Baikari Khal

In the Baikari Khal, the boundary should be demarcated on the agreed basis and principles, namely, that the ground shall prevail, i.e. as per the agreement reached between the directors of Land Records and Surveys of West Bengal and erstwhile East Pakistan in 1949. The boundary will be a fixed boundary.

12. Enclaves

The Indian enclaves in Bangladesh and the Bangladesh enclaves in India should be exchanged expeditiously, excepting the enclaves mentioned in paragraph 14 without claim to compensation for the additional area going to Bangladesh.

13. Hilli

The area will be demarcated in accordance with Radcliffe Award and the line drawn by him on the map.

14. Berubari

India will retain the southern half of South Berubari Union No. 12 and the adjacent enclaves, measuring an area of 2.64 square miles approximately, and in exchange Bangladesh will retain the Dahagram and Angarpota enclaves. India will lease in perpetuity to Bangladesh as area of 178 metres x 85 metres near 'Tin Bigha' to connect Dahagram with Panbari Mouza (P.S. Patgram) of Bangladesh.

....5/-

15. Lathitilla-Dumabari

From point I (the last demarcated boundary pillar position), the boundary shall run southwards along the Patharia Hills RF boundary upto the point where it meets the western boundary of Dumabari Mouza. Thence along the same Mouza boundary upto the tri-junction of Mouzas Dumabari, Lathitilla and Bara Putnigaon through the junction of the two Mouzas Dumabari and Lathitilla. From this point it shall run along the shourtest distance to meet the mid-stream of Putni Chara. Thence it shall run generally southwards along the midstream of the course of Putni Chara at the time of demarcation, till it meets the boundary between Sylhet (Bangladesh) and Tripura (India).

Article 2

The Governments of India and Bangladesh agree that territories in adverse possession in areas already demarcated in respect of which boundary strip maps are already prepared, shall be exchanged within six months of the signing of the boundary strip maps by the pleni-potentiaries. They may sign the relavent maps as early as possible and in any case not later than the 31st December, 1974. Early measures may be taken to print maps in respect of other areas where demarcation has already taken place. These should be printed by 31st May 1975 and signed by the plenipotentiaries thereafter in order that the exchange of adversely held possessions in these areas may take place by the 31st December, 1975. In sectors still to be demarcated, transfer of territorial jurisdiction may take place within six months of the signature by plenipotentiaries on the concerned boundary strip Maps.

....6/-

Article 3

The Governments of India and Bangladesh agree that when areas are transferred, the people in these areas shall be given the right of staying on where they are, as nationals of the State to which the areas are transferred. Pending demarcation of the boundary and exchanged of territory by mutual agreement, there should be no disturbance of the status que and peaceful conditions shall be maintained in the border regions. Necessary instructions in this regard shall be issued to the local authorities on the border by the two countries.

Article 4

The Government of India and Bangladesh agree that any dispute concerning the interpretation or implementation of this Agreement shall be settled peacefully through mutual consultations.

Article 5

This Agreement shall be subject to ratification by the Governments of India and Bangladesh and Instruments of Ratification shall be exchanged as early as possible. The Agreement shall take effect from the date of the exchange of the Instruments of Ratification.

....7/-

(7)

Signed in New Delhi on May 16, 1974, in two originals each of which is equally authentic.

For the Government of the Republic of India

(INDIRA GANDHI)
Prime Minister of India

For the Government of the People's Republic of Bangladesh

(SHEIKH MUJIBUR RAHMAN)
Prime Minister of Bangladesh

Annexure - IV

Letters Exchanged between the Indian Foreign Secretary and the Bangladesh Additional Foreign Secretary on the transfer of Tin Bigha.

New Delhi, March 26, 1992

Letter of the Indian Foreign Secretary :

Excellency,

I have the honour to refer to item 14 of Article 1 of the Agreement of 16th May, 1974,[1] signed by the Prime Ministers of India and Bangladesh concerning the demarcation of the land boundary between India and Bangladesh and related matters, and the Exchange of Letters dated 7th October, 1982,[2] between the Minister of External Affairs of India and the Minister of Foreign Affairs of Bangladesh regarding the terms of lease in perpetuity of the Tin Bigha area. This is to confirm that in the subsequent discussions regarding the modalities for leasing out the above mentioned area, the following understanding has been reached :

1. Indian flags will fly at the four corners of the Tin Bigha corridor as a manifestation of India's sovereignty over the area:
2. An East-West road to connect Dahagram (Bangladesh) with Patgram (Bangladesh) will be constructed by India before 26th June, 1992 roughly at right angles to the existing North-South road. The new East-West road is to conform to the specifications and width of the existing North-South road;
3. Landscaping (horticulture) protected by fencing, on both sides of the proposed road, is to be carried out and maintained by India, so as to prevent the possibility of encroachment and infiltration, keeping adequate provision for drains, laying of cables, water-supply etc., in future:
4. Two check points each are to be set up at both ends of the East-West road where it touches the Bangladesh boundary. They will be separately manned by Indian and Bangladesh authorities with a view to regulating the movement of traffic:
5. Traffic in the corridor will be regulated by the Indian authorities, and the opening and closing of the check points on the East-West road will be coordinated accordingly in such a manner that there is no intermixing of Indian and Bangladeshi streams of traffic;

6. All the intersection, i.e., the specific point where East-West road will cross the North-South road, there will be an Indian traffic Police control to direct the traffic movement:
7. Indian traffic movement on the North-South road will continue as heretofore. Bangladesh traffic will use the East-West road in the corridor at alternate hours during the day-light period. However, exceptions will be made at the local level to the above arrangements in cases of emergency, such as natural calamities, movement of civil administrators and medical emergencies;
8. Suitable lighting arrangements will be made for the entire corridor in order to facilitate monitoring by security agencies on both sides;
9. Differences, if any, regarding modalities for implementing the terms of lease will be resolved in the first instance through consultations between the Deputy Commissioner of Cooch Behar (India) and the Deputy Commissioner of Lalmonirhat (Bangladesh). Remaining differences, if any, will be referred to their respective Governments for resolution;
10. India and Bangladesh will provide mutual judicial assistance to each other to the extent necessary, in all matters relating to the prosecution, trials, etc. concerning incidents constituting offences in the leased area;
11. Agreed arrangements will come into effect from 26th June, 1992. 1 shall be grateful if your Excellency could confirm that the above sets out correctly the understanding reached between our two Governments.

Please accept. Excellency, the assurances of my highest consideration.

Sdl-

(J. N. Dixit)

Foreign Secretary

His Excellency Mr. A. H. Mahmood Ali,
Additional Foreign Secretary,
Ministry of Foreign Affairs,
Government of People's Republic of Bangladesh.

♦♦♦♦♦

Letter of Bangladesh Foreign Secretary :

Excellency,

I have the honour to refer to item 14 Article 1 of the Agreement of 16th May, 1974 between the Government of the People's Republic of Bangladesh and the Government

2

of the Republic of India concerning the Demarcation of the Land Boundary between Bangladesh and India and Related Matters; the Exchange of Letters dated 7 October, 1982, between the Minister of Foreign Affairs of Bangladesh and the Minister of External Affairs of India regarding the terms of lease in perpetuity of the Tin Bigha Area; and to acknowledge your letter dated 26th March, 1992, setting out the modalities for leasing out the Tin Bigha Area to Bangladesh.

I have the honour to confirm that the following correctly sets out the understanding reached between our two Governments regarding the: modalities for leasing out the Tin Bigha Area :

1. Indian flags will fly at the four corners of the Tin Bigha corridor as a manifestation of India's sovereignty over the area;
2. An East-West road to connect Dahagram (Bangladesh) with Patgram (Bangladesh) will be constructed by India before 26th June, 1992 roughly at right angles to the existing North-South road. The new East-West road is to conform to the specifications and width of the existing North-South road;
3. Landscaping (horticulture) protected by fencing, on both sides of the proposed road, is to be carried out and maintained by India, so as to prevent the possibility of encroachment and infiltration, keeping adequate provision for drains, laying of cables, water-supply etc., in future;
4. Two check points each are to be set up at both ends of the East-West road where it touches the Bangladesh boundary. They will be separately manned by Bangladesh and Indian authorities with a view to regulating the movement of traffic;
5. Traffic in the corridor will be regulated by the Indian authorities, and the opening and closing of the check points on the East-West road will be coordinated accordingly in such a manner that there is no intermixing of Bangladeshi and Indian streams of traffic;
6. At the intersection, i.e., the specific point where East-West road will cross the North-South road, there will be an Indian traffic Police control to direct the traffic movement;
7. Indian traffic movement on the North-South road will continue as heretofore. Bangladesh traffic will use the East-West road in the corridor at alternate hours during the day-light period. However, exceptions will be made at the local level to the above arrangements in cases of emergency, such as natural calamities, movement of civil administrators and medical emergencies;

8. Suitable lighting arrangements will be made for the entire corridor in order to facilitate monitoring by security agencies on both sides;
9. Differences, if any, regarding modalities for implementing the terms of lease will be resolved in the first instance through consultations between the Deputy Commissioner of Lalmonirhat (Bangladesh) and the Deputy Commissioner of Cooch Behar (India). Remaining differences, if any, will be referred to their respective Governments for resolution;
10. Bangladesh and India will provide mutual judicial assistance to each other to the extent necessary, in all matters relating to the prosecution, trials, etc. concerning incidents constituting offences in the leased area;
11. Agreed arrangements will come into effect from 26th June, 1992. Please accept, Excellency, the assurances of my highest consideration.

Sdl-
(A.H. Mahmood Ali)
Additional Foreign Secretary

His Excellency Mr. J.N. Dixit,
Foreign Secretary
Ministry of External Affairs,
Government of Republic of India,
New Delhi

♦♦♦♦♦

4

Annexure - V

PROTOCOL TO THE AGREEMENT BETWEEN THE GOVERNMENT OF THE REPUBLIC OF INDIA AND THE GOVERNMENT OF THE PEOPLE's REPUBLIC OF BANGLADESH CONCERNING THE DEMARCATION OF THE LAND BOUNDARY BETWEEN INDIA AND BANGLADESH AND RELATED MATTERS

The Government of the Republic of India and the Government of the People's Republic of Bangladesh,

Bearing in mind the friendly relations existing between the two countries,

Desiring to define more accurately at certain points and to complete the demarcation of the land boundary between India and Bangladesh,

Having regard to the Agreement between the Government of the Republic of India and the Government of the People's Republic of Bangladesh concerning the demarcation of the land boundary between India and Bangladesh and related matters, May 16, 1974 and Exchange of Letters dated December 26, 1974; December 30, 1974; October 7, 1982; and March 26, 1992 (hereinafter referred to as the 1974 Agreement),

Have agreed as follows:

ARTICLE 1

The provisions of this Protocol shall form an integral part of the 1974 Agreement.

ARTICLE 2

(I) Article 1 Clause 5 of the 1974 Agreement shall be implemented as follows:

Muhuri River (Belonia) sector

Boundary in this segment shall be drawn westwards from the existing Boundary Pillar No. 2159/48-S along the agreed line as depicted in the index map prepared jointly till it meets the southern limit of the Burning Ghat as shown in jointly surveyed map of Muhuri river area in 1977-78. Thereafter it shall follow the external limit of the Burning Ghat in South-West direction and then turn northwards along the external limit of the Burning Ghat till it meets the centre of the existing Muhuri River. Thereafter it shall run along the mid stream of the existing Muhuri River upto Boundary Pillar No. 2159/3-S. This boundary shall be the fixed boundary. The two Governments should raise embankments on their respective sides with a view to stabilising the river in its present course as Stipulated in the 1974 Agreement. The Parties agree to fencing on 'zero line' in this area.

(II) Article 1 Clause 12 of the 1974 Agreement shall be implemented as follows:

Enclaves

111 Indian Enclaves in Bangladesh and 51 Bangladesh Enclaves in India as per the jointly verified cadastral enclave maps and signed at the level of DGLR&S, Bangladesh and DLR&S. West Bengal (India) in April 1997, shall be exchanged without claim to compensation for the additional areas going to Bangladesh.

(III) Article 1 Clause 15 of the 1974 Agreement shall be implemented as follows:

Lathitilla and Dumabari

Line drawn by Radcliffe from Boundary Pillar 1397(point Y) i.e. the last demarcated boundary pillar position, straight southward to the tri-junction of Mouzas Dumabari, Lathitilla and Bara Putnigaon i.e. upto iron bridge, and thence it shall run generally southwards along the midstream of the course of Putni Chara as already demarcated on the ground, till it meets the boundary between Sylhet (Bangladesh) and Tripura (India) i.e. Boundary Pillar No. 1800.

(IV) The land boundary in the area mentioned below shall be demarcated in the following manner:

Daikhata 56 (West Bengal-Jalpaiguri)/Panchagarh

Boundary in this segment shall be drawn as fixed boundary from existing Boundary Pillar 774/32-S in the strip sheet 444/6 along the mouza boundary of Daikhata-56 as surveyed in 1997-98 and thereafter will follow the southern boundary of Daikhata-56 (from east to west) upto Point No 18 and therefrom it will follow the western boundary of Daikhata-56 (from south to north) till it meets the center of River Sui at Point No 15 and thereafter, will run along the center of the River Sui upto Point No 1, the point as depicted in the sketch map jointly prepared and mutually agreed on August 3, 2011. Thereafter the international Boundary shall follow the already delineated boundary through Main Pillar (MP) 775.

ARTICLE 3

(I) Article 2 of the 1974 Agreement shall be implemented as follows:

The Government of India and the Government of Bangladesh agree that the boundary shall be drawn as a fixed boundary for territories held in Adverse Possession as determined through joint survey and fully depicted in the respective adversely possessed land area index map (APL map) finalized by the

Land Records and Survey Departments of both the countries between December 2010 and August 2011, which are fully described in clause (a) to (d) below.

The relevant strip maps shall be printed and signed by the Plenipotentiaries and transfer of territorial jurisdiction shall be completed simultaneously with the exchange of the enclaves. The demarcation of the boundary, as depicted in the above-mentioned index Maps, shall be as under:-

(a) **West Bengal Sector**

(i) **Bousmari — Madhugari (Kushtia-Nadia) area**

The boundary shall be drawn from the existing Boundary Pillar Nos. 154/5-S to 157/1-S to follow the centre of old course of river Mathabanga, as depicted in consolidation map of 1962, as surveyed jointly and agreed in June 2011.

(ii) **Andharkota (Kushtia-Nadia) area**

The boundary shall be drawn from existing Boundary Pillar no 152/5-S to Boundary Pillar No 153/1-S to follow the edge of existing River Mathabanga as jointly surveyed and agreed in June 2011.

(iii) **Pakuria (Kushtia-Nadia) area**

The boundary shall be drawn from existing Boundary Pillar No 151/1-S to Boundary Pillar No 152/2-S to follow the edge of River Mathabanga as jointly surveyed and agreed in June 2011.

(iv) **Char Mahishkundi (Kushtia-Nadia) area**

The boundary shall be drawn from existing Boundary Pillar No 153/1-S to Boundary Pillar No 153/9-S to follow the edge of River Mathabanga as jointly surveyed and agreed in June 2011.

(v) **Haripal/ Khutadah/ Battoli/ Sapameri/ LNpur (Patari) (Naogaon-Malda) area**

The boundary shall be drawn as line joining from existing Boundary Pillar No 242/S/13, to Boundary Pillar No 243/7-S/5 and as jointly surveyed and agreed in June 2011.

(vi) **Berubari (Panchagarh-Jalpaiguri area)**

The boundary in the area Berubari. (Panchagarh-Jalpaiguri) adversely held by Bangladesh, and Berubari and Singhapara-

Khudipara (Panchagarh-Jalpaiguri), adversely held by India shall be drawn as jointly demarcated during 1996-1998.

(b) **Meghalaya Sector**

(i) **Lobachera-Nuncherra**

The boundary from existing Boundary Pillar No 1315/4-S to Boundary Pillar No 1315/15-S in Lailong - Balichera, Boundary Pillar No 1316/1-S to Boundary Pillar No 1316/11-S in Lailong-Noonchera, Boundary Pillar No 1317 to Boundary Pillar No 1317/13-S in Lailong- Lahiling and Boundary Pillar No 1318/1-S to Boundary Pillar No 1318/2-S in Lailong- Lubhachera shall be drawn to follow the edge of tea gardens as jointly surveyed and agreed in Dec 2010.

(ii) **Pyrdiwah/ Padua Area**

The boundary shall be drawn from existing Boundary Pillar No 1270/1-S as per jointly surveyed and mutually agreed line till Boundary Pillar No 1271/1-T. The Parties agree that the Indian Nationals from Pyrdiwah village shall be allowed to draw water from Piyang River near point No 6 of the agreed Map.

(iii) **Lyngkhat Area**

(aa) **Lyngkhat -I/Kulumcherra & Lyngkhat-II/Kulumcherra**

The boundary shall be drawn from existing Boundary Pillar No. 1264/4-S to Boundary Pillar No 1265 and BP No 1265/6-S to 1265/9-S as per jointly surveyed and mutually agreed line.

(ab) **Lyngkhat-III/Sonarhat**

The boundary shall be drawn from existing Boundary Pillar No 1266/13-S along the nallah southwards till it meets another nallah in the east-west direction, thereafter it shall run along the northern edge of the nallah in east till it meets the existing International Boundary north of Reference Pillar Nos.1267/4-R-B and 1267/3-R-1.

(iv) **Dawki/Tamabil area**

The boundary shall be drawn by a straight line joining existing Boundary Pillar Nos 1275/1-S to Boundary Pillar Nos 1275/7-S. The Parties agree to fencing on 'zero line' in this area.

(v) **Naljuri/Sreepur Area**

(aa) **Naljuri I**

The boundary shall be a line from the existing Boundary Pillar No 1277/2-S in southern direction upto three plots as depicted in the strip Map no 166 till it meets the nallah flowing from Boundary Pillar No 1277/5-T, thereafter it will run along the western edge of the nallah in the southern direction upto 2 plots on the Bangladesh side, thereafter it shall run eastwards till it meets a line drawn in southern direction from Boundary Pillar No 1277/4-S.

(ab) **Naljuri III**

The boundary shall be drawn by a straight line from existing Boundary Pillar No 1278/2-S to Boundary Pillar No 1279/3-S.

(vi) **Muktapur/Dibir Hawor Area**

The Parties agree that the Indian Nationals shall be allowed to visit Kali Mandir and shall also be allowed to draw water and exercise fishing rights in the water body in the Muktapur/Dibir Hawor area from the bank of Muktapur side.

(c) **Tripura Sector**

(i) **Chandannagar-Champarai Tea Garden area in Tripura/Moulvi Bazar sector**

The boundary shall be drawn along Sonaraichhera river from existing Boundary Pillar No 1904 to Boundary Pillar No 1905 as surveyed jointly and agreed in July 2011.

(d) **Assam Sector**

(i) **Kalabari (Boroibari) area in Assam sector**

The boundary shall be drawn from existing Boundary Pillar No 1066/24-T to Boundary Pillar No 1067/16-T as surveyed jointly and agreed in August 2011.

(ii) **Pallathal area in Assam sector**

The boundary shall be drawn from existing Boundary Pillar No. 1370/3-S to 1371/6-S to follow the outer edge of the tea garden and from Boundary Pillar No. 1372 to 1373/2-S along outer edge of the pan plantation.

ARTICLE 4

This Protocol shall be subject to ratification by the Government of the Republic of India and the Government of the People's Republic of Bangladesh and shall enter into force on the date of exchange of Instruments of Ratification.

Signed at Dhaka on the Sixth day of September, 2011, in two originals in the English language.

For the Government of the Republic of India

For the Government of the People's Republic of Bangladesh

Annexure - VI

Annexure - VI

Exchangeable Bangladesh enclaves in India with Area

A. Enclaves with Independent chhits

Sl No.	Name of Chhits	Lying within Police Station		J.L. No	Acres in Scres
		W. Bengal/	Bangladesh		
1	2	3	4	5	6
1.	Chhit Kuchlibari	Mekliganj	Patgram	22	370.64
2.	Chhit Land of Kuchlibari	-do-	-do-	24	1.83
3.	Balapukhari	-do-	-do-	21	331.64
4.	Chhit Lend of Panbari No. 2	-do-	-do-	20	1.13
5.	Chhit Panbari	-do-	-do-	18	108.59
6.	Dhabalsati Mirgipur	-do-	-do-	15	173.88
7.	Bamandal	-do-	-do-	11	2.24
8.	Chhit Dhabalsati	-do-	-do-	14	66.58
9.	Dhabalsati	-do-	-do-	13	60.45
10.	Srirampur	-do-	-do-	8	1.05
11.	Jote Nijama	-do-	-do-	3	87.54
12.	Chhit Land of Jagatber No. 3	Mathabhanga	-do-	37	69.84
13.	-do- No. 1	-do-	-do-	35	30.66
14.	-do- No. 2	-do-	-do-	36	27.09
15.	Chhit Kokoabari	-do-	-do-	47	29.49
16.	Chhit Bhandardaha	-do-	-do-	67	39.96
17.	Dhabalguri	-do-	-do-	52	12.50
18.	Chhit Dhabalguri	-do-	-do-	53	22.31
19.	Chhit Land of Dhabalguri. No. 3	-do-	-do-	70	1.33
20.	-do- No. 4	-do-	-do-	71	4.55
21	-do- No. 5	-do-	-do-	72	4.12
22.	-do- No. 1	-do-	-do-	68	26.83
23.	-do- No. 2	-do-	-do-	69	13.95
24.	Mahishmari	Sitalkuchi	-do-	54	122.77

25.	Bura Saradubi	-do-	Hatibandha	13	34.96
26.	Falnapur	-do-	Patgram	64	505.56
27.	Amjhol	-do-	Hatibandha	57	1.25
28.	Kismat Batrigachh	Dinhata	Kaliganj	82	209.95
29.	Durgapur	-do-	-do-	83	20.96
30.	Bansua khamar Gitaldaha	-do-	Lalmonirhat	1	24.54
31.	Poaturkuthi	-do-	-do-	37	589.94
32.	Paschim Bakalir Chhara	-do-	Bhurungamari	38	151.98
33.	Madhya Bakalir Chhara	-do-	-do-	39	32.72
34.	Purba Bakalir Chhara	-do-	-do-	40	12.23
35.	Madhya Masaldanga	-do-	-do-	3	136.66
36.	Madhya Chhit Masaldanga	-do-	-do-	8	11.87
37.	Paschim Bakalir Chhara	-do-	-do-	7	7.60
38.	Uttar Masaldanga	-do-	-do-	2	27.29
39.	Kachua	-do-	-do-	5	119.74
40.	Uttar Bansjani	Tufanganj	-do-	1	47.17
41.	Chhat Tilei	-do-	-do-	17	81.56
B.	Enclaves with fragmented Chhits				
42.	(i) Nalgram	Sitalkuchi	Patgram	65	
	(ii) -do- (Fragment)	-do-	-do-	65	1397.34
	(iii) -do- -do-	-do-	-do-	65	
43.	(i) Chhit Nalgram	-do-	-do-	66	49.50
	(ii) -do- (Fragment)	-do-	-do-	66	
44.	(i) Batrigachh	Dinhata	Kaliganj	81	577.37
	(ii) -do- (Fragment)	-do-	-do-	81	
45.	(i) Karala	-do-	Phulbari	9	269.91
	(ii) -do- (Fragment)	-do-	-do-	9	
	(iii) -do- -do-	-do-	-do-	9	
46.	Sipprasad Mustati	-do-	-do-	8	373.20
	(ii) -do- (Fragment)	-do-	-do-	8	
47.	(i) Dakshin Masaldanga	-do-	Bhurungamari	6	571.38
	(ii) -do- -do- (Fragment)	-do-	-do-	6	
	(iii) -do- -do- -do-	-do-	-do-	6	
	(iv) -do- -do- -do-	-do-	-do-	6	
	(v) -do- -do- -do-	-do-	-do-	6	
	(vi) -do- -do- -do-	-do-	-do-	6	

48.	(i) Paschim Masaldanga	-do-	-do-	4	29.49
	(ii) -do- -do- (Fragment)	-do-	-do-	4	
49.	(i) Purba Chitt Masaldanga	-do-	-do-	10	35.01
	(ii) -do- -do- (Fragment)	-do-	-do-	10	
50.	(i) Purba Masaldanga	-do-	-do-	11	153.89
	(ii) -do- -do- (Fragment)	-do-	-do-	11	
51.	(i) Uttar Dhaldanga	-do-	-do-	14	24.98
	(ii) -do- (Fragment)	-do- -do-	-do-	14	
	(iii) -do- -do-	-do- -do-	-do-	14	
	Total Area:				7,110.02

The above given details of encleves have been jointly compared and reconciled with records held by India and Bangladesh during the Indo-Bangladesh Boundary Conference held at Calcutta during 9th-12th Oct. 96 as well as during joint field inspection at Jalpaiguri (West Bengal) - Panchagarh (Bangladesh) sector during 21-24 Nov. 96.

Brig J N Poter

Directer Land Records & Survey
Ex-Official West Bengal, India
Director, Eastern Circle
Survey of India, Calcutta

Md. Shafi Uddin

Director General, Land Records and
Surveys, Bangladesh

Annexure - VII

Annexure - VII

Exchangable Indian enclaves in Bangladesh with area

A. Enclaves with Independent chitts

Sl No.	Name of Chhits	Chhit No.	Lying Within Police Station		Area in Acres
			Bangladesh/W. Bengal		
1	2	3	4	5	6
1.	Garati	75	Pochagar	Haldibari	58.23
2.	-do-	76	-do-	-do-	0.79
3.	-do-	77	-do-	-do-	18.00
4.	-do-	78	-do-	-do-	986.66
5.	-do-	79	-do-	-do-	1.74
6.	-do-	80	-do-	-do-	73.75
7.	Bingimari part - I	73	-do-	-do-	6.07
8.	Nazirganja	41	Bodo	-do-	58.32
9.	-do-	42	-do-	-do-	434.29
10.	-do-	44	-do-	-do-	53.47
11.	-do-	45	-do-	-do-	1.07
12.	-do-	46	-do-	-do-	17.95
13.	-do-	47	-do-	-do-	3.89
14.	-do-	48	-do-	-do-	73.27
15.	-do-	49	-do-	-do-	49.05
16.	-do-	50	-do-	-do-	5.05
17.	-do-	51	-do-	-do-	0.77
18.	-do-	52	-do-	-do-	1.04
19.	-do-	53	-do-	-do-	1.02
20.	-do-	54	-do-	-do-	3.87
21.	-do-	55	-do-	-do-	12.18
22.	-do-	56	-do-	-do-	54.04
23.	-do-	57	-do-	-do-	8.27
24.	-do-	58	-do-	-do-	14.22

25.	-do-	60	-do-	-do-	0.52
26.	Putimari	59	-do-	-do-	122.80
27.	Daikhata Chhat	38	-do-	-do-	499.21
28.	Salbari	37	-do-	-do-	1188.93
29.	Kajal Dighi	36	-do-	-do-	771.44
30.	Nataktoka	32	-do-	-do-	162.26
31.	-do-	33	-do-	-do-	0.26
32.	Beuladanga Chhat	35	-do-	-do-	0.83
33.	Balapara lagrabar	3	Debiganj	-do-	1752.44
34.	Bara Khankikharija Dimla	30	Boda	-do-	7.71
35.	-do-	29	-do-	-do-	36.83
36.	Barakhangir	28	-do-	-do-	30.53
37.	Nagarjikobari	31	-do-	-do-	33.41
38.	Kuchlibari	26	Patgram	Mekliganj	5.78
39.	-do-	27	-do-	-do-	2.04
40.	Bara kuchlibari	Fragment of J. L. 107 of P.S. Mekliganj	-do-	-do-	4.35
41.	Jamaldaha-Balapukhari	6	-do-	-do-	5.24
42.	Uponchowki Kuchlibari	115/2	-do-	-do-	0.32
43.	-do-	7	-do-	-do-	44.04
44.	Bhothnri	8	-do-	-do-	36.83
45.	Balapukhari	5	-do-	-do-	55.91
46.	Bara Khangir	4	-do-	Mekliganj	50.51
47.	-do-	9	-do-	-do-	87.42
48.	Chatt Bogdokra	10	-do-	-do-	41.70
49.	Ratanpur	11	-do-	-do-	58.91
50.	Bogdokra	12	-do-	-do-	25.49
51.	Fulker Dabri	Fragment of J.L. 101 of P.S. Mekliganj	-do-	-do-	0.88
52.	Khalkharia	15	-do-	-do-	60.74
53.	-do-	13	-do-	-do-	51.62
54.	Lotamari	14	-do-	-do-	110.92
55.	Bhotbari	16	-do-	-do-	205.46
56.	Komat Changrabandha	16A	-do-	-do-	42.80

57.	-do-	17A	-do-	-do-	16.01
58.	Panisala	17	-do-	-do-	137.66
59.	Dwarikamari Khasbash	18	-do-	-do-	36.50
60.	Panisala	153/P	-do-	-do-	0.27
61.	-do-	153/O	-do-	-do-	18.01
62.	-do-	19	-do-	-do-	64.63
63.	-do-	21	-do-	-do-	51.40
64.	Lotamari	20	-do-	-do-	283.53
65.	-do-	22	-do-	-do-	98.85
66.	Dwarikamari	23	-do-	-do-	39.52
67.	-do-	24	-do-	-do-	45.73
68.	Chhat Bhothat	24	-do-	-do-	56.91
69.	Baakata	131	-do-	Hathabhanga	22.35
70.	-do-	132	-do-	-do-	11.96
71.	-do-	130	-do-	-do-	20.48
72.	Bhokramguri	133	-do-	-do-	1.44
73.	Chenataka	134	-do-	Mekliganj	7.81
74.	Banskata	119	-do-	Mathabanga	413.81
75.	-do-	120	-do-	-do-	30.75
76.	-do-	121	-do-	-do-	12.15
77.	-do-	113	-do-	-do-	57.86
78.	-do-	112	-do-	-do-	315.04
79.	-do-	114	-do-	-do-	0.77
80.	-do-	115	-do-	-do-	29.20
81.	-do-	122	-do-	-do-	33.22
82.	-do-	127	-do-	-do-	12.72
83.	-do-	128	-do-	-do-	2.33
84.	-do-	117	-do-	-do-	2.55
85.	-do-	118	-do-	-do-	30.98
86.	-do-	125	-do-	-do-	0.64
87.	-do-	126	-do-	-do-	1.39
88.	-do-	129	-do-	-do-	1.37
89.	-do-	116	-do-	-do-	16.96
90.	-do-	123	-do-	-do-	24.37
91.	-do-	124	-do-	-do-	0.28

92.	Gotamari Chhit	135	Hatibandha	Sitalkuchi	126.59
93.	-do-	136	-do-	-do-	20.02
94.	Banapachai	151	Lalmonirhat	Dinhata	217.29
95.	Banapachai Bhitarkhuthi	152	-do-	-do-	81.71
96.	Dasiar Chhara	150	Fulbari	-do-	1643.44
97.	Dakurhat - Dakinirkuthi	156	Kurigram	-do-	14.27
98.	Kalmati	141	Bhurungamari	Dinhata	21.21
99.	Bhahobganj	153	-do-	-do-	31.58
100.	Baotikursa	142	-do-	-do-	45.63
101.	Bara Coachulka	143	-do-	-do-	39.99
102.	Gaochulka II	147	-do-	-do-	0.90
103.	Gaochulka I	146	-do-	-do-	8.92
104.	Dighaltari II	145	-do-	-do-	8.81
105.	Dighaltari I	144	-do-	-do-	12.31
106.	Chhoto Garaljhora II	149	-do-	-do-	17.85
107.	Chhoto Garaljhora I	148	-do-	-do-	35.74
108.	1 Chhit without name ~~and JL No.~~ at the southernend of JL No. 38 and ~~southwesternend~~ of JL No.39 (Asokbari)		~~Patgram~~ Dalia	~~Mekliganj~~ Mathabhanga	~~1.00~~ 3.50

B. Enclaves with Fragmented Chhits

109.	(i) Bewladanga	34	Haldibari	Boda	862.46
	(ii) Bewladanga	Fragment	-do-	Debiganj	
110.	(i) Kotbhajni	2	-do-	Debiganj	2012.27
	(ii) Kotbhajni	Fragment	-do-	-do-	
	(iii) Kotbhajni	-do-	-do-	-do-	
	(iv) Kotbhajni	-do-	-do-	-do-	
111.	(i) Dahala Khagrabari	1	-do-	-do-	2650.3[illegible]
	(ii) -do-	Fragment	-do	-do-	
	(iii) -do-	-do-	-do-	-do-	
	(iv) -do-	-do-	-do-	-do-	
	(v) -do-	-do-	-do-	-do-	
	(vi) -do-	-do-	-do-	-do-	
	Total Area				~~47,160~~ 7,[illegible]

The above given details of enclaves have been jointly compared and reconciled with records held by India and Bangladesh during the Indo-Bangladesh Boundary Conference held at Calcutta during 9th-12th Oct.96 as well as during joint field inspection at Jalpaiguri (West Bengal) Panchagarh (Bangladesh) sector during 21-24 Nov.96.

Note:

Name of enclave in Sl. no. 108 above has been identified as "Ashokabari" by Joint ground verification durign field season 1996-97.

Brig. J.R.Peter
Director Land Records & Survey
(Ex-Officio) West Bengal, India & and
Director, Eastern Circle
Survey of India, Calcutta.

Md.Shafi Uddin
Director General, Land Records
and Surveys, Bangladesh.

Annexure - VIII

Adverse possession	
Territory to be transferred to India (in acres)	
West Bengal	
Berubari and Singhpara-Khudipara (Panchagarh- Jalpaiguri)	1374.99
Pakuria (Khustia-Nadia)	576.36
Char Mahishkundi	393.33
Haripal/ LNpur (Patari)	53.37
Total	2398.05
Meghalaya	
Pyrdiwah	193.516
Lyngkhat i	4.793
Lyngkhat ii	0.758
Lyngkhat iii	6.94
Dawki / Tamabil	1.557
Naljuri i	6.156
Naljuri iii	26.858
Total	240.578
Tripura	
Chandannagar (Moulvi Bazar-Uttar Tripura)	138.41
Total	138.41
Grand Total (APs)	2777.038

Annexure - IX

Adverse possession	
Territory to be transferred to Bangladesh (in acres)	
West Bengal	
Bousmari-Madhugari (Khustia-Nadia)	1358.25
Andharkota	338.79
Berubari (Panchagarh- Jalpaiguri)	260.55
Total	1957.59
Meghalaya	
Lobachera-Nuncherra	41.702
Total	41.702
Assam	
Thakurani Bari- Kalabari (Boroibari) (Kurigram-Dubri)	193.85
Pallathal (Moulvi Bazar -Karimganj)	74.54
Total	268.39
Grand Total (aps)	2267.682

Frequently Asked Questions

Q. Is Bangladesh in illegal occupation of Indian land?

Ans. There is no illegal occupation of indian land by bangladesh. Since independence, there have been pockets along the india- bangladesh border that have traditionally been under the possession of people of one country in the territory of another country. These are known as adverse possessions. during the visit of the prime minister to bangladesh in September 2011, a protocol to the 1974 land boundary agreement between india and bangladesh was signed. The protocol addresses outstanding land boundary issues, including the issue of adverse possessions, between the two countries.

Q. We understand that an Agreement on land boundary issues has been signed between India and Bangladesh during the visit of the Prime Minister to Bangladesh in September 2011. What are the main elements of this agreement?

Ans. India and bangladesh concluded a land boundary agreement in 1974, soon after the independence of bangladesh, to find a solution to the complex nature of border demarcation. The agreement was implemented in its entirety with the exception of three issues pertaining to (i) un-demarcated land boundary of approximately 6.1 km in three sectors, viz. daikhata-56 (west bengal), muhuri river-belonia (tripura) and lathitila- dumabari (assam); (ii) exchange of enclaves; and (iii) adverse possessions. Although the agreement was not ratified by india, its implementation, except for the outstanding issues mentioned above, represented significant progress, given the fact that the two countries share an approximately 4,096.7 km long land boundary.

The outstanding issues, however, contributed to tension and instability along the border and adversely impacted on the lives of people living in the areas involved. Those living in the enclaves could not enjoy full legal rights as citizens of either country and infrastructure facilities such as electricity, schools and health services were deficient. for those in adverse possessions, it meant an unsettled existence between two countries without the certainty of being able to cultivate their lands or lead normal lives. The need for a settlement of the outstanding land boundary issues between india and bangladesh was, therefore, acutely felt and articulated by the people involved, the concerned state governments and others. Several attempts have been made to address the outstanding land boundary issues. it was, however, only with the signing of the protocol to the 1974 lba during the visit of the prime minister to bangladesh on 6th September 2011 that a settlement to the outstanding land boundary issues between the two countries was achieved. The 2011 protocol will result in a fixed demarcated boundary in all the un-demarcated segments, exchange of indian enclaves in bangladesh with bangladesh enclaves in india and a resolution of all adversely possessed areas. This historic agreement will remove a major irritant in relations between the two neighbouring countries. it will contribute to a stable and peaceful boundary and create an environment conducive to enhanced bilateral cooperation. it will result in better management and coordination of the border and strengthen our ability to deal with smuggling, illegal activities and other trans-border crimes.

In concluding the protocol, the two sides (india and bangladesh) have taken into account the situation on the ground, the wishes of the people residing in the areas involved and the views of the concerned State governments. as such, the protocol does not envisage the dislocation of populations and ensures that all areas of economic activity relevant to the homestead have been preserved. The protocol has been prepared with the full support and concurrence of the concerned State governments (assam, meghalaya, tripura and west bengal).

Q. Will signing of the Protocol to the 1974 Land Boundary Agreement lead to surrender of Indian land to Bangladesh?

Ans. The implementation of the protocol will result in the exchange of 111 indian enclaves in bangladesh with 51 bangladesh enclaves in india and preservation of the status quo on territories in adverse possession. in implementing the protocol, 111 indian enclaves with a total area of 17,160.63 acres in bangladesh are to be transferred to bangladesh, while 51 bangladesh enclaves with an area of 7,110.02 acres in india are to be transferred to india. moreover, with the adjustment of adverse possessions in the implementation of the protocol, india will receive 2777.038 acres of land and transfer 2267.682 acres of land to bangladesh.

In reality, however the exchange of enclaves and adverse possessions denotes only a notional exchange of land. The actual situation on the ground is that the enclaves are located deep inside the territory of both countries and there has been no physical access to them from either country. Thus the exchange of enclaves will legalise a situation which already exists de facto. Similarly, in the case of adverse possessions, the reality is that the area to be transferred was already in the possession of bangladesh and the handing over of this area to bangladesh and india respectively. The exchange of adverse possessions confirms that each country will legally possess the territories it is already holding.

Q. How will the three un-demarcated segments be demarcated?

Ans. With the signing of the protocol, the un-demarcated land boundary in three sectors, viz. daikhata-56 (west bengal), muhuri river-belonia (tripura) and dumabari (assam) have been demarcated. The demarcation of boundary in daikhata-56 is based on status quo; in belonia, demarcation has taken place along the muhuri river charland while retaining the traditional cremation grounds on the indian side of the boundary; and in lathitila-dumabari, demarcation has followed a mutually acceptable line. Joint survey of the boundary demarcation in the three un-demarcated segments was carried out by the Survey departments of the respective State governments. The demarcation has been carried out keeping in view the situation on the ground and the wishes of the people involved.

Chapter 2 (Appendix B)

MOST IMMEDIATE

No. 12/63/2014-BADP

Government of India/Bharat Sarkar Ministry of Home Affairs/Grih Mantralaya

Department of Border Management (Seema Prabandhan Vibhag)

5th Floor, NDCC-II building,

Jai Singh Road, New Delhi-110001

Dated 29 June 2015

Subject: Modified Guidelines of the Border Area Development Programme (BADP), June, 2015.

A copy of the Modified Guidelines of the Border Area Development Programme (BADP), June, 2015 as approved by the competent authority is forwarded for information.

Sd/- (Suresh Kumar)

Deputy Secretary to the Government of India

Tele: 23438131

PSs to HM/MOS(R)/MOS(C)

PSs to HS/Secy (BM) PS to AS & FA (Home)

Adviser (MLP), NITI Aayog, Parliament Street, New Delhi

Joint Secretary (PF), Department of Expenditure, Ministry of Finance, North Block. Joint Secretary (K)/Joint Secretary (NE), Ministry of Home Affairs, North Block.

Joint Secretary, Ministry of DoNER, Vigyan Bhawan Annexe, Joint Secretary, Ministry of Rural Development,

Joint Secretary, Ministry of Human Resource Development, Joint Secretary, Ministry of Youth Affairs and Sports,

Joint Secretary, Ministry of Health & Family Welfare. IGs (Ops), BSF/ITBP/SSB/ Assam Rifles.

PS to JS(BM)/DS(BM-I)

Copy to SO (IT) with the request the Border Area Development Programme (BADP): Modified Guidelines (June, 2015) may please be uploaded on the MHA's website, immediately.

(SueshKua!)

Deputy Secretary to the Government of India

Government of India
Ministry of Home Affairs
Department of Border Management

Border Area Development Programme (BADP): Modified Guidelines (June, 2015)

Objective:

The main objective of the BADP is to meet the special developmental needs and well-being of the people living in remote and inaccessible areas situated near the international border and to saturate the border areas with the entire essential infrastructure through convergence of Central/State/BADP/Local schemes and participatory approach.

Coverage:

The BADP will continue to be a 100% centrally funded programme. The programme will cover all the villages which are located within the 0-10 kms of the International Border, irrespective of the border block abutting on the International Border or not, in 381 Blocks (approx.) and come under 106 border districts of 17 States viz. Arunachal Pradesh, Assam, Bihar, Gujarat, Himachal Pradesh, Jammu & Kashmir, Manipur, Meghalaya, Mizoram, Nagaland, Punjab, Rajasthan, Sikkim, Tripura, Uttar Pradesh, Uttarakhand and West Bengal, which constitute the International Land Borders. Priority will be given to those villages which are located within 0-10 Km from the International Border and within that the villages identified by the Border Guarding Forces (BGF) shall get uppermost priority and will be known as strategic villages. Only after saturation of 0-10 kms villages, State Governments may take up the next set of villages within the 0-20 kms distance. After saturation of 0-20 kms villages, the State Government may take up the next set of villages within 0-30 kms distance and so on up to 0-50 kms. The State Government shall obtain a certificate from the DLC and after due satisfaction, send the same to the Department of Border Management, MHA that all villages within the 0-10 kms/0-20 kms/0-30 kms/0-40 kms distance have been saturated and respectively next set of villages 0- 20/0-30/0-40/0-50 kms distance are considered under BADP. Aerial distance will be taken into account. There too the BGFs will identify villages. For the purpose of drawing the priority, the first habitation/village from the international border shall be treated as "Zero:/"0" line distance and next distance shall be calculated from this Village only. The term 'strategic village will be applied to those villages as identified by the BGFs.

Saturation of a Village: District Level Committees (DLCs) shall make their own definition for "saturation of a village' infrastructure. However, for saturation of a Village," the minimum facilities will include road connectivity, schools along with facilities like separate toilets for girls, sports facilities, health services, electricity, water supply, community centre, public toilets particularly for women, houses for teachers and health staff, etc. But it would be incumbent on the DLCs to decide the definition of saturation on villages keeping in view their local conditions.

Allocation of Funds to the States.

Budgetary allocation shall be divided into two components: viz. (i) First component being 40% of total allocation for the eight North-Eastern (NE) States (including Sikkim); and (ii) Second component 60% of total allocation for the States other than the eight NE States. Funds shall be distributed separately for eight NE States and other than NE States respectively on the basis of: (i) Length of International border; (ii) Population of the Border Blocks; (iii) Area of the Border blocks *(all the above three criteria shall have equal weightage).* Fifteen weightages will be given to hilly/desert and Rann of Kutch area on account of difficult terrain and scarcity of resources and higher cost of construction. The smaller States which have less International Border and small population shall be given fixed allocation. The State Governments shall manage the funds, within the allocation made to the States as per the above formula, for the villages located within the permissible distance from the international land border but are not in the blocks which touch the international border.

District Administration, first of all, will find out the resources and do the spatial mapping of the border block(s) covered under the BADP by taking into account the following and prepare block-wise plan accordingly:

a) The BADP funds will be utilized for undertaking developmental scheme in villages close to the Zero line on the border on first priority.

b) BGFs shall draw a list of strategically prioritized villages in their respective areas and forward the same to the District Authorities, State Government and Ministry of Home Affairs. The Strategically border villages, as drawn by BGFs and endorsed by MHA, would be saturated first with respect to developmental activities such as road connectivity, electricity, drinking water supply, sanitation, health, agriculture & allied sectors, etc.

c) After saturating the strategically prioritized villages, other village will be taken up for development.

Guiding principles:

BADP funds shall ordinarily be used for meeting the critical gaps and to meet the immediate needs of the border population. Planning and implementation of BADP schemes should be on participatory and decentralized basis involving the Panchayati Raj Institutions/Autonomous Councils/Other Local Bodies/Councils.

The State Governments may consider creating/nominating a Nodal Department/Cell within the existing administrative arrangement for implementation of the BADP. The Nodal Department dealing with the BADP in the State shall hold individual meetings with line departments of the States such as Power, Rural Development, Electricity, Roads & Buildings, Water Supply, Social Welfare, Public Distribution, Civil Supplies etc. in order to ensure the implementation of the respective State/Central schemes within the 0-10/0-20/0-30/0-40/0-50 Km border villages. Utilization of funds under the Centrally Sponsored Schemes/Flagship Schemes of Govt. of India and the State plan schemes to the maximum possible extent in these areas in the border blocks should be ensured. To avail funds under the various Centrally Sponsored Scheme/flagship programmes of Government of India and for relaxation in guidelines, if any, the State Departments concerned may forward suitable proposals to the Ministries/ Departments of Government of India concerned with a copy thereof to the Department of Border Management, MHA for information.

A baseline survey shall be carried out in border villages in order to assess the gaps in basic physical and social infrastructure. For filling up these gaps preparation of a village-wise plan shall be ensured duly indicating the projects/funding through State Plan Schemes/the Centrally Sponsored Schemes (CSS)/Flagship Schemes of Government of India and the BADP. This plan should be a guide map for selection of projects. Such a plan shall also ensure the convergence and dovetailing of various Central/State schemes with the BADP. For example, various infrastructure schemes may be dovetailed with MGNREGA so as to have more coverage of projects taken up under BADP. All-out effort must be made to take up those projects on topmost priority which are not covered under any scheme of Government of India or the State Government.

Assets created under BADP must be maintained and kept under good repairs by the State Government. An amount of up to 15% of annual allocation under BADP may be utilized and the balance amount required for maintenance should be provided by the State Government.

Selection of schemes'

An illustrative list of schemes, which can be taken up under BADP, is at *Annexure-I.* A List of schemes not permissible under BADP is at Annexure-II. Schemes can also be suggested by BGFs concerned and expenditure on the same shall be 10% of the annual allocation made to the State. A list of permissible and non-permissible security related schemes is at *Annexure-III*

Schemes should be planned to take care of the special problems faced by people living in the border areas. State Government shall draw the annual plan for the BADP by keeping in view the objectives of overall balanced development of the region and assessment made by the State Government in the gaps in basic physical and social infrastructure in the border areas by taking into account the other resources available with the State Government for developmental activities in the border areas. Emphasis must be laid on schemes for employment promotion, production-oriented activities, skill up gradation to create a sense of security amongst the people in border areas so that the people do not migrate to other areas in search of livelihood. State Government should ensure that no single sector get disproportionately large share of the allocation of the State. Hence, to facilitate the same, the maximum/minimum limit is suggested in the table below.

Table: *Allocation of the State*

Sector	Scheme	Limit	%age allocation
Infrastructure (I)	(i) Link roads, bridges, culverts, footpaths, helipads in hilly and inaccessible areas having no road connectivity	Maximum	35
Infrastructure (II)	(ii) Safe Drinking Water Supply	No limit	
Health	PHCs buildings, medical equipment, mobile dispensaries/ambulance, houses for doctors and para-medics	Minimum	10
Agriculture	All activities under Agriculture and allied sector	Maximum	10
Social Sector	(a) Community center, common shelters for old and handicapped etc. Electricity, tracks, transit camps, kissan sheds with toilet facility, etc.	Maximum	15
	(b) Capacity building and skill development including tourism and hospitality etc.	Minimum (50% share should be for women)	10
	(d) Sanitation, Swatch Bharat Abhiyan, construction of toilets particularly for ladies, rural sanitation, etc.	Minimum	5
Education	Buildings of schools, residential schools, libraries, computer, science and laboratory rooms, construction of houses for teachers and other staff engaged in schools.	Minimum	10

Sports Activities	Sports activities includes play fields, mini open stadium, indoor stadium, auditorium, adventure sports and other sports related infrastructure (on suggestion of BGFs)	Minimum	5
Special/ Specific area schemes.	Model Villages, construction of dispensaries, mobile dispensary, Community based infrastructure for livelihood, Promotion of organic farming, New and Renewable energy, tourism, Swatch Bhara Abhiyan, warehouses for food grains and fodder, e-chaupal, mobile media etc.	Minimum (may be kept reserved by States)	10
Maintenance	15% share of each sector may be utilized on maintenance/repairs, if required, of the assets created under BADP.	Maximum	15
Schemes to be suggested by BGFs.	All the above sectors shall include the schemes of 10% of the amount as suggested by the BGFs. No scheme inside the BOPs or COBs shall be taken up under BADP.	maximum	10
To be kept reserved for various services.	Implementation of MIS, Monitoring, administrative expenditure, survey, media publicity, logistic support (excluding purchase of vehicles etc.)	Maximum	1.5 with maximum limit of Rs. 50 lakhs only.

The maximum/minimum limit suggested in para 5.2 above is for guidance only and not mandatory for the State Government. If the State Governments feel that particular sector has already been developed and there is no scope for further development in that sector, State Government may utilize the funds meant for that particular sector on permissible scheme under the BADP for development of any other under-developed sector under intimation to the Department of Border Management, Ministry of Home Affairs.

A detailed village-wise long-term action plan prioritizing the projects must be prepared for filling up the gaps as identified under para 4.3. Out of the long term plan every Annual Action Plan may be prepared picking up the prioritized projects. The Annual Action Plan of the BADP should be prepared three months in advance and submitted to Department of Border Management, Ministry of Home Affairs by April/ May after taking the approval of the State Le\/el Screening Committee. The process of completion of formalities, if any, such as forest, environment and other local clearances, availability of land etc. should be planned in advance, while recommending various projects under the BADP.

There shall be a Committee called District Level Committee (DLC) headed by District Magistrate/Deputy Commissioner and comprised of District Forest Officer, District Planning Officer, Superintendent of Police of concerned District and Commandant or Deputy Commandant of the Border Guarding Force (BGFs) present in the area, which would be responsible for planning and implementation of the BADP in the border block covered under the BADP guidelines;

As indicated in para 5.4 the District Level Committee shall prepare village- wise plans through a Base Line Survey of the villages in the block. It will assess the gaps in the existing physical and social infrastructure sectors and work out the overarching sectoral priorities, within which the various department schemes will be selected in a systematic manner e.g. if it is the school infrastructure in a particular village then the construction of the school building/additional class rooms, laboratories, toilets, school boundary wall, library/reading room, playground/sports infrastructure,, computer room, teachers quarters etc. should be included according to the need/gap.

The District Level Committee shall ensure that there is no overlapping of the schemes taken up under BADP with that of other ongoing schemes of Central Governments/ State Plan and give certificate to the effect while submitting the Annual Action Plan to the State Government for onward transmission to Ministry of Home Affairs.

The District Level Committee shall look into the convergence and dovetailing with on-going development programmes and schemes of different Ministries/Departments of Central /State Government and funds coming through various channels e. g.: PMGSY, MNREGA, SSA, Water Supply Schemes, Health Schemes, Social Development Schemes, Rural Development Schemes, Health Schemes, Social Development Schemes, Rural Development Schemes ,Panchayati Raj Schemes, skill development, and other schemes for the well-being of the people.

The District Level Committee shall have consultation with the local Members of Parliament, MLA, Members of PRIs, Autonomous Councils, community leaders and development agencies to know the felt-needs of the people and will give due consideration to their proposals. The DLCs shall take final decision keeping in view the people's priorities, and its own assessment for bridging the gaps in public infrastructure and services for selection of works within the overall sectoral priorities.

As indicated in para 5.4 the State Governments should prepare a shelf of projects/ schemes well in advance for inclusion in the Annual Action Plan of the Border Area Development Programme (BADP) so that they can obtain all requisite clearances and may avail of the funds in the beginning of the year. The District Level Committee shall discuss the schemes with all the concerned including BGFs and ensure critical gaps in the infrastructure are addressed and the convergence/dovetailing with other Central/State Schemes is done and then forward the Annual Plan of BADP to the State Government latest by February every year for consideration of the State Level Screening Committee (SLSC). While formulating schemes/projects, DLCs shall ensure that priority has been given to the strategically located villages as provided by the BGFs. The Annual Plan of BADP duly approved by the State Level Screening Committee (SLSC) headed by the Chief Secretary of the State should be submitted to the Department of Border Management, Ministry of Home Affairs latest by the month of March/April. In case, the Annual Action Plan is not submitted by the month of April, the State Governments will not be able to implement the same in that particular year and will not get allocated funds under BADP for that year.

State Government shall adhere to the following timeline for preparing the Annual Action Plan (AAP) of the BADP:

Table: Timeline for preparing the Annual Action Plan (AAP) of the BADP

Activity	**Timeline**
Identifying the work by Block authorities, BGFs etc. and submission to DLCs	Up to January
Consultation, approval and forwarding the approved schemes by DLCs to the State Nodal Department.	Up to February/March
Examination by the State Nodal Department and approval of the SLSC and submission to the Ministry of Home Affairs.	Up to March/ April.
Examination of the AAP by Ministry of Home Affairs subject to fulfillment of all the conditions as per the guidelines of the BADP	Within one month of receipt of the Annual Action Plan
Preparation, examination and release of funds to executive agencies by States.	Within one month of receipt of funds from GOI.

The BGFs will also devise a clear schedule for preparing their schemes for inclusion in the Annual Action Plan of the BADP and furnish the same to the DLCs and Nodal Department of the States with copy to the Department of Border Management, Ministry of Home Affairs well in advance and the concerned Commandant/Deputy Commandant will attend the meetings of DLCs for close synergy and ensure that their proposals are included, if found feasible.

District Level Committee shall ensure that no schemes below the estimated cost of 5 lakh are included in the Annual Action Plan of the BADP, except sport activities and construction of toilets.

Empowered Committee

The policy matters such as the guidelines of BADP, the geographical areas within which the BADP is implemented, allocation of funds, modalities of execution of schemes etc. will be laid down by an Empowered Committee of BADP constituted under the Chairmanship of the Secretary, Department of Border Management, Ministry of Home Affairs. The composition of the Empowered Committee of the BADP is as under:

Composition:

1.	Secretary (BM), Department of Border Management-	Chairman
2.	Secretary, Department of Expenditure -	Member
3.	Representative of NITI Aayog (Not below the rank of Joint Secretary) -	Member
4.	Additional/Special Secretary & F.A. (Home), MHA -	Member
21	Chief Secretaries of the 17 BADP States or their nominees (not below the rank of JS to GOI in their respective States)	Members
22.	Joint Secretary (K), MHA-	Member
23.	Joint Secretary (NE), MHA-	Member
24.	Joint Secretary, Ministry of DONER-	Member
25.	Joint Secretary, Ministry of Rural Development-	Member
26.	Joint Secretary, Ministry of Sports & Youth Affairs-	Member
27.	Joint Secretary, Ministry of Health & Family Welfare-	Member
28.	Joint Secretary, Ministry of Human Resource Development-	Member
29-32	A representative each of BSF, ITBP, SSB & Assam Rifles (not below the rank of IG).	Special Invitees
33.	Joint Secretary (BM), MHA- Secretary	Member

The Empowered Committee (EC) within the frame work of these guidelines will be responsible for policy matters relating to the scope of the BADP prescription of geographical limits in the States concerned within which the BADP will be implemented, modalities of implementation, arriving at a formula for allocation of funds to States etc. The Committee shall meet, at least, thrice in a financial year and may co-opt such members, considered as necessary to facilitate its deliberation/decision making. In the rare cases of exigencies of situation/operational difficulties and keeping in view the urgent requirement to redress the immediate grievances of the border population, the Chairman of the Empowered Committee is authorized to make State/area/ scheme/ project relaxation in the BADP guidelines.

An amount not exceeding 5% of the budgetary allocation of the BADP in a particular year will be kept reserve and will be placed at the disposal of the Ministry and the same shall be sanctioned by the Chairman, Empowered Committee with the approval of the Minister for urgent schemes/projects, contingencies and other unforeseen circumstances. If such circumstances do not occur this amount shall be released to the needy States at the end of the year along with the savings, if any.

State Level Screening Committee:

There shall be a State Level Screening Committee (SLSC) on Border Area Development Programme (BADP) under the Chairmanship of the Chief Secretary of the State, as indicated below:

Composition:

1.	Chief Secretary-	Chairman
2.	Secretary, Planning Department of the State-	Member
3.	Secretary, Department of Home of the State-	Member
4.	Secretary, Finance Department of the State-	Member
5.	Secretary, Rural Development Department of the State-	Member
6.	Secretaries concerned of the line Departments of the State Implementing various Central/State Schemes in the border Blocks/Districts.	Member
7.	Representative of Government of India, Ministry of Home Affairs (Department of Border Management)-	Member
8.	Representative of NITI Aayog	Member
9.	Representative of Government of India, Ministry of DoNER (in case of North-Eastern States)-	Member
10.	District Magistrates of the Border Districts of the State	Members
11.	Nodal officer of the Border Guarding Force(s) deployed along the international border of the State-	Member
12.	Secretary, Nodal Department of BADP in the State-	Member Secretary

Within the framework of these guidelines and subject to such general/special directions as may be given by the Empowered Committee, the State Level Screening Committee (SLSC) shall finalize the list of Scheme for implementation under the BADP and approve the Annual Action Plan (AAP) for submission to the Department of Border Management, Ministry of Home Affairs. The Chairman of the SLSC (viz. Chief Secretary) may co-opt such members on the Screening Committee, considered as necessary to facilitate deliberation/ decision making in the SLSC.

An amount not exceeding 2.5% of the allocation of the State under the BADP in a particular year will be kept reserve and will be placed at the disposal of the Chairman, State Level Screening Committee (SLSC) for urgent schemes/projects, contingencies and other unforeseen circumstances. If such circumstances do not occur this amount shall be released to the border blocks at the end of the year.

The SLSC shall meet at least twice in a year. The first meeting shall be convened in March/April in order to finalize and approve the schemes recommended by the DLCs, etc. as stipulated in the guidelines for the following year. The Annual Action Plan (AAP) is required to be finalized in the first meeting and communicated to the Department of Border Management, Ministry of Home Affairs, Government of India by April.

The schemes/projects for a particular year once approved by the Department of Border Management, Ministry of Home Affairs, Government of India, as recommended in the Annual Action Plan (AAP) shall ordinarily be not changed. However, any change in the schemes will be considered in the Department of Border Management, Ministry of Home Affairs, only after it is recommended by the States (viz. the Chief Secretary) on account of operational difficulties/special circumstances.

The 2nd meeting of the SLSC shall be held in November/December to review the progress of schemes under the BADP, submission of Utilization Certificates (UCs) & Quarterly Progress Reports (QPRs) etc.

The respective BGF shall nominate State-wise nodal officers for co-ordination with the States and such nodal officers shall be invited for the SLSC meetings.

The State Government shall furnish the Annual Action Plan of BADP as approved by the SLSC to the Department of Border Management, Ministry of Home Affairs, Government of India, latest by the month of April every year as in the proforma given at Annexure-V (a) to Annexure V.

Works/schemes suggested by BGFs out of their 10% allotment, shall be shown separately as indicated in the formats

Flexibility in execution of programme

To provide flexibility, schemes under the BADP can be executed by any of the following agencies:

i) State Government agencies such as PWD, PHE, Rural Development agencies, other line department agencies and State Government PSUs;

ii) Central Government agencies such as CPWD, Central Government PSUs, Border Guarding Forces located in the border areas;

iii) Panchayati Raj Institutions/Autonomous District Councils/Traditional Councils, other Local Bodies & Village Authorities/Councils.

Due emphasis should be given to effective involvement of local population, voluntary agencies comprising of local NGOs/Self Help Groups which are not receiving foreign aid/assistance may be engaged for executing schemes in order to inspire mutual trust and confidence between the Government and the border population.

Funds flow:

Before the commencement of the financial year, the Department of Border Management would convey the quantum of funds allocated to the States during the next year under the BADP. The Annual Action Plan consisting of schemes, duly approVed by State Level Screening Committee (SLSC) haVe to be forwarded to the Department of Border Management, Ministry of Home Affairs as in the proforma at Annexures-IV (a) to IV(I) for release of funds through MIS application along with the information as in proforma at Annexures-V (a) and Annexure -V(b).

Funds will be released to States in two installments. Funding for the subsequent year will be based on confirmation of expenditure and receipt of approved list of schemes. The 1'" installment of 90% of the allocation of the State, will be released to the State only after the receipt of Utilization Certificates (UCs) for the amount released in the previous years except the preceding year; If there is any shortfall in furnishing the UCs for the amount released during the previous years, except the preceding year, the same would be deducted at the time of release of the 1st installment. The 2' d installment of the remaining 10% of the allocation of the State will be released to the State in the month of October only after furnishing of UCs to the extent of not less than 50% of the amount released during the preceding year, and furnishing of Quarterly Progress Reports (Physical & Financial) up to the quarter ending September. (i.e. 2nd quarter of the financial year)

To the extent of submission of pending UCs pertaining to the previous years, deduction, if any, made in the release of 1'"installment for non-submission of UCs will be made good at the time of release of 2' d installment.

The State Governments are required to have a separate budget head for the BADP. Funds should be released by the State Governments to the implementing agencies immediately upon receipt of the same from Government of India and as per the directions of Government of India, Ministry of Finance; parking of funds at any level is strictly prohibited.

Monitoring and review:

The State Governments shall develop an institutional system for inspection of the BADP schemes/projects and submit reports to the Department of Border Management, Ministry of Home Affairs. Each border block should be assigned to a high-ranking State Government

Nodal Officer who should regularly visit the block and take responsibility for BADP schemes. A quarterly report should be sent to the Ministry of Home Affairs on the MIS application, indicating the number of inspections conducted and highlighting the important achievements/ lacunae pointed out in the reports of the inspecting officers. Third party inspections also need be commissioned by the States for an independent feedback on the quality of work and other relevant issues. An appropriate 'Social Audit System' should also be put in place by the State Governments.

There will be a Third Party Inspection and Quality Control Mechanism under the Department of Border Management, Ministry of Home Affairs, which shall appoint independent Monitors (Individual/Agency) for random inspections of the BADP schemes. This independent Monitors shall be designated as National Quality Monitors (NQMs), who shall be given free access to all administrative, technical and financial records. The NQMs shall submit their reports to the Department of Border Management as well as the State Governments on a quarterly basis. The NQMs shall also suggest improvements in the execution of schemes, if required

The District Level Committee shall take responsibility of monitoring of implementation of Works under BADP as well as quality of works and submit a report on quarterly basis to State Government for onward transmission to Ministry of Home Affairs along with the photos of the works/schemes.

State Governments shall have the monitoring of the BADP schemes by the existing District Level Monitoring/vigilance Committee where local Members of Parliament and MLAs are represented

Quarterly progress reports should be submitted scheme-wise to the Department of Border Management latest by 15'h day of closure of the quarter through MIS application (as in the proforma at Annexure-VI). The year-wise consolidated utilization certificates should be sent in the prescribed proforma (GFR- 19A) of the General Financial Rules within one month of the closure of the financial year as given at Annexure-VII. A display board may be kept at project sites indicating that the work is being done/has been completed under the BADP of Government of India.

State Government shall issue Utilization Certificates (UCs) and Completion Certificates in respect any scheme/project suggested by the BGFs after consulting the concerned BGF.

The State Governments shall develop an inventory of assets created under the BADP in border villages/hamlets, for analytical purposes etc. Such details may be communicated to the Department of Border Management, Ministry of Home Affairs with a write-up on important schemes/projects (with photographs) implemented by the States through GIS application.

The District Magistrate/Deputy Commissioner and Chief Secretaries of the State shall be responsible for uploading of photographs on the website of all the complete projects just after their completion.

Management Information System (MIS):

An appropriate "Management Information System (MlS)" has been developed in the Ministry of Home Affairs by treating village as well as scheme/project as the basic unit. It will be implemented w.e.f. the year 2015-16 and all the activities, including submission of the Annual Action Plans, release of funds, monitoring and e- filing will strictly be through MIS application.

To this end, the State Governments shall identify a Nodal Officer of sufficient seniority at the State as well as District level who has adequate knowledge of Information Technology to function as State IT Nodal Officer and District IT Nodal Officer to oversee the regularity and accuracy of the data being furnished by the Districts to the States and by the States to the Ministry of Home Affairs. The Nodal Officer so identified shall be responsible to oversee the upkeep of the Hardware, Software and Internet connectivity as well as computer training requirements of the personnel engaged to work for BADP. He will regularly interact with the NIC Coordinator at State Headquarter. The District Magistrate shall fix responsibility for uploading the data on the application and its uninterrupted maintenance at District level as well as block level as the case may be.

Utilization of Interest Earned on Deposits: Interest accrued on deposits on BADP funds at any level shall be treated as additional resources under the BADP and would be utilized on the works/projects drawn by the District Level Committee for the areas covered under the guidelines of the BADP in priority Villages.

C &AG audit: The State Government shall have the regular audit of works taken up under BAD P carried out by the C &AG and furnish the observations of C& AG on expenditure under the head BADP after completion of C & AG Audit to Ministry of Home Affairs.

Annexure-I

Illustrative List of Schemes/Projects permissible under the Border Area Development Programme.

The BADP funds shall ordinarily be used for meeting the critical gaps after utilizing funds under the various Central/State schemes and to meet the immediate needs of border population. A base line survey shall be carried out in border villages in order to assess the gap in basic physical and social infrastructure and convergence of various Central/State schemes with the BADP should be ensured

Various schemes/projects that can be taken up under BADP sectors are as illustrated below:

1. (A) Infrastructure (I)

i) Construction and strengthening of approach roads, link roads bridges, culverts, foot bridges, Foot Suspension Bridges, foot paths, pathways, ropeways, Steps/ masonry steps, helipads in hilly and inaccessible areas having no road connectivity;

(B) Infrastructure (II)

i) Safe Drinking Water Supply.

(C) Other Infrastructure

i) Development of infrastructure for weekly haats/bazaars and also for cultural activities etc. in border areas.

ii) Creation of new tourist centers.

iii) New and Renewable electricity- Bio gas/Biomass gasification, Solar and Wind energy and Mini Hydel Projects - systems/devices for community use and related activities

iv) Development of infrastructure for Industries — Small Scale with local inputs viz handloom, handicraft, furniture making, tiny units, black smith works etc. and food processing industry.

v) Promotion of Rural Tourism/Border tourism.

vi) Protection of heritage sites.

vii) Retaining walls in hilly areas to protect the link roads, public buildings;

viii) Drains/Gutters as a part of water disposal system etc.

2. Health

i) Construction of houses for Doctors, paramedics and other officials engaged in health sector in border Villages.

ii) Building infrastructure (PHC/CHC/SHC)

iii) Provision of medical equipment of basic/elementary Type.

iv) X-Ray, ECG machines, equipment for dental clinic, pathological labs. etc. can also be purchased.

v) Setting up of mobile dispensaries/ambulances in rural areas by Govt./ Panchayati Raj Institutions including Tele medicine.

vi) Construction of Boundary walls/barbered wire fencing around HSCs/ dispensaries in border villages.

3. Agriculture and allied sectors

i) Animal Husbandry and Dairying

ii) Pisciculture

iii) Sericulture

iv) Poultry farming/Fishery/Pig/Goat/Sheep farming

v) Farm forestry, horticulture/floriculture

vi) Construction of irrigation embankments, or lift irrigation or water table recharging facilities (including minor irrigation works).

vii) Water conservation programmes

viii) Social Forestry, parks, gardens in government and community lands or other surrendered lands including pasturing yards.

ix) Veterinary aid Centers, artificial insemination Centers and breeding Centers. Area specific approach keeping in view the economy of Scale — Backward-Forward integration.

x) Skill development training to farmers for the use of modern/ scientific technique in farming.

4. Social Sector

i) Construction of community centers

ii) Construction of *Anganwadies*

iii) Cultural Centers/Community Halls

iv) Construction of common shelters for the old or Handicapped

v) Construction of Transit Camps/staging huts/waiting sheds/rain shelters with toilets. *Kissan* sheds with toilets at the gates of fencing, etc.

vi) Construction of boundary walls/barbed wire fencing around public buildings including *Anganwadies*.

vii) Rural Sanitation/Toilet blocks in border villages particularly for women and public places including in slum areas and in SC/ST habitations and at tourist centers, bus stands etc. Thrust should be on separate toilets particularly for women

viii) Swatch Bharat Aabhiyan in border villages.

ix) Capacity building programme by way of vocational studies &training for youth for self-employment and skill up gradation of artisans, weavers, farmers etc. skill development in Tourism and hospitality, etc. focused attention should be given to women workers.

x) Provisions for civic amenities like electricity, water etc.

5. Education

i) Construction of houses for Teachers and other officials engaged in education sector in border villages.

ii) Primary/Middle/Secondary/Higher secondary school buildings (including additional rooms)

iii) Construction of hostels/dormitories

iv) Public libraries and reading rooms

v) Construction of computer labs with necessary infrastructure and internet connectivity

vi) Construction of science labs with necessary infrastructure

vii) Construction of residential schools and construction of hostels in existing in Hilly areas and remote and inaccessible areas, wherever feasible

viii) Construction of school/strengthening of infrastructure in existing schools such as rooms, laboratories, computer rooms, sports facilities, hostel accommodation etc. for girls.

ix) Construction of toilets in schools including toilets for girls

x) Construction of boundary wall/barbed wire fencing around the schools, hostels/ dormitories, play grounds, libraries and reading rooms.

6. Activities in the field of sports

i) Development of play fields.

ii) Sports infrastructure in border villages for activities such as boxing, Archery, shooting, martial arts, judo karate and other popular games including adventure sports.

iii) Development of infrastructure for Sports: Tourism/Sports/Adventure Sports Scheme — creation of world class infrastructure for tourism and sports in border block where ever feasible- like rock climbing, mountaineering, river rafting, forest trekking, skiing and safaris (car/bike race, camel safaris, yak riding, boating in Rann of Kutch.

iv) Construction of buildings for recognized District or State Sports Associations and for Cultural and Sport Activities or for hospitals (provision of multi-gym facilities in gymnastic centers, sports association, physical education training institutions, etc.)

v) Construction of mini open stadium, indoor stadium, auditoriums, etc.

7. Special/Specific area schemes

i) Model Village: Composite Development of at least one village of sizeable population surrounded by five-six or more villages close to the border.

ii) Health: Construction of Dispensaries, Mobile dispensary/ambulance fitted with necessary portable equipment.

iii) Livelihood: Community based infrastructure like pasture land, sheds for livestock (Only for BPL), Fishery ponds, multi-utility community centers, Marketing yards, mini *haat*, common industrial sheds for cottage/small scale industry for local artisans, small organic manure units with linkage to *goshala*

iv) Promotion of Organic Farming

v) Power New and Renewable energy such as solar and mini hydel projects, bio- gas, bio-mass gasification, wind energy, hydro energy, etc.

vi) Tourism: Tourist guest houses, adventure tourism facilities, canteen at tourist places, parking, public conveniences facilities for Rural Tourism, protection of heritage sites, skill development in Tourism and hospitality, etc.

vii) Swatch Bharat Abhiyan: Construction of toilets in schools, public places particularly for women.

viii) Warehouses for food grains and fodder in hilly areas particularly in snow bound areas of Arunachal Pradesh, Sikkim, Uttarakhand, Himachal Pradesh and Jammu & Kashmir.

ix) E-chaupals, agrishops, mobile media vans etc.

Annexure-II

List of the works which are not permissible under the Border Area Development Programme:

Creation of tangible assets should be given priority under the BADP. The smaller schemes, which are of direct benefit in nature to specific villages/individuals, need to be addressed by the State Governments under their own development initiatives.

The following schemes/projects/works are not permissible under the BADP.

Infrastructure:

i) Any schemes of individual benefit (such as roads to private *basties*, *dera*'s and *dhanies* established in private agricultural fields, farm houses, etc.)

ii) Boundary walls and construction of cremation sheds in graveyards/*samsan* ghats

iii) Cleaning of *cools/naias/khalas*.

iv) Boundary/retaining walls of ponds.

v) Construction of building for Offices of local bodies, patwarkhana, panchayat ghar, BDOs, DCs, and residences for officials (except the official engaged in schools in border areas and houses for para medics in border villages), circuit houses, Inspection Bungalows, etc.

vi) Any type of earth work which can be undertaken under the Mahatma Gandhi National Rural Employment Guarantee Scheme (MNREGA).

Health:

i) Health Awareness Programme

ii) Eye Camps

iii) RCH Programme

iv) Blood banks

v) Control of Malaria, Filaria, Leprosy, Al DS, etc.

vi) First aid kit for midwives

Agriculture and allied sectors:

i) Desilting of ponds in villages, towns and cities

ii) Drainage facilities

iii) Soil conservation-protection of erosion-flood protection

iv) Use of improved seeds, fertilizers and improved technology

v) Organic farming

Education:

i) Buying of school dresses/books

ii) Adult Education

iii) Books/Journals

iv) TV/Dish antennas

Annexure-III

List of permissible and non-permissible items of works to be undertaken under BADP by the Border Guarding Forces:

Following schemes of developmental nature and for the well-being of the border population can be recommended/implemented by the Border Guarding Forces under the Border Area Development Programme. The expenditure on these schemes shall not exceed 10% of the annual allocation made to the State under the Programme:

a) Porter tracks, suspension bridges, roads needed for border guarding forces for their movements

b) Drinking water supply in border villages. It will include setting up of water purifier/R.0. systems;

c) Electricity including new and renewable energy, mini hydel projects etc. in the border villages.

d) Link Roads to villages.

e) Construction of Transit Camps/staging huts/waiting sheds/rain shelters with toilets along the patrol roots and near the landslides prone areas in hilly regions and *Kissan* sheds with toilets at the gates of fencing etc. or wherever necessary from BGFs point of view and for local population;

f) Any other item relating to the benefit of the border population within the purview of the Guidelines of the Border Area Development Programme.

Border Guarding Forces (BGFs) shall encourage sports activities amongst the youths in border villages. These activities may be boxing, archery, shooting, martial arts, judo, karate etc. and other popular games including adventure sports, camel/horse riding training in schools, mountaineering, rock climbing, tracking, etc. of which the youth like to take training. The BGFs shall provide platform and coaches for this purpose and groom children under sports sector.

Development/creating of Infrastructure such as play grounds, stadium, indoor stadiums, auditoriums, shooting ranges etc. as per the requirements shall be provided under the BADP on the recommendation of the Border Guarding Forces. Necessary sports articles, equipment/kits etc., except Arms and ammunition, can also be provided under the Border Area Development Programme. For this purpose, an amount up to 10% of allocation of the State may be utilized w.e.f. the year 2015-16 onwards. This expenditure would be over and above the 10% of allocation earmarked for the schemes enumerated in para 1 above.

However, approval of the State Level Screening Committee is a pre-requisite for implementing such schemes and it shall form part of the Annual Action Plan of the State. Such schemes recommended and implemented by the BGFs under the BADP are open for inspection by the District Level Committee, State/Central Government Officers concerned and also by the Third-Party Inspection Agency appointed for the purpose by the State Government/Government of India.

Following works/activities are not permissible under BADP:

a) Any type of Civic Action Programme for which funds are released by the Ministry of Home Affairs from other schemes/programmes such as purchase of medicines, eye camps etc.

b) Purchase of vehicles/night vision devices/other equipment, etc.

c) Any type of infrastructure inside the BOPs including Constructions of barracks, machan, watch tower, residences, common infrastructure, etc.

Annexure-IV (a)

Border Area Development Programme (BADP)

ANNUAL ACTION PLAN OF BADP FOR THE YEAR

Name of the State:

Meeting of the SLSC held on:____

N0.	Name of the Sector and Schemes/ Project	Location			Approved outlay of the scheme for current year	Target for completion of the Scheme	Whether scheme is new	Whether scheme is on-going from the previous years		Funds Remarks required in the current year
		District	Block	Village				Year of commencement	Funds already utilized (Year-wise)	
1	2	3	4	5	6	7	8	9	10	11 | 12
1(A)	Infrastructure (I)									
(B)	Infrastructure (II)									
(C)	Other INF Rastructure									
2	Health									
3	Agriculture and Allied Sectors									
4	Social Sector "									
5	Education									
6	Sports Acti Vities									
7	Special/ Specific area schemes.									
	Total:									

Annexure-IV (b)

Border Area Development Programme (BADP)

ANNUAL ACTION PLAN OF BADP FOR THE YEAR

Name of the State

Meetinq of the SLSC held on:

Format showing the works/schemes suggested by the Border Guarding Forces

No.	Name of the Sector and Schemes/ Project	Location			Approved outlay of the scheme for current year	Target for completion of the scheme	Whether scheme is new	Whether scheme is on-going from the previous years		Funds required in the current, year	Remarks
		District	Block	Village				Year of commen-cement	Funds already utilized (Year-wise)		
	2	3	4	5	6	7	8	9	10		12
(A)	Infrastructure (I)										
(B)	Infrastructure (II)										
(C)	Other infrastructure										
2	Health										
3	Agriculture and allied sectors										
4	Social sector										
5	Education										
6	Sports Activities										
7	Special/ Specific area schemes.										
	Total										

Annexure-IV (c)

Border Area Development Programme (BADP)

ANNUAL ACTION PLAN OF BADP FOR THE YEAR

Name of the State:

Meeting of the SLSC held on

Format showing the works/schemes of maintenance of the assets created under the BADP:

No.	Name of the Sector and Schemes/Project	Location			Approved outlay of the scheme for current year	Target for completion of the scheme	Whether scheme is new	Whether scheme is on-going from the previous years		Funds required in the current year	Remarks
		District	Block	Village				Year of commencement	Funds already utilized, (Year-wise)		
1	2	3	4	5	6	7	8	9	10	11	12
1(A)	Infrastructure (I)										
(B)	Infrastructure (II)										
(C)	Other Infrastructure										
2	Health										
3	AGR IC Ulture And Alli Ed Sectors										
4	Social Sector										
5	Education										
6	Sports Activities										
7	Special/Specific area schemes.										
	Total										

Annexure-IV (d)

Border Area Development Programme (BADP)

ANNUAL ACTION PLAN OF BADP FOR THE YEAR

Name of the State:

Meeting of the SLSC Cheldon:

Format showing the Projects/schemes/Activities under Sports Sector

No	Name of the Sector and Schemes/ Project	Location			Approved outlay of the scheme for current year	Target for comple-tion of the scheme	Whether scheme is new	Whether scheme is on-going from the previous years		Funds requi-red in the current year	Re-marks
		District	Block	Village				Year of commen-cement	Funds already utilized (Year-wise)		
1	2	3	4	5	6	7	8	9	10	11	12
1	Play Fields										
2	Indoor Stadiu M										
3	Audit Orium										
4	Sports Areicles										
6	Other Spor+S Activities (Each Activ Qty Be Shown Separately)										
7	Miscellaneous (Details may be given)										
	Total										

Annexure-IV (e)

Border Area Development Programme (BADP)

ANNUAL ACTION PLAN OF BADP FOR THE YEAR

Name of the State:

Meeting of the SLSC held on

Format showing the schemes Capacity building, Skill development etc.

No.	Types of training to be given.	Location			Approved outlay of the scheme for current year	Target for completion of the scheme (i.e. number of persons to be benefitted)	Name of the Agency which would impart training	Remarks
		District	Block	Village				
1	2	3	4	5	6	7	11	12
	Total:							

Annexure- IV (f)

Border Area Development Programme (BADP)

ANNUAL ACTION PLAN OF BADP FOR THE YEAR

Name of the State:

Meeting of the SLSC held on

Format showing the details of expenditure on items of works on which 15% of allocation/ maximum 50 lakhs only) kept reserved for Monitoring Training of staff, evaluation of BADP, administrative expenditure, survey, logistic support media publicity,etc.

No.	Details of items on which funds will be utilized	Location			Approved outlay	Target for completion	Expenditure booked during the current year	Remarks
		District	Block	Village				
1	2	3	4	5	6	7	11	12
	Total:							

Annexure-V(a)

Ministry of Home Affairs
Department of Border Management
Border Area Development Programme

ANNUAL ACTION PLAN FOR THE YEAR:____________________

*Name of the State:*____________________

Meeting of the State Level Screening Committee (S LLC) held on: __________

Name of the District: ____________________

Name of the Block ____________________

Scheme- wise Break up of Funds to be utilized in the border block.

II. No	Name of the Scheme	AmountI to be utilized in the Block	Remarks
1.	Out of State Resources (Specify sectors in which funds will be utilized during the year.)		
	a State-Plan		
	b District Plan		
2.	Flagship Sche me of Government of India (Specify thescheme-wise amount to be utilized in the block during the year)		
	i) Prime Minister Gram Sadak Yojana (PMGSY)		
	iii) Accelerated Rural Water Supply (ARWS)		
	iv) Accelerated Irrigation Benefit Programme (AIBP)		
	v) Rural Telephon y		
	vi) Rajiv Gandhi Gramin Vidyutikaran Yo|ana (RGGVY)		
	vii) Mahata ma Gandhi National Rural Employment Guarantee Scheme (MNREGA)		
	viii) Total Sanitation Campaign (T&C)- Nirmal Bharat		
	ix) National Rural Health Mission (NHRM)		
	x) Sarva Siksha Abhiyan (SLA)		
	xi) Mid-day meal Programme		
	xii) Integrated Child Development Scheme (ICDS)		
	xiv) Backward Regions Grant Fund (BRGF)		
	xv) Ra|iv Gandhi Khel Abhiyan (RGKA)		
	xvi) Skill Development schemes etc		
3.	Other Centrally Sponsored Schemes(CSS		
4.	Any other source (such as loans etc.)		
5.	Border Area Development Programme (BADP)		

Annexure-V(b)

Ministry of Home Affairs
Department of Border Management
Border Area Development Programme

ANNUAL ACTION PLAN FOR THE YEAR:

Name of the State:____________________

Meeting of the State Level Screening Committee (SLSC) held on: __________

Name of the District: ____________________

Name of the Block ____________________

Sector-wise break of funds utilized under Border Area Development Programme (BADP) in the Annual Action Plan.

S. No.	Name of the Sector	Number of assets created.	Amount utilized. (Rs. In lakh)
	i) (A) Infrastructure (I) a) Roads/Link Road (in km length) b) Bridges/culverts/FSBs (span in metres) c) Foot paths/pathways/ropeways d) Steps/masonry steps e) Helipads. (B)Infrastructure (II) Safe Drinking Water supply (C) Other Infrastructure ii) Health i) Houses for doctors and para medics. ii) Buildings iii) Medical equipment iv) Mobile dispensary/Ambulance v) Boundary wall. (in metres) iii) Agriculture and allied sector iv) Social Sector; a) Community centers b) Cultural centers c) Tourism, d) *Anganwadies*, e) Common shelters for Old and handicapped, etc. f) Capacity building/skill development/employment generation including tourism and hospitality. g) Rural Sanitation/Swatchh Bharat Abhiyan h) Construction of toilets i) Men ii) Women i) Others v) Education i) Houses for teaching and other staff. ii) Number of rooms in schools/Laboratory/computer rooms.		

	iii)Residential School iv) Library v) Boundary walls (in metres.) v) Sports Activities i) Play fields ii) Mini Open Stadium. iii) Indoor stadium/auditorium iv) Adventure sports v) Sports articles vi) Special/Specific area schemes: a) Model villages b) Mobile dispensary c) Livelihood d) Promotion of organic farming. e) Power f) Tourism g) Swatch Bharat Aabhiyan h) Warehouses vii) Maintenance of assets: viii) [Schemes suggested by Border Guarding Forces (BGFs) and other security forces in above sectors may be shown separately sector-wise.] ix) Works/schemes taken up under reserve fund i) Monitoring ii) Administrative expenditure. iii) Implementation of MIS iv) DEOs. v) Others.	
	Total:	

Annexure-VI

Border Area Development Programme (BADP)

BADP Quarterly Progress (Financial And Physical) Report For The Quarter Ending

Name of the State:

SI. No	Name of the Sector and Schemes/ Project	Location			Year of commencement of the scheme	Approved outlay	Physical Target with date for completion of the work	Expenditure till now (Year-wise)	Expenditure during the quarter	Commulative expenditure upto the quarter	Physical progress		Remarks
		District	Block	Village							During the quartern %age	Commulative upto the quarter in %age	
1	2	3	4	5	6	7	8	9	10	11	12	13	14
1(A)	Infrastructure (I)												
(B)	Infrastructure (II)												
(C)	Other NF RAST RUCT URE												
2	Health												
3	Agriculture and Allied Sectors												
4	Social Sector												
5	Education												
6	Sports Activities												
7	Special/ Specific area schemes.												
	Total:												

Note: (i) Schemes of Capacity building, skill development, employment generation, relating to sports activities and schemes suggested by the BGFs may be shown separately on separate sheets.

Annexure-VII

BORDER AREA DEVELOPMENT PROGRAMME(BADP) Form GFR 19 A

(See Government of India's Decision (1) below Rules (150) FORM OF UTILIZATION CERTIFICATES

SI.No.	Letter No. and Date	Amount	
	(give number of letter of Government of India sanctioning the fund with date)	(give amount and year for Which sanctioned)	Certified that out of Rs. of grants-in-aids sanctioned during the year ----------- in favour of ---------- under Ministry/Department letter No. given in the margin and Rs. ---------on account of unspent balance of the previous year, a sum of Rs. -----------has been utilized for the purpose of ----- -------------- for which it was sanctioned and that the balance of Rs. ----------- remaining unutilized at the end of the year has been surrendered to Government (vide No.-----------------dated--------) will be adjusted towards the grant-in-aid payable during the next year-----.
	TOTAL		

Certified that I have satisfied myself that the conditions on which the grants-in-aid was sanctioned have been duly fulfilled/are being fulfilled and that I have exercised the following checks to see that the money was actually utilized for the purpose for which it was sanctioned

Kinds of Checks exercised:

1. ____________________

2. ____________________

3. ____________________

Signature------------------

Designation------------------

Date------------------

Appendix C

Pakistan/Gujarat and Rajasthan (India) Ground Rules, 1960

The military sub-committees of India and Pakistan were directed to frame the Ground Rules with regard to Border areas adjoining Gujarat, Rajasthan and Punjab. These Ground Rules were implemented in 1961. The importance of maintaining an impartial view by both Border Forces while implementing these Rules was emphasized.

Important Provisions of Rules

a) No armed force be deployed within 150 yds distance from IB, temporarily or permanently. No OP or BOP be established within this distance.

b) Security Forces of either country may pursue trans-border criminals up to IB.

c) Security Forces of both countries may patrol/ operate in areas within this range of 150 yds, provided:

  i) Prior info to counterpart is given if patrol were to operate within 50 yds of IB.

  ii) Str of tps does not exceed one sec in this case.

  iii) Patrols/ OP party to carry flags of specified colour and size:

    (aa) Colour: India- orange, Pak- blue.

    (ab) Size of flag: 2 x 2 ½ feet.

    (ac) Length of pole: 4 feet

  iv) Patrol/ ops party not to carry LMG, etc. only personal weapons be carried.

d) All existing posts within 150 yds to remain in existence but no new post should be established without agreement of counterpart.

e) No such defence work be carried out within 150 yds of IB, which is not part of inventory of existing posts.

f) Security forces of both countries would be duty bound to pursue armed infiltrators up to 150 yds from IB in own territory.

g) Local comdrs of security forces would jointly conduct enquiry into any incident/ complaint of nibbling.

h) In case of rivers changing their course there would be no change in the alignment of IB.

i) Commanders at all levels of border guarding forces of both sides to ensure observance of these rules and hold periodic meetings in case of any problems.

j) Military commanders of both sides to meet regularly to review situation on border.

k) SPs of border districts to take part in monthly meetings.

l) Hot line communication be established between commanders at appropriate levels to resolve bilateral issues.

Duties of Sub Sector Commander/Wing Commander

They will perform the following duties:

a) They will maintain close liaison with members of counterpart forces.

b) They will obtain information about each other through meetings.

c) On complaints of Border crossing/tensions, they will conduct an on the spot enquiry, followed by a joint enquiry within 24 hrs.

d) They should hold Flag Meetings to improve mutual understanding and sort out minor problems.

e) To aim at reduction of tension and to take decisions in the National and Forces interest.

Conduct of Flag Meetings

Post commanders and sector commanders should have meetings with their counterparts of equal rank to investigate and resolve peculiar problems. The procedure of holding border meeting would be as follows:

a) When posts are located in proximity of each other.

  i) The commander desiring to have a meeting will have a flag displayed, the specifications of which are as given below. He will proceed to a pre-determined location on the IB without guard or any weapons. The opposite commander will also have his flag displayed in acceptance and proceed to the same spot without any escort or weapons.

  ii) The specifications of the flag for a meeting are:

    (aa) <u>Colour</u>: India – Orange, Pakistan – Blue.

    (ab) Pole – 7 feet.

    (ac) Flag – 4 * 3 feet.

b) When posts are far away.

  i) An armed party consisting of 1 UO and 6 *jawans*, carrying the correct flag will come to 300 yds of opposite post. They will then halt there. Two of the *jawans*, unarmed will then move forward, holding the flag and establish contact.

  ii) Normally, the use of civilians has been made to establish contact. However, the Ground Rules makes no reference of this fact.

c) Contact during night. When posts are close by, due to a misunderstanding, a normal situation can worsen very speedily. Therefore, an emergency meeting can be held between the two counterparts. A pre-decided torch signal or illumination by VLP can be made for drawing attention. If the posts are far off, it is advisable to wait till morning. It would be foolhardy to send patrol party to establish contact in the night.

Other Important Points

a) Security forces would desist from interfering in the work of farmers who happen to be working in their fields close to the border.

b) If a citizen of one country stakes a claim over property in the other country, the matter, if objected to, would be resolved with an on-the-spot enquiry.

c) In case of an incident of firing it would not be retaliated by fire. Joint enquiry be conducted to identify guilty and suitable actions be taken against him.

d) Press and media on either side should desist themselves from publishing such news which may create tension between the forces of two sides.

Western Pakistan/Punjab (India) Ground Rules 1961

The representatives of the Governments of India and Pakistan met in New Delhi from 22 Aug till 27 Aug 1961. It was in this meeting that the Western Pakistan/Punjab (India) Ground Rules were framed. These are similar to the Ground Rules for Rajasthan and Gujarat, although some additional issues have been added. These Rules are applicable to those parts of the demarcated IB over which there is no dispute.

Maintenance of Boundary Pillars

The procedure for maintenance of boundary pillars will be:

a) The responsibility of looking after even numbered pillars lies with India, and odd numbered with Pakistan.

b) The whole of IB will be inspected jointly twice a year, in April/May & in Oct/Nov. Every pillar will be jointly checked by the concerned DCs of both countries.

c) Replacement of missing pillars will be dealt with by revenue authorities of both countries.

d) Disputes due to pillars being destroyed/swept away/removed - Local officials to maintain liaison with each other till matter is sorted out by appropriate senior officials, assisted by the civilian officials.

Main Provisions

a) Armed Forces of both countries will not be deployed permanently or temporarily within 150 yards of the IB.

b) All existing OP towers, pickets forward posts within 150 yds of the IB will be destroyed. However, those towers specifically approved will remain, their height remaining under 12 feet.

c) All OP points/pickets from 150 – 250 yards of the IB will not be more than 12 feet in height.

d) All OP points/pickets from 250 – 1000 yards of the IB will not be more than 30 feet in height.

e) Any construction work already undertaken with the consent of counterpart would be completed and accepted up to agreed limits of height.

Patrolling and Other Provisions

Irrespective of the provisions in Para 11, both Security Forces are duty bound to:

a) Pursue criminal's right up to IB, but they will not enter into counterpart territory.

b) They are permitted to send patrols within 150 yds of IB provided:

   i) The patrolling party of counterpart will be fore-warned in case patrolling is to be carried out within 150 yds of IB.

   ii) Strength of patrol will not exceed one section.

   iii) Patrol will carry flags as prescribed. Patrol will only carry personal weapons.

c) Joint check posts will remain. However, no defense work/OP pickets will be established here unilaterally.

d) Security Forces of both countries are duty bound to stop armed infiltrators from crossing over to the counterpart territory before 150 yds of IB.

e) If any civilian inadvertently crosses IB, he should be arrested and handed over to an officer of counterpart on receipt after ascertaining reasons of his illegal entry.

f) If any Security Force personnel inadvertently crosses the IB, information should be passed to the nearest post of counterpart. He is to be handed/taken over with all arms/amn at officer's level.

g) No unmanned cattle grazing should be allowed along IB. Stray cattle should be intercepted and handed over to owner in presence of counterpart on proper receipt.

h) In case of cattle smuggling, info should be given to nearest post of counterpart and track and other details be handed over. The post commander will in turn hand over this information to the nearest police station. The animals will be returned on proper receipt.

i) Clearing of elephant grass, burning of dried grass along IB will be done after information to counterpart at least 48 hours in advance.

j) Civil authorities will be permitted to perform their duties along IB. Information will be given to counterpart and their programme conveyed.

Duties of Commanders

Flag meetings are a way of maintaining liaison and sorting out minor problems. Adherence of these Ground Rules will help in subduing potentially troublesome happenings.

Appendix D

East Pakistan Border Ground Rules 1959

The East Pakistan Ground Rules were framed in a joint sitting of a military sub-committee. These papers are in two parts. Basic requirements have been enumerated in Part I. Ground Rules have been enumerated in Part II. These ground Rules were applicable to the Indo-East Pakistan (Now Bangladesh Border).

Part 1

Basic Requirement

a) Following completion of demarcation, handing/taking over of territory should follow after completion of legal requirements.

b) Territory will be handed/taken over only after standing crops have been cut.

Part II

Ground Rules: The Security Forces of both countries are deployed in close proximity. Sometimes there are instances of cross border firings, the reasons of which are:

a) *Jawans* of both Forces are unaware of layout of IB. There are instances of inadvertent straying across the IB, leading to firing instances.

b) Riverine boundaries are not easily identifiable.

c) Char lands are claimed by both countries, leading to disputes.

d) Infringement of fishing/sailing rights.

e) During the night, on suspicion.

Measures to avoid firing incidents

The Ground Rules are an effective means to curb incidents of firings. Some of the salient features are:

a) In the absence of a De-Jure boundary, commanders of both sides to fix a working boundary.

b) This working boundary is not to be violated.

c) Once this boundary is decided, no post to be constructed within 150 yds of this boundary.

d) However, patrolling can be carried out up till the IB. The followings will have to be kept in mind:

   i) The counterpart should be informed in advance.

   ii) Strength of patrol should not be more than a section.

   iii) Patrol party should not carry automatics.

e) Security Forces on both sides are duty bound to prevent smuggling.

f) In case of Thalweg boundary, fishing can be done by citizens of both the nations, provided the under mentioned procedure is adhered:

   i) A joint check post (JCP) be made on the riverbank.

   ii) Transitional items should be kept under observation by the JCP. A manifest should be made, signed by the JCP and should be considered as a permit.

   iii) Water vessels of one country being used in main channel of the river, will not be permitted to move up to the river bank on the counterpart side. Neither will goods be exchanged in mid-stream with a vessel from the counterpart side.

   iv) Security Forces will not involve themselves in problems /issues of locals.

Other provisions

Sub Sector commanders will maintain contact with each other to develop goodwill and cooperation. Flag meetings and monthly meetings will be held to resolve the following minor issues beforehand:

a) Communication system between commanders of counterpart.

b) Minor skirmishes between civilians on both sides.

c) Media should desist from publishing news items of inflammatory nature.

Appendix E

"Joint India Bangladesh Guidelines for Border Authorities – 1975"

Since the liberation war in 1971, the relations between the Border Security Forces of India and Bangladesh have been extremely cordial. A few border incidents of a minor nature have occurred since then. Whenever they occurred a quick and amicable settlement was reached by mutual discussion and cooperation. However, since the two Border Security Forces operate in close proximity of each other, it is desirable to lay down clear and precise rules and procedures to guide the two forces employed to look after the common border, this would also obviate the possibility of minor frictions which cannot be ruled out altogether at the lower levels. With this aim in view and to guard against undesirable trans-border activities, a set of guidelines a set of guidelines for the Border Security Force of India and Bangladesh have been framed and recorded hereunder.

The trans-border problems are:

a) Unauthorised movement of persons across the borders.

b) Inadvertent crossing of the land and riverine boundaries by the nationals of either countries.

c) Smuggling.

d) Private claims overland, cattle, fisheries etc.

e) The possibility of a clash occurring when border security forces reach border line in hot pursuit of criminals.

f) Traffic in illicit arms and ammunition.

g) Border crimes, particularly armed dacoities, cattle lifting, kidnapping etc.

There may be occasional border incident which may occur because of a variety of reasons:

a) Often Border Security Forces on both sides do not know where the international boundary lies on the ground and nationals of the other country may cross what they think is their territory;

b) Where boundary in the riverine area runs criss-cross and portions of the land on both sides of the river are owned by the other country, incidents may occur when these are cultivated or attempts made to dispossess their rightful owners;

c) When the 'Char Land' is formed after the floods, whether in the bed of the river or as an accretion to the mainland and when attempts are made by nationals of both the countries to seize the newly formed char land leading to claims and counter claims;

d) Sometimes fishing and navigational disputes occur when the river falls on the international boundary;

e) When attempts are made to stop cattle lifting or trespass by local inhabitants on either side;

f) When locals try to take over the adverse possessions as soon as they come to light during the process of joint boundary demarcation on the ground.

There should be frequent contacts between the border authorities of the two countries concerned to discuss matters of immediate administrative concern, which have been mentioned above. Needless to say, co- operation between the two border security forces and police forces should be close and everything possible should be done to ensure eradication of trans- border crimes smuggling etc. by mutual and timely exchange of information and intelligence at the appropriate levels. The Border Security Force of the two countries should also ensure that strict check is kept on illicit trading whether of currency or goods, creation of dumps of agriculture produce and illicit arms and ammunition. If any information is received of the commission of crime by the criminals of one country in the other country, the country to which the criminals belong should take appropriate action against the criminal according to the law of the land. Whenever a criminal commits a crime in his own country and crosses over to the other country and is apprehended. He should be handed over to the Border Security Forces of the other country, at an officer level after he had been dealt with according to the law of the land.

Pending final settlement of the borders between India and Bangladesh, the status quo as on 25th March 1971 should be maintained. This does not preclude routine joint inspection by the respective Directorates of Land Records and Surveys and Border Security Forces officials of either country of any portion of the boundary between Bangladesh and India. Wherever boundary pillars are missing or displaced, they should be replaced as early as possible. An inspection of the pillars will be done annually (February – march) jointly by the Border Security Force and the Bangladesh Rifles.

All border problems should be amicably settled by mutual consultation as early as possible by authorities of the border districts. The problems, the solution of which cannot be found at the local level, should be immediately referred to the respective Government.

On receipt of information, that a border incident has taken place the Commandant, Border Security Force or Wing commander, Bangladesh Rifles will contact his counterpart for consultation and for holding an immediate on the spot joint enquiry that may be necessary to settle the problems expeditiously. If considered necessary, this meeting may be followed by a meeting between the district Magistrates/ Deputy Commissioners.

The border security forces on both sides shall observe following simple rules to avoid the possibility of unpleasant incidents:

a) If there is disagreement in any area regarding the interception of these guidelines or the working boundary on the 25 March, 1971 or on account of missing international boundary pillars, an easily identifiable working boundary should be decided between the respective border security force authorities without prejudice to the de-jure boundary.

b) Working boundary may or may not coincide with the international boundary and its acceptance by both sides will not commit the two governments in any manner in respect of the de- jure boundary. The working boundary wherever necessary will be marked in a simple manner and delimitation shown only and recorded on large scale maps agreed upon.

c) After the identifiable boundary line, whether 'real' or 'working' has been fixed, neither side will have any permanent or temporary border security force or any other armed personnel within 150 yds on either side of this line. No permanent post will be constructed till the final demarcation has been done and the problem is resolved.

d) The above will not prevent either side from patrolling up to the real or working boundary provided.

    i) Where possible adequate warning is given to the other side.

    ii) Patrols are small in number, i.e. not exceeding a section (1 and 10):

e) If defensive work of any nature, including trenches, exists in the stretch of 300 yds (150 yds on each side of the boundary) these must destroyed or filled up.

f) It will be the duty of the border security force on either side to prevent armed civilians entering the 300 yds stretch of the border (150 yds on either side of the boundary).

g) Border Security Force of both sides are charged with the responsibility of preventing smuggling in their respective areas. Therefore, it is incumbent upon them to arrest smugglers of any nationality, armed or unarmed, and to deal with them under the law of the land.

h) Wherever the boundary real or working runs through the midstream of a river, the facilities to use the main channel will be adopted to regulate traffic and ensure that nationals of both the countries are not harassed.

   i) Joint check posts will be established on the river bank if possible or in the main channel where it levels or enters the midstream boundary.

   ii) A check will be made and manifests of commodities will be prepared at the joint check posts. Manifests signed by joint check posts will be accepted along with the permit to use the main channel for the navigation purpose only.

   iii) The boats using the main channel in the other country will not be allowed to touch the bank or exchange goods or engage in any other transaction with the national or other side.

i) Border Security Force on both sides shall on no account participate in any quarrel between nationals of the two countries living on the border. If nationals of one country ingress the working boundary and enter illegally and commit or attempt to commit an offence, the Border Security Forces would be at liberty to take appropriate action in the exercise of the "Right to private defence" preferably without resorting to fire. In case, fire has been opened the local commander will intimate his action to the opposite commander and to his own higher authorities.

j) In case of inadvertent crossing, after satisfying themselves that the crossing was done inadvertently the border security forces shall immediately return the persons concerned to the opposite commanders at the officer's level.

k) Certain bonafide governmental bodies e.g., survey parties forest guards, etc. will be operating in the near vicinity of the international borders, Border Security Force shall not interfere with their working in fact, they are expected to help. The existence of such parties will be notified to both sides, by the department concerned.

l) Grazing of unattended cattle on the border must be discouraged. In the case of cattle straying across the border, the border post commanders shall return such cattle immediately to their counterparts, after having satisfied themselves that the cattle have in actual fact strayed from across the borders, and a receipt obtained. The post commanders must maintain proper record of such cases.

m) Whenever any cattle are alleged to have been lifted across the border, a report with the opposite post comdr to whom the details, such as the tracks of the cattle and the criminals involved etc., will be handed over. The Border Post Commander concerned will acknowledge receipt of the report and then inform the nearest police station in his own country, who will make all efforts to recover, the cattle and apprehended the criminals. After recovery, the cattle must be handed over to the Post Commander concerned who will arrange to hand them over immediately to his opposite number on a proper receipt. Pound charged should be waived, if Government concerned permits.

For the practical implementation of the above, border on both sides shall be divided into sectors/ sub- sectors. The existence and the Headquarters of the sub- sectors will be intimated to each other and attempt should be made to link the Headquarters of both sides with telephone.

The sub- sector Commander should be of the rank of Capt/Major or of equivalent ranks in the police.

The duties of sector/sub sector/post commanders in their respective area of responsibility shall be:

a) They will maintain close liaison with their opposite number.

b) They will, by frequent visits make themselves known to both the Border Security Forces of the opposite side and to own local population.

c) They shall receive all complaints regarding territorial dispute referring to title to any land, immovable property lying on the other side of the border, char lands, navigation facilities and difficulty of harvesting. They will immediately hold a joint enquiry not later than 24 hours of the information report.

d) They will immediately enforce a status quo e.g., if a national of one country lays a fresh claim to land and takes any step in furtherance of that claim which is objected to by the other side, then the two commanders will hold a joint enquiry on the spot and restrain the person from enforcing his claim until the matter is settled at appropriate level.

e) The two commanders shall be responsible for referring the problems to the appropriate authorities and for seeing that they are progressed with a view to bringing them to a final settlement.

Great importance is attached to contact at all levels as this would contribute subsequently towards the good relations between the two Border Security Forces and help in removing any misunderstanding about moves by both sides.

Appendix F

India-Bangladesh Coordinated Border Management Plan (CBMP)

Border Security Force - Border Guard Bangladesh Introduction

India and Bangladesh share a long and densely populated border. The need to address issues related to cross-border activities and crimes as well as incidents of firing has been recognized. The Prime Ministers of the two countries in the Joint Communiqué in 2010 had underscored the need for both countries to cooperate actively on security issues. They had directed their respective Ministries and agencies to cooperate closely and implement all decisions taken during the talks. While recognizing the need to check cross border crimes, both Prime Ministers agreed that the respective border guarding forces exercise restraint and underscored the importance of regular meetings between the border guarding forces to curtail illegal cross border activities and prevent loss of lives.

These issues have been discussed in details in Home Secretary level meetings and they agreed to have a Coordinated Border Management Plan (CBMP) for vulnerable areas including riverine areas. Aim

The aim of CBMP is to synergize the efforts of both the Border Guarding Forces (BSF and BGB) for more effective control over cross-border illegal activities and crimes as well as for maintenance of peace and harmony along India-Bangladesh Border.

Vulnerable Areas

Identification: The areas along the India-Bangladesh border prone to cross border activities and crimes are considered vulnerable areas. A Joint India-Bangladesh team, will visit the vulnerable stretches and make an initial list for the purpose of the CBMP. The first of such list shall be prepared within three months of signing of the CBMP. Each Border Guarding Force thereafter will identify the vulnerable areas from their perspectives and share with each other. The list may be updated from time to time.

Coordination and Modalities

Close coordination and an appropriate approach is required to curb illegal cross-border activities and crimes by both BSF and BGB. The level of coordination, responsibility and the allied modalities are highlighted in subsequent paragraphs.

Nodal Officers: The following will act as Nodal Officers nominated with appropriate rank:

Serial	Indian (BSF)	Bangladesh (BGB)
1.	Nodal Officer, BSF HQ DIG (Staff Officer)	Nodal Officer, BGB HQ GSO-1 (Operation)
2.	South Bengal Frontier DIG/Comdt (Staff Officer)	South - West Region Sector 21C/GS0-2 (Staff Officer)
3.	Malda/North Bengal Frontier DIG/ Comdt (Staff Officer)	North - West Region Sector 21C/GS0-2 (Staff Officer)
4.	Guwahati, Meghalaya & Cachar Frontier (less Mizoram Sector) DIG/Comdt (Staff Officer)	North - East Region Sector 21C/GSO-2 (Staff Officer)
5.	Region Tripura Frontier and Mizoram Sector DIG/Comdt (Staff Officer)	South — East Sector 21C/GS0-2 (Staff Officer)

Responsibilities of Nodal Officers:

a. Immediate intervention into any border issue, if deemed necessary, for prevention and peaceful settlement of the problem.

b. Share understanding of problem with counterpart Nodal Officer and solve the issue in question.

c. Ensure timely implementation of all developmental works (except military) within 150 yards of IB.

d. Promote confidence building measures between the two border forces.

e. Refer major issues to appropriate level.

Discuss any other matter as deemed appropriate for attaining the goal of CBMP.

Contact Method: Communication through landlines and cell phones forms the prime means of contact between Nodal Officers of respective BSFBGB Hqs, Regions/ Frontiers. Besides, e-mail address and a facsimile number are to be designated to exchange documents. The information is to be intimated to all concerned promptly. They will keep record of the communications referred to above.

Frequency of Meeting: The Nodal Officers would meet frequently and report to Hqs about progress through proper channel, following guidelines below:

a) BSF-BGB Hqs' Nodal Officers, may meet as and when required

b) Region/Frontier level Nodal Officers may meet minimum twice in every quarter.

c) Meetings at any level may be arranged on any special issues other than the quarterly meeting.

Issues to be Dealt with by Nodal Officers

a. Trans Border Activities and Crimes

i) Human trafficking

ii) Drug smuggling/trafficking

iii) Arms/Ammunition I Explosive trafficking

iv) Dealing of fake currency

v) Any trespassing (armed/unarmed) of Border

vi) Smuggling, theft, terrorism, etc.

vii) Straying of animals/cattle smuggling

viii) Incidents resulting in deaths and injury at border

ix) Illegal immigration Inadvertent/ Accidental crossing of land and riverine borders

x) Any air violation

xi) Kidnapping

xii) Any other related issues

Border Issues

1. Coordinated patrolling.
2. Coordinated Pillar checking.
3. Flag meeting.
4. Border violations.
5. Implementation of developmental works within 150 yards of IB
6. Coordinate screening of persons crossing border for trade purposes on the basis of lawful documents.
7. Any other points deemed appropriate.

Working Modalities

To check crimes, following to be carried out in coordination by the two border forces:

Coordinated Patrolling

1. Coordinated Patrolling will be carried out simultaneously on both sides of border which will create a greater sense of security among the border population and also build greater coordination and confidence between the Border Guarding Forces.
2. Area of Coordinated Patrolling may be decided upon jointly by both the Sector Commanders for their respective sectors. The battalion commanders will be consulted and kept informed in whose jurisdiction the patrolling is needed.
3. **The Coordinated Patrolling should be done at frequent intervals. It should continue till the purpose is achieved.**
4. Coordinated Patrolling should be conducted simultaneously along plain/hilly areas and water bodies. Rearward communication shall always be maintained by respective Headquarters of the two forces.
5. Any apprehension/seizure during the patrol will be dealt with under the laws of the land where the crime occurs.
6. Review to adjust/modify modalities based on ground requirements as and when deemed necessary.
7. Details of deployment, time, weapon, AOR, etc. would be decided by Sector Commanders locally.
8. All such coordinated patrol shall always maintain communication with counter part by radio, cell phone, walkie talkie, etc.
9. During patrol, only personal weapons ie Sub Machine Gun (SMG)/Rifle/ Pistol/ Revolver with first line pouch ammunition will be carried.
10. Patrol will remain restricted to its own territory and will not cross over to the other side of 1B under any circumstance.
11. Neither side will resort to use of lethal weapons except in self defence against terrorists or smugglers. Patrols on both sides shall exercise maximum restraint; and only after clear warning, may use force.
12. Patrol Commanders of respective country will carry out debriefing of own patrol.

Establish Standing Patrol:

Respective Border Guarding

Forces may establish standing patrol if deemed necessary.

Exchange of intelligence:

Intelligence in respect of border crimes may be exchanged by Nodal Officers/concerned Sector/Battalion Commanders on the ground.

Dialogue and Meetings:

Both forces shall mutually address the issues through dialogue and meetings.

Joint Action in Case of a Serious incident:

1. Immediate holding of a Flag Meeting.
2. Establish contact at the BOP, Company, Battalion and Sector level.
3. Exchange lessons learnt.

Conclusion

To maintain peace and tranquility along the vulnerable patches/areas, close cooperation is imperative. Introduction of CBMP regarding vulnerable patches is a key step in ensuring close understanding between the two Border Guarding Forces considering the decision taken during Home Secretary level talks.

(Raman Srivastava)

Director General

Border Security Force

India

(Major General MAR ar Hussain ic, psc)

Director General

Border Guard

Bangladesh

Chapter 3 (Appendix G)

No. F.20/130/67-BSF-.I

Government of India
Ministry of Home Affairs
5th April 1968

To

The Director General,

Border Security Force

NEW DELHI

Sub:- **UTILIZATION OF BSF IN WAR SITUATION**

Sir,

The Study Group on para Military Forces, whose report was the basis on which Government took certain decisions regarding the formation of the Border Security Force, gave an idea of the role of the BSF in peace time as also in times of an emergency. Relevant extracts from the report are enclosed in the appendix to this letter. Keeping in view the original aims as also the specific requirements of the Army and the capabilities etc; certain conclusions have been reached by Government regarding the utilization of the BSF in a war situation. These are indicated below so that planning for tackling emergency situation can proceed on the Army side, and the local BSF Commanders know the rationale of it.

Except for the requirements of internal security for which some units of the BSF may have to be earmarked, in a war situation the bulk of the BSF units will in one form or another be expected to play a role complementary to the Army. The exact availability at any given point of time would have to be worked out with reference to the situation then prevailing. It has, however, been assumed that a minimum of 50 battalions of the BSF would be available to the Army and, in any case, the units already deployed on the border would form a part of these 50 battalions.

It is visualized that once a decision is taken by Government to place the Border Security Force in any sector under the operational control of the Army, the units of the BSF concerned will come under the command and control of the concerned Army commanders. To ensure that the utilization of the BSF is made in the best interests of the country, it is necessary that even in peace time there should be close coordination and co-operation between the Army and BSF Commanders. BSF Commanders may make any suggestions which would be of use with regard to operational plans. The Army Commanders would consider them and make appropriate use of them in the operational plans.

It has been agreed in principle that the utilization of the BSF by the Army would be done keeping in view the state of training, equipment and overall strength of the BSF in a particular sector along with the requirements dictated by the prevailing tactical situation. Generally speaking, tasks in excess of the capabilities of the BSF will not be planned for by Army Commanders but, obviously, no hard and fast rule in this regard can be laid down, particularly as flexibility will be needed in any developing situation.

Against the above back-ground the following main role for the BSF are envisaged:-

(i) Holding ground in less threatened sectors so long as the main attack does not develop in a particular sector, and it is felt that the local situation is within the capability of the BSF to deal with. The BSF units can continue to remain deployed in particular sector even in a war situation to release the Army for offensive tasks. In the event of a major attack developing, which is not within the capacity of the BSF to deal with, the Army can be expected either to reinforce the BSF with Artillery or other support, or relieve the BSF from its role in the particular sector.

(ii) Protection of vital installations particularly air-fields against enemy commandos/ para troopers or raids. This role can be entrusted to the BSF Units which are placed under the Army's operational control.

(iii) Providing extensions to the flanks of main defence line by the holding of strong points in conjunction with other units.

(iv) Limited aggressive action against para military or irregular forces of the enemy within the overall plan of the Armed Forces.

(v) Performing special tasks connected with intelligence including raids. These are tasks which might be entrusted to BSF Units by the Army in a war situation according to local necessity. It would, however, be expected that the state of training and equipment of the particular BSF Units would be kept in view in assessing their adequacy for the tasks.

(vi) Acting as guides in an area of responsibility where routes are known. This is a task which the BSF should be able to perform.

(vii) Maintenance of law and order in enemy territory administered under the control of the Army. Normally, ordinary civil police force would be utilised for this task but the BSF could be used to supplement the civil police or to act in lieu thereof in a situation where civil police is not readily available.

(viii) Provision of escorts.

(ix) Guarding of prisoners of war cages.

(x) Assistance in control of refugees. It is the intention to utilise civil police force and armed Home Guards etc. for these tasks but again depending upon local exigencies, the BSF might be entrusted with these tasks.

(xi) Anti – infiltration duties in specified area. This is an important responsibility which will have to be performed by security forces. The exact responsibility of the BSF in this matter is still under consideration and separate instructions are expected to be issued.

This letter is being issued to acquaint the BSF Commanders about the Government thinking on the role of the BSF in a war situation that operational planning by local military commanders may be facilitated and the BSF commanders are aware of their responsibilities. It is necessary for successful operational planning that there should be close liaison and co-operation between the BSF and Army in the field both to facilitate preparation of operational plans and to ensure their successful implementation. In the matter of specific training which may be desirable for local BSF units to fit them for the planned operational tasks also, close liaison and co-operation between the army and the BSF would be necessary. BSF Units would be included in exercises conducted by the Army formations.

These instructions are issued with the concurrence of the Ministry of Defence.

Sd/-
(T P Issar)
Deputy Secretary to the Govt. of India

(*For details, see: http://www.mea.gov.in/Uploads/PublicationDocs/24529_LBA_MEA_Booklet_final.pdf; https://www.mha.gov.in/; https://www.mea.gov.in/; https://bsf.gov.in/; https://idsa.in/)

Appendix H

Extracts of Army HQ Letter No. 12795/SD 5 dt 31/1/76

Subject: Command and Control : BSF/Police and Other Paramilitary Forces

General

In view of the large number of BSF/Police and other paramilitary units coming under operational command/control in a war situation, it is imperative that the demarcation of responsibility is clearly defined and strictly enforced. These are laid down in the succeeding paragraphs.

Operational

(a) On units/sub-units of the BSF/Police being placed under operational command of the army, the responsibility for the security of the border to the extent to which it rested on these units/sub-units will, from the time they are placed under operational command, fall on the army. The security of the border shall include prevention of trans-border crime, un-authorised entry into or exit from the territory of India, prevention of smuggling and any other illegal activity and promotion of a sense of security among the people living in the border areas. Any regrouping/redevelopment will ensure that at no time is the security of the border jeopardized.

(b) All directions for deployment and assignment of missions and tasks will emanate from the Army. The smallest self-contained unit in the paramilitary force which is capable of operating independently for any length of time is a battalion. However, in an emergency companies may be detached for limited periods. Normally all orders to such troops shall be given through the Commandant concerned. Where it becomes necessary to issue orders to a sub-unit direct, commanding Officer of the battalion concerned will be informed of the position by the Army. Companies in forward areas will be employed on company tasks. The platoons in forward area will not normally be detached and placed under army sub-units. However, in rear areas when they are employed purely on protection duties on VAs and VPs, PLs may be employed detached but as far as possible remain under command of their own companies. It will be the responsibility of the Army to ensure that the communications of Paramilitary Forces are integrated with the controlling Headquarters of the Army that the Command and control by Comdt is maintained and at the same time information and orders can be speedily disseminated.

(c) The following procedure will be followed for the movement of armed police battalions under the operational control of the Army.

   (i) Normally no change will be made in the original role and area of operation of the armed police battalions placed under the operational control of the Army.

   (ii) When a change in the role/area of deployment is contemplated, prior concurrence of the Ministry of Home Affairs will be obtained by Army Headquarters through the Ministry of Defence. However, in cases where moves have to be carried out urgently to meet operational requirements, MO Directorate and SD Directorate will be informed by Headquarters COMMANDS immediately on occurrence, so that the ministry of Home Affairs can, in turn, be informed accordingly.

   (iii) In the event of any change in the area of deployment, the Ministry of Home Affairs may consider releasing other armed Police battalions except where it is felt that the battalions originally placed at the Army's disposal will be more useful because of their previous experience/knowledge of the terrain.

(d) The Army will ensure that tasks allotted to the paramilitary units are commensurate with the capability of the force to execute them. Fire support/air support/engineer support/additional communications resources and additional administrative support should be arranged where necessary.

Training

The BSF units will be responsible for the normal training of their units in order to ensure that all the BSF battalions would at all time be able to play the role that is being envisaged for them in a war situation. Police Bns placed under the Army's operational control would be trained in their operational tasks according to the directions of the concerned formation Comdrs. One Company from a battalion which is under the operational control of the Army should be kept free for training during peace time. Normal police training will also be covered in the training Programme.

Guidelines will be issued by other HQrs Command or Headquarters Corps to concerned IsG laying down the requirements from the Army point of view on training and other administrative matters, which may have a close bearing on the operational requirements. Those in turn will be incorporated in the instructions/orders issued by the IsG concerned.

Equipping Policy

(a) The parent force will equip their units to the laid down by the Ministry of Home Affairs. Army authorities will not transfer any equipment from these units.

(b) When operational requirements demand, additional transport, defence stores and equipment will be issued to these units by the Army. These items will be returned by the units when relieved of the operational commitments for which they were issued.

(c) The replacement of arms and other war like stores destroyed or rendered unserviceable as a direct consequence of operations, will be the responsibility of army.

(d) Replacement of ammunition expended in operations in training by the Army will be an Army responsibility.

Clothing

Normal and extra clothing and equipment will be provided by the parent forces concerned. The special items of clothing required in the sector or theatre concerned will be issued by the Army, and withdrawn on de-induction. Conditioning of special items of equipment and ECC clothing will be carried out by the BSF.

Accommodation

Paramilitary Forces will make use of their own accommodation where available. Otherwise, accommodation will be provided as per the scales and specifications applicable to regular troops subject to availability. Licence fee for the accommodation provided will be assessed by the authorities providing the accommodation as charged against the user. Bashas, Bunkers, shelters etc. provided for operations will not be charged for.

Ration and Pol

Items of Rations and POL which include extra rations and fuel for warming and drying purposes will be issued by ASC Supply Depots to units of paramilitary forces as per scale laid down for Army personnel similarly located. Demands will be placed to the supply Depot concerned on the appropriate indent form.

Rations will be issued on book debit at payment issue rates from the supply Depots or will be delivered at mutually agreed centers under the arrangement of the Army. Further transportation to these units will be the responsibility of the force concerned.

Additional transportation and incidental charges will be recovered wherever stores are delivered beyond Rail Head Supply Depots. Such charges will be fixed by the local Army authorities in consultation with the regional CDA.

Transport

The Army will provide hired transport, animal transport and porters in accordance with operational necessity.

Supply and Services Imprest

The orders regarding provision, sanction and maintenance of supply and services imprest for the purchase of supplies, stores locally and for the payment of hire charges for porters, ponies, camels, labour and civil transport as applicable to regular Army units will supply.

Inspection, Repair and Recovery

All paramilitary forces other than BSF units. Inspection repair and recovery of vehicles, arms and radio equipment whenever required and asked for by the police units concerned when the units are placed under operational control of the Army be provided by the Army. EME workshops providing cover will be authorized to procure by local purchase spares, special maintenance tools and technical literature (i.e., hand books, workshops and spare parts lists etc) required for the repair of such equipment as are not of standard make, model and type with the Army, the local market and/or the makers. Certificate regarding non-availability of such spares, tools and literature from the ordnance will not be required. Officers Commanding EME workshops concerned may also at their discretion maintain a stock of moving spares for vehicles of make, model and type not standard with the Army to enable prompt repairs. Where necessary the vehicles/equipment may be got repaired locally under the arrangement of the Ministry of Defence letter No.95046/EME-6/1397-S/D(dated 25 Sep 68 as amended or revised from time to time.

BSF UNITS: BSF will normally be responsible to carry out their own inspection and repair of vehicles, arms and signal and power equipment under the command/ control of the Army in war situation. BSF workshops supporting units operating under the Army, if located in an area under the operational control the Army will be placed under the Army. The BSF has no recovery facilities and hence recoveries may be undertaken by the Army on request from the BSF.

Remount and Veterinary

(a) The BSF will ordinarily provide veterinary cover for its own animals. Where it is unable to do so, it may request the Army for provision of necessary facility in respect of veterinary cover, stores, evacuation treatment of sick and wounded animals in mobile veterinary sections/Military veterinary Hospitals.

(b) Evacuation of animals to mobile veterinary section for treatment, as far as practicable, will be done under arrangements of units concerned.

Leave

The Army authorities in consultation with the concerned Deputy Inspector General will lay down from time to time the policy in regard to the number of persons that may be sent on leave at one time. While evolving the leave policy, the Army authorities will bear in mind the fact that leave entitlement of the persons belonging to the different police forces is different and several police forces whose units are under the Army's operational control might have already worked out their leave percentage, authority for sanctioning leave in respect of all ranks except himself will vest in the officer Commanding. The leave programme of officer commanding and second in Command of the battalions would be approved by the formation Commanders concerned.

Applications for earned and casual leave of the Officers of these Battalions under the operational control of the Army will be sanctioned by the appropriate authority of the unit concerned. However, before proceeding on leave the officers Commanding and second-in-command of police/BSF Battalions will inform the superior Army formation headquarters.

Move of Police Officers:

The following procedure will be followed regarding move of police officers:-

(a) In each case where the officer commanding of a Battalion deployed under the operational Control of the Army has to move from the area of his operational responsibility under instructions from his departmental superiors, he must ensure prior concurrence of the Army formation Commander concerned.

(b) In case of a temporary move of an Officer other than the Officer commanding of a Battalion from area of his operational responsibility the order regarding such move issued by the officer commanding should be made known to the Army authorities concerned.

(c) Order of permanent transfer of officer commanding and other officers of such Battalions serving under the operational control of the Army should be made known to the Army authorities concerned by marking copies of such orders to the concerned Brigade Commander.

(d) With regard to the number of personnel to remain at any post, number of personnel to remain on leave, courses and so on, formation commanders will lay down restrictions for police/BSF personnel in consultation with their Battalion Commanders and affiliated DIsG. These restrictions will, however, be within the scope of similar restrictions as applicable to Army units employed on similar duties.

Medical

The Army will be responsible for :-

(a) Provision of medical stores, evacuation (from ADS onwards) and treatment of all sick and wounded in medical Battalions, field hospitals and Military Hospitals except special form of treatment, deep X-ray treatment and so on. The location of BSF/Police persons evacuated beyond ADS should be intimated to the parent unit in order to enable them to prepare connected documents and forward their emoluments.

(b) Issue of Military railway warrants for conveyance of sick patients of police units, serving under the operational control of the Army from their units to field medical units and military hospitals and back to their units on discharge therefrom.

(c) Disposal of the police personnel found unfit for field service or service in forward areas by the military hospitals to which they are admitted for treatment should be as follows:-

(i) In the case of serving Army Officer/personnel on deputation to police Battalions the medical categorization orders in respect of serving officers/personnel of the Army will apply.

(ii) In the case of all BSF Officers/personnel the hospital concerned will inform the officer Commanding of the Battalion concerned of the individual who will arrange for a Medical Board of the individual in a civil hospital as per existing procedures prevalent in the Unit. Should the civil Medical Board recommend his removal from the field/forward areas the officer Commanding of the Battalion will then take further necessary action. The formation under which the battalion is serving will be informed accordingly.

Canteen Facilities:

Army Headquarters letter No.43809/Q/CN/Vol IV dated 27 Mar 65 lays down facilities in this regard.

Postal Facilities

Postal facilities and concessions will be provided to the Police Battalions by the Army Postal Service on the same scale and conditions as are applicable to the Army units.

Provisioning Policy

The requirements of police units will be vetted and as far as possible, provided by the local Army authorities. Where such provisioning is not possible the police units will approach the Ministry of Home Affairs through their IsGP to provide for these requirements, supported by the vetting report of the local Army authorities. Police must keep the Army informed about changes in their establishments and as to the equipment they would be bringing into use.

Pay and Allowances:

The following will be the exclusive responsibilities of Central and state Governments concerned:-

(a) Pay and allowances including deputation allowances

(b) Clothing, other than special items referred to in paragraph 6 above.

(c) Cost of the postal concessions to the posts and Telegraphs Departments.

(d) Items not covered in paragraphs 5 to 15 and 19 to 21 above.

Rendition of Confidential Reports:

The channel for rendition of annual confidential reports on officers serving with paramilitary and police units placed under the operational control of the Army will be as follows:-

a) Officer Commanding Unit

b) Deputy Inspector General

c) Brigade Commander

d) General Officer Commanding Division

e) Inspector General

As regards the confidential reports of the Commandants, the same procedure as outlined above will be followed except that the annual confidential reports will be initiated by the DIG concerned and endorsed by the Brigade and Divisional Commanders.

Accounting

Hospital stoppages under paragraphs 46 of Appendix 5 to Regulations for the Medical Services of the Armed Forces 1962 will be adjusted by book debit. The current rates of hospital stoppages are as under :-

(a) Gazetted Officers : Rs. 8/- per day

(b) Non Gazetted Officers : Rs. 4/- per day

(c) Charges for conveyance to military Hospital/medical Battalion will be levied at normal rates laid down in AI 928/45.

(d) Warrants issued to sick police patients will be superscribed on the tip in red ink "Armed Police personnel at public Tariff Rates". The cost of warrants will be debited according to paragraph 28 below.

The charges will be recovered at the following rates :-

(a) Proportionate charges at public tariff rates, when the police patients share a ward, coach with Army personnel.

(b) Charges at public Tariff Rates when a ward half coach is used exclusively for conveyance of police personnel only. Charges on account of hire, haulage and maintenance etc. will also be recovered.

(c) Charges for inspection, light and field repairs and recovery of vehicles and equipment will be calculated in accordance with the annual flat rates laid down in the Ministry of Defence letter No.38674/MG/ME 3(a)/8289-D(C&D) dated 30 Oct 53 as amended and No.3517/212/MG/ME-3(c)/14323/D(O&D) dated 9 Jan 56 as amended vide corrigendum No.3517/21/EME org 2/1938-S/D(O-II) dated 4 Nov 71 and letter No.3517/21/EME org 2/750-S/D(O-II) dated 24 Apr 72

(d) When only recovery cover is provided by the Army, hire charges for recovery vehicles will be calculated in accordance with the Ministry of Defence letter No.91371/EME org 2/8697/1/D(O-II) dated 16 Dec 69 as amended from time to time and extended by the Ministry of defence letter No.9137/EME org 2/3922/D (O-II) dated 5 Jun 73 or as revised separately iln case inspection and repair cover is also being provided by the Army.

All issues made to police units placed under the operational control of the Army will be on payment-book debit basis Vouchers or contingent bills in regard to the issues of stores, rations, POL, spares, accommodation, repair of vehicles and equipment hiring of civil/military transport/porters, remount and veterinary cover with reference to para 15 above. Postal facilities and concessions with reference to para 21 above and medical treatment will be enfaced "AID TO POLICE' and will be debited from the following Budget Heads:-

(a) **Border Security Force:** Grant No.49-Police-A, 2-Border Security Force-A, 2(1)-Directorate General of Border Security Force. Debit is to be raised against AGCR New Delhi under intimation to the Deputy Director (Accounts), Pay Accounts Division, BSF New Delhi-11001.

(b) **Central Reserve Police:** Grant number (Police-Minor Head-Central Reserve Police in the account of the Battalion concerned.

Debit in respect of the CRPF battalions will be forwarded to the Accountant General who is responsible for maintaining the accounts of the Battalion concerned for adjustment of expenditure on the account head of the CRP under intimation to the respective officers.

State Police Battalions: Debits will be forwarded initially to the parent state to whom the Battalion belongs for acceptance. The parent state may claim reimbursement from the borrowing state/authorities in due course if admissible.

Instructions regarding discipline and honours and awards will be issued later. Till the issue of the revised instructions, the existing instructions regarding honours and awards will continue to be followed.

This issues with the concurrence of the Ministry of Home Affairs, the Ministry of Defence and the Ministry of Finance (Defence) vide UO No.11/29/75-G&Q dated 13 Nov 75, UO No.243-D/D(GS-I) dated 30 Jan 76 and UO No.2253/Addl FA(J)/75 respectively.

Our letter No.57447/Gen/PC 4/SD 5 dated 30 Sep 66 as amended from time to time is hereby cancelled.

References

Rajya Sabha Secretariat, New Delhi. (April, 2017). Parliament of india rajya sabha department-related parliamentary standing committee on home affairs two hundred third report border security: capacity building and institutions. http://164.100.47.5/committee_web/ReportFile/15/15/203_2017_4_11.pdf

Agarwal, A. K. (2014). *The Third Dimension: Air Power in Combating the Maoist Insurgency*. VIJ Books (India) Pty Ltd.

Annual Report Border Management. (2019). New Delhi: Government of India, Ministry of Home Affairs. https://www.mha.gov.in/documents/annual-reports.

Vifindia.org. (2001). Report of the Group of Ministers on national security. https://www.vifindia.org/sites/default/files/GoM%20Report%20on%20National%20Security.pdf

The Law Department J and K (n.d.). Instrument of accession of Jammu and Kashmir State. http://jklaw.nic.in/instrument_of_accession_of_jammu_and_kashmir_state.pdf

Sanajaoba, N. (August 18, 2016). Problem of 1949 annexation of Manipur

Part 3 – (Instrument of Accession executed on 11-8-47 between governor-general of India and his highness the maharajah of Manipur). *E-PAO*. http://e-pao.net/epSubPageExtractor.asp?src=news_section.Oja_Naorem_Sanajaoba.Sanajaoba_Articles.Problem_of_1949_Annexation_of_Manipur_Part_3_By_Naorem_Sanajaoba.

Ministry of External Affairs (1956). Treaty establishing de jure cession of French establishments in India. https://mea.gov.in/bilateral-documents.htm?dtl/5302/Treaty+establishing+De+Jure+Cession+of+French+Establishments+in+India

United Nations, Peacekeeping United Nations. (1965). Agreement between the government of India and the government of Pakistan relating to cease-fire and the restoration of the status quo as on 1 January 1965 in the Gujarat/west Pakistan border and determination of the border in that area. https://peacemaker.un.org/sites/peacemaker.un.org/files/IN%20PK_650630_Agreement%20to%20CeaseFire%20and%20Restoration%20of%20the%20Status%20Quo.pdf.

Misra, A. (2010). The Rann of Kutch Dispute and the Resolution Process. In: *India-Pakistan*. Palgrave Series in Asian Governance. Pp. 81-106. Palgrave Macmillan, New York. https://doi.org/10.1057/9780230109780_5

Lagergen, G., Entezam, N. and Bebler, A. (1968). The Indo-Pakistan Western Boundary (Rann of Kutch) between India and Pakistan (India, Pakistan). *legal.un.org. Reports of international arbitral awards, United Nations*. pp. 336–357. https://legal.un.org/riaa/cases/vol_XVII/1-576.pdf.

Treaties United Nations. (n.d.). Treaties and international agreements filed and recorded from 28 March 1979 to 8 August 1979 No. 838. https://treaties.un.org/doc/Publication/UNTS/Volume%201142/volume-1142-II-838-English.pdf.

Laine, J. and Kolosov, V. (2015). Introduction to Border Studies. *absborderlands, Far Eastern Federal University*, pp. 14–61. https://absborderlands.org/wp-content/uploads/2013/04/Introduction-to-Border-Studies-2.pdf.

Farinelli, F. (2000). Friedrich Ratzel and the nature of (political) geography. *Political Geography, 19*(8), pp. 943–955. https://www.sciencedirect.com/science/article/pii/S0962629800000366.

Abrahamsson, C. (2013). On the genealogy of Lebensraum. *Research Gate*. https://www.researchgate.net/publication/274054319_On_the_genealogy_of_Lebensraum.

Blake, G. (1998). The objective of Land Boundary Management. *Durham University*. https://www.dur.ac.uk/ibru/publications/download/?id=137.

Singh, P. (2001). Border management. *BSF Journal.*

Department of Border Management, Ministry of Home Affairs. (2015). Border Area Development Programme (BADP): Modified guidelines. https://badp.mha.gov.in/sites/default/files/Guidelines_badp.pdf.

Kargil Review Committee. (2000). From surprise to reckoning: The Kargil Review Committee report. New Delhi: Sage Publications.

The Border Security Force Act (1968). Constitution of the force and conditions of service of the members of the force. New Delhi. http://legislative.gov.in/sites/default/files/A1968-47.pdf

Ministry of Home Affairs. (2004). *The Border Security Force Rules, 1969*. https://mha.gov.in/sites/default/files/bsfAct&Rules_2.pdf.

Deshpande, A. (ed.). (2015). *The First Line of Defence glorious 50 years of the border security force.* Delhi: Shipra publications, pp. 15. http://bsf.nic.in/doc/history/01.pdf

Sherlock, S. (2001). The Indian railways strike of 1974: A study of power and organised labour. New Delhi: Rupa.

Report of the Group of Ministers on National Security. (2000). GoI: New Delhi p. 62. https://www.vifindia.org/sites/default/files/GoM%20Report%20on%20National%20Security.pdf

Babu, J. (2018). An insight into the intricacies of BSF Law: An anatomy of BSF Law by a GD officer for GD officers. Notion Press.

Khan, H., Tandon, L. R., and Hooda, Y. (2017). *Internal security*. McGraw Hill Education; First edition.

Rajgopal, P. V. (Ed.). (2010). *The British, The Bandits and The Bordermen: From the diaries and articles of K F Rustamji*. Wisdom Tree Publishers.

Index

L

M

T

U

V

W

Y

Z

Books of Similar Interest

ISBN: 9788187393689
PRICE: 795/-

ISBN: 9788187393160
PRICE: 895/-

ISBN: 9788187392026
Price: 450/-

ISBN: 9788187393627
Price: 595/-

ISBN: 9788187393795
Price: 595/-